Urban Multilingualism in Europe

Contributions to the Sociology of Language

Edited by
Ofelia García
Francis M. Hult

Founding editor
Joshua A. Fishman

Volume 110

Urban Multilingualism in Europe

Bridging the Gap between Language Policies and Language Practices

Edited by
Giuditta Caliendo
Rudi Janssens
Stef Slembrouck
Piet van Avermaet

DE GRUYTER
MOUTON

ISBN 978-1-5015-2667-1
e-ISBN (PDF) 978-1-5015-0320-7
e-ISBN (EPUB) 978-1-5015-0300-9
ISSN 1861-0676

Library of Congress Control Number: 2019945594

Bibliographic information published by the Deutsche Nationalbibliothek
The Deutsche Nationalbibliothek lists this publication in the Deutsche Nationalbibliografie;
detailed bibliographic data are available on the Internet at http://dnb.dnb.de.

© 2021 Walter de Gruyter Inc., Boston/Berlin
This volume is text- and page-identical with the hardback published in 2020.
Typesetting: Integra Software Services Pvt. Ltd.
Printing and binding: CPI books GmbH, Leck
Cover image: sculpies/shutterstock

www.degruyter.com

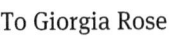
To Giorgia Rose

Acknowledgements

The editors of this volume would like to express their thanks to the Royal Flemish Academy of Belgium for Science and the Arts (Brussels), which sponsored in 2014 the organisation of the International Symposium "Urban Multilingualism in the European Union: Bridging the Gap between Language Policies and Language Practices" within the framework of an EURIAS research fellowship granted to Giuditta Caliendo. Without the constructive debates and the vigorous exchange of ideas that took place before, during and after the symposium, this book would have never been conceived.

Contents

Acknowledgements —— VII

Giuditta Caliendo, Rudi Janssens, Stef Slembrouck and Piet Van Avermaet
Introduction —— 1

Part 1: Tensions between language policies and language practices

Rudi Janssens
1   Language policies versus language practices: A new language conflict? —— 13

Paola Catenaccio and Giuliana Garzone
2   Multilingualism and immigration in the educational system: The case of Italian schools —— 37

Part 2: Responses to multilingual challenges in the field of societal practices

Stef Slembrouck
3   Rescaling the problem of language difference: Some observations for policy and practice of language support in an era of globalisation —— 71

Kathelijne Jordens, Kris Van den Branden and Koen Van Gorp
4   "Only dirty things!" Functions of mother tongue use in collaborative group work —— 91

Part 3: Responses to multilingual challenges in the context of family policies and practices

Elizabeth Lanza
5   Urban multilingualism and family language policy —— 121

Luk Van Mensel
6 Multilingual family practices: An interactional study —— 141

Part 4: New ways of mapping multilingual proficiency

Giuditta Caliendo and Annarita Magliacane
7 Sociopragmatic competence and second language acquisition: Learners of English in a study abroad context —— 167

Patrizia Giuliano
8 The building of textual cohesion in the narrations of bilingual children: Implications for bilingualism and multilingual societies —— 191

Elizabeth Lanza, Giuditta Caliendo, Rudi Janssens, Stef Slembrouck and Piet Van Avermaet
Conclusion —— 217

Index —— 227

Giuditta Caliendo, Rudi Janssens, Stef Slembrouck
and Piet Van Avermaet
Introduction

This book has a dual focus. It observes the complexities of contemporary multilingualism in its various manifestations, while focusing on the current dynamics between language policy and communicative practice. This dual orientation was also at the core of the international event that inspired this volume, the symposium "Urban multilingualism in Europe: Bridging the gap between language policies and language practices", which was held at the Royal Flemish Academy of Belgium for Science and the Arts of Brussels in 2014. The event was a unique opportunity to bring together a significant number of scholars and researchers from various disciplinary backgrounds, including sociolinguistics, cognitive and developmental linguistics, education, language policy and planning, (second) language acquisition and linguistic ethnography. The discussion focused on the interface between language policy, language beliefs, language planning and actual practices in the current panorama of linguistic diversity within Europe. In particular, the symposium reflected on the impact of current policy on language practices and on the changes that would need to be brought about in order to valorise linguistic diversity and promote social inclusion in a context of globalisation-affected and migration-related multilingualism.

In today's complex urban settings, monolingual policies which originate in a historically-inherited rational and Romantic ideal of "one nation-one community-one language" in many respects prevail and arguably continue to dominate debate and regulations, although this has become subject to different forces which are currently at play. Stressing observations recurrently being made at the level of micro practices, it is clear that language policies are under "bottom-up" pressure for a number of reasons. Firstly, existing policies are not ready to accommodate and respond to recent and currently emerging realities of widespread, though still widely unregulated, multilingual practice. This might be related to the fact that, although multilingual practices in situated activities have become increasingly translingual in nature, language policies appear to hold on

---

Giuditta Caliendo, Université de Lille, Domaine Universitaire du Pont de Bois, Villeneuve-d'Ascq, France.
Rudi Janssens, Vrije Universiteit Brussel, VUB-BRIO, Pleinlaan 5, Brussels, Belgium.
Stef Slembrouck, Piet Van Avermaet, University of Ghent, Department of Linguistics, Faculty of Arts and Philosophy, Blandijnberg 2, Ghent, Belgium.

https://doi.org/10.1515/9781501503207-001

to an older, dated view of multilingualism in which languages are exclusively perceived as separable behaviours, which exist next to each other. In this view, multilingualism is one-sidedly perceived in terms of "parallel monolingualisms" (Heller 1999: 5). This compartmentalised view fails to do justice to the many different forms and manifestations of multilingual practice in today's world – forms of code-switching and mixing, as well as new variants and varieties emerging out of language contact. This is a point which extends to the characteristics which are indicative of processes of second language acquisition and/or foreign language learning. Secondly, where bilingual or multilingual policies do occur at the national level, the scope of these tends to be restricted to a country's "national" or "official" languages – as inherited historically, rather than as representative of the current multilingual dynamics. The languages brought by immigrants are mostly left out of the picture. This is particularly salient in contexts where the debate has been strongly mediatised, e.g. immigration/education and immigration/integration. The debate about multilingualism in schools is indeed still widely framed within a dominant monolingual (or, in some cases, a dominant bilingual) system, in spite of the widely divergent multilingual practices being noted "on the ground", and in spite of more recent studies of how one may invest strategically in children's plurilingual repertoires, for instance, making the most of their "home languages" as didactic capital for learning the host language (Hélot and Young 2005; Auger 2014; Sierens and Van Avermaet 2014; Slembrouck, Van Avermaet, and Van Gorp 2018). This book's aim is to critically address the divide between multilingual and second language acquisition policies and practices and to move beyond the binaries in this respect.

Within Europe and elsewhere, globalisation has triggered a series of dynamics that have complicated the policy-making process at the national level even further. A case in point is the fact that while transnational mobility for study and employment is actively promoted within the European Union (EU), how to deal with its effects remains a problem left to be handled by national authorities. For instance, with the Bologna process, the EU sought to increase the compatibility between different national/regional educational systems in order to encourage exchange and mobility and promote excellence. All applications to take part in one of the exchange initiatives and international research programmes must be written in English, the lingua franca of education in the European space. However, where mobility results in more diverse classrooms, local institutions are expected to deal with this within a national framework of policy. One can note a similar lack of harmonisation in how the EU promotes free movement of people, without saying anything at all about the role of language in this. Similarly, the EU documents on the recent refugee crisis stress the need for integration and language learning, but it is effectively left to the national level to determine how this is accomplished. These examples underline how little harmonisation exists within the EU in the domain of language policies, which continue to fall within the territorially-defined jurisdiction of nation-states. Here the EU principle of subsidiarity holds, which implies that political power is exercised at the level of citizenship. Not surprisingly, various authors (e.g. Davis 2014; Shohamy 2015) have raised the question of how EU policy can become more "engaged language policy". The larger question thus raised – the EU providing just one instance of this – is that of the absence of language policy spaces beyond the nation in which to thematise transnational multilingualism and its language policy dimensions. The triennial Programme for International Student Assessment (PISA) by the Organisation for Economic Co-operation and Development (OECD) provides one of the few exceptions, but its data still constitutes a collection of national results.

Globalisation has often been described as a "crisis of level", especially the scale of the national or local level being eviscerated by transnational or global events and tendencies (Herod 2011: vii). This comes with fundamental questions and challenges for policy. These include questions about the level at which policy can be developed and articulated most effectively, questions about how to translate successful policy initiatives which have been developed at one level into wider- or higher-scale implementations, etc. Especially for a book dealing with multilingual policy and practice in and across Europe, the question must be raised about the conditions for successful "re-scaling" (e.g. from local to national, to the European level, and vice versa). If it turns out that developing language policy at a more local, city- or even neighbourhood-specific level comes with the advantages of being "more effective" and "easier to manage" because of "improved context-sensitivity" (especially since globalisation has resulted in patchy landscapes), then one of the questions is how such a dynamics can be translated successfully into national or transnational (e.g. EU) policy. And, how can one do so without losing out on the advantages that have been noted? Current work in language planning certainly advocates approaches which are more oriented to smaller-scale implementations which are domain-specific (e.g. health, education, administration, etc.) and which are organised in cycles of intervention and assessment (Jernudd and Nekvapil 2012; see also Roels et al. 2015: 163). This constitutes a major departure from post-World War II *big* language planning efforts which were mostly oriented to the scale of the nation-state and prioritised single and uniform solutions for all domains of social activity. The assumption was that macro change administered through a national legislative framework would provide sufficient guarantees for success at the level of micro behaviours. This, however, does not mean that we can now afford to deny the national and transnational levels. The level of the nation-state may have "eroded" in a number of ways in the era of globalisation; it certainly has not disappeared (Collins and Slembrouck 2015). For instance, the state's gatekeeping role in the regulation of citizenship has pretty much remained in place (Van Avermaet 2009) and the application of resources that are mobilised to attend to multilingual provisions are mostly confined to and managed within territorial boundaries. In sum, the position adopted in this volume is that new challenges have emerged at both ends, *below* the national level – e.g. how to formulate/develop national language policy in a way which accords with contemporary "productions of locality" (Appadurai 1996), as well as *above* the national level – e.g. how to organise transnational levels, such as that of the EU, as a much-needed stratum of policy development and implementation.

Against this general background, the urban context of cities ("global cities" [Sassen 2001] and other-scaled urban entities; see Derudder, De Vos, and Witlox 2012) occupies a central position in a debate on language policy. Cities provide privileged sites for recording and observing globalisation processes, their implications and effects. The emphasis on cities is a nodal one. In urban contexts different flows of national and international mobility converge, physically and linguistically. Cities are deeply affected by globalisation-induced diversity, although the question of "super-diversity" itself (Vertovec 2007) needs to be handled more carefully than has been the case so far in the (sociolinguistics) literature. At the same time, an urban-focused approach needs to account for the specificity of interactions within and across spaces, i.e. the range from informal/private spaces (e.g. chat in family settings) over semi-formal/semi-public spaces (e.g. community interpreting in a medical consultation room) to more formal/public ones (university lecturing, classroom education, service encounters, etc.). The dynamics of globalisation-affected multilingualism cuts across spheres of activity, both public and private. And, so do the processes of foreign language learning and second language acquisition. This raises the question of how processes of language learning permeate multilingual contexts of language use, as well as that of how multilingual contexts are often organised, researched or understood in terms of "language learning" (e.g. city authorities using posters to encourage clients to treat a service transaction as an opportunity to practice the locally dominant language; e.g. perceptions of the immigrant as the "eternal language learner"). There is a need to chart multilingual practice in its multiple manifestations in the different fabrics of social existence, including the level of private contact between individuals. The disciplinary frameworks of sociolinguistic enquiry and investigation into processes of language learning count as complementary and interdependent perspectives in such an exercise. In addition, there are notable and significant differences between cities themselves, and between cities and their outskirts or hinterland, where monolingual models of the past continue to be borne out more clearly by empirical realities. Multilingualism is not evenly distributed within national territories. The multilingual and multicultural nature of cities often clashes with the realities of other parts of the country, where monolingualism is taken for granted and remains unchallenged by the (socio)linguistic experiences on the ground. The development of language policy is therefore increasingly confronted with a complex and multi-faceted puzzle, which may well be the harder to solve in urban contexts. The challenge to respond adequately to today's complex and multi-faceted sociolinguistic landscapes is one of the motivations behind the compilation of this volume.

Migration and mobility have also evolved, since the early 1990s when the first key publications on globalisation became widespread. The migration and mobility flows of the current century are generated by a wider variety of reasons and motivations (study, work, retirement, political exile and asylum, etc.), with specific linkages to age groups and units of travelling people involved. The length of stay in the host context also varies considerably, compared to the past. Experiences of mobility no longer necessarily represent a single, permanent life change. In addition, the traditional distinction between "sending" and "receiving" countries is no longer as dichotomic and rigid as it used to be. Boundaries have become more fluid (e.g. through social media) and movements more unpredictable. All these different and diverse movements which often converge into city life, and may spread out inland from the urban centres, affect the hosting context and render local realities even more complex. As a matter of fact, in some cities it has become unclear what the terms "local", or "being/acting locally" exactly mean from a sociolinguistic point of view. This applies to the range of languages identified as "local" and their share of the population as noted in surveys (Brussels is a case in point, see Janssens in this volume). It also applies to how the practices that can be observed in situated conversational activity invite a perspective on code switching, shifting and mixing within and across contexts. Within the same remit are the challenges posed at the level of what can be identified as "local features" of a dominant language (see e.g. Rampton's 2012 detailed account of local London varieties of English). A final important element of mobility to be taken into consideration are the technological evolutions which have radically changed our ways of communicating across boundaries. Widespread use of social media such as Facebook has in many cases meant that the context of ancestry and its characteristic forms of language use continue to be "nearby" – accessible on a smartphone and this is true irrespective of where the user is located physically. For instance, diasporic Facebook communities simultaneously subscribe to networks of "friends" in the country of origin and in the host country.

The various contributions to this book address different aspects of the complex relationships between policy and practice at the crossroads of different levels of social organisation. The book is divided in four parts, with clear links between them. Part 1 deals with tensions between language policy and practice, illustrated through a situation of language conflict and through multilingual classrooms (Chapters by Janssens and by Catenaccio and Garzone). The next two parts address responses to multilingual challenges in institutional contexts (part 2; Chapters by Slembrouck and by Jordens, Van den Branden and Van Gorp) and in the context of family policy and practice (part 3; Chapters by Lanza and by Van Mensel). Part 4 presents novel ways of mapping multilingual proficiency in different contexts (Chapters by Caliendo and Magliacane, and by Giuliano). In the conclusion of the book, Lanza and the editors stress the need to reappraise our view of language and reframe the policies based on this reappraisal.

The opening Chapter by Janssens entitled "Language policies versus language practices: A new language conflict?" draws our attention to a language conflict in the very heart of Europe – Brussels. Language has always been a contested issue in Belgium since its independence, with four different language areas: Dutch-speaking, French-speaking, German-speaking and a number of bilingual (Dutch/French) areas. While there is no national language as an official language for the country, the official language of each municipality is constitutionally protected. Municipalities surrounding the distinct areas offer language facilities, while the Brussels Capital Region is the only officially bilingual area in Belgium. A "pacification model" has been in place in order to avert conflict between the two main language communities – Dutch and French. Increased mobility contributes to the complex process of temporary and permanent migration, resulting in linguistically mixed neighbourhoods and growing multilingualism in the capital, as mapped by language barometer studies over time. The sustainability of the pacification model based on two "imagined communities" can now be questioned in the light of language practices that have become much more diverse and complex. As Janssens concludes, multilingualism in Brussels "presupposes a radical change in the way of thinking about language, administration and education, and last but not least the concept of integration and inclusion".

Tension between language policy and practice are also highlighted in the contribution by Catenaccio and Garzone – "Multilingualism and immigration in the educational system: The case of Italian schools". Due to the accessibility of its borders, Italy has become one of what the authors call "immigration hotspots", resulting in the need for a variety of new language policies. Policies affecting new immigrant languages need to be considered with the backdrop of current policies concerning minority languages in Europe. In their Chapter, Catenaccio and Garzone focus on the linguistic needs of children with an immigrant background in schools in Milan, an urban area with the highest immigration figures in the country. Their investigation of schools with a high percentage of students with a non-Italian background includes interviews with teachers and headmasters in schools ranging from primary over junior high school to secondary schools. What they discovered is that while policies may exist, how these policies are practised can vary widely. Indeed the effects of such policies are left up to the "craftsmanship" and good will of the educators.

The two articles of section 2 highlight institutional and domain-specific responses to multilingual challenges. A "scaled" perspective on urban multilingualism is presented in Slembrouck's Chapter, "Rescaling the problem of language difference: Some observations for policy and practice of language support in an era of globalisation". Space and "scale" play an important role for understanding language practices in situations of occupational and professional service provision, allowing us to grasp the impact of the global with the local, through the distribution of languages. Such a perspective on urban multilingualism brings out the fact that while an individual may have competence in one or several languages, the actual use of these languages in an institutional setting may be constrained by the multilingual affordances of particular spaces and activities in these spaces, as Slembrouck points out. In the article, the author reports on the language regimes of two neighbourhood health centres in Ghent and the local solutions the centres developed and adopted, at two points in time, in addition to a cross-sectorial study on the use and distribution of strategies of language support. Ideologies of language (use) are clearly at play in all of these spaces. In conclusion, a number of recommendations for policy and practice are discussed, each seeking to "re-scale" the problem of language differences.

The role of mother tongues or "home languages" in classrooms with a different medium of instruction has been studied extensively in the literature. However, in Flanders the mother tongues of students with an immigrant background have been willingly excluded from the classroom as there is mostly a strict Dutch-only policy. Jordens, Van den Branden and Van Gorp explore the functions of the mother tongue in peer conversations during collaborative group work among Turkish-speaking pupils in their Chapter "'Only dirty things!' Functions of mother tongue use in collaborative group work". While the teachers normally did not allow the use of Turkish in the classroom, the students were exceptionally allowed to use it in group work. Results of the study indicate that the mother tongue was employed for a range of sociocognitive functions, including talk on content in the collaborative group work and management-related talk. Language ideologies are clearly evoked as the Turkish-speaking students felt that their language was perceived as dirty.

Lanza's contribution to the volume, "Urban multilingualism and family language policy", opens the next section. An appeal is made to investigate family language policy in regards to burning educational issues concerning immigration in contemporary urban spaces. Data from Norway are drawn on to illustrate how language ideologies operate on the local level and may even be contradictory. While Norway has been considered a sociolinguistic paradise in the widespread tolerance of dialectal variation, with no diglossia at play, the use of other immigrant languages is not looked upon as favourably. Drawing on media data following a report that school students with a Pakistani background did poorly in schools because they did not master sufficient knowledge of Norwegian at the start, the study shows how family spaces and practices, traditionally considered private domains, have become public spaces. Political pressures to instantiate a policy attempt to coerce families with an immigrant background into speaking Norwegian in the home, thus promoting monolingualism in society. A comparison is made with other similar cases in Europe. The article calls for greater attention to be paid to the study of family language policies and practices within a larger socio-political context.

In the second contribution to this section, "Multilingual family practices: An interactional study", Van Mensel points out the tension between the sociolinguistic reality of multilingual practices involving the deployment of the multilingual speaker's entire linguistic repertoire and the macro-perspective taken by policy-makers in their use of top-down categories such as "Dutch-speaking" and "French-speaking". Indeed while policies may recognise the sociolinguistic reality, they nonetheless manage linguistic reality as bounded entities, that is, as named languages. Using interactional data recorded by parents in multilingual families in Brussels in various settings, the author highlights how the parents deploy their diverse repertoires in everyday social interactions as they negotiate various identities. Rather than going in and out of languages, the interactants can be said to be translanguaging (García and Li 2014), using their entire linguistic repertoires. Defining proficiency in a language can be challenging, as it calls upon the necessity to define what we mean by a language, especially since multilingual practices draw upon various elements from several languages. In conclusion, the author calls for policy makers to refrain from language-based categorisations and instead move towards an appreciation of multilingual practices.

The fourth section focuses on new ways of mapping multilingual proficiency. Caliendo and Magliacane's Chapter "Sociopragmatic competence and second language acquisition: Learners of English in a study abroad context" examines the micro level of communication to investigate socio-pragmatic competence in second language acquisition. The target group is second language learners of English who spent a semester abroad in Ireland. More subtle aspects of sociolinguistic competence such as the appropriate use of discourse markers and other conversational phenomena are highlighted as potential indicators of the attainment of multilingual proficiency. Their results indicate that various contextual parameters such as place of residence were deemed important in some cases, but not in others. Although the sample was small, as the authors point out themselves, the longitudinal aspect of the study and the in-depth inquiry into the functions of the linguistic markers provide a rich display of ways in which to map multilingual proficiency.

In the second Chapter of this last section, Giuliano follows up on the mapping of multilingual proficiency through the investigation of textual cohesion in the narratives of bilingual (Italian/French) teenagers resident in Italy in her Chapter "The building of textual cohesion in the narrations of bilingual children: Implications for bilingualism and multilingual societies". The bilinguals as well as monolingual control groups were asked to retell the story in a video clip with the bilinguals recounting in both of their languages. As the authors clearly show, multilingual proficiency involves more than just knowledge of the lexicon and syntax of a language. Perspective-taking is an essential part of creating cohesion in a text and socio-pragmatic norms for each language may have different means for performing this. The results of the study indicate that the bilingual speakers creatively draw on both of their languages in different ways in order to perform the tasks at hand, thus providing evidence for a multilingual repertoire as opposed to a conception of the bilingual as two monolinguals in one and the same person.

The volume ends with the concluding remarks by Lanza and the four book editors, who reflect upon the main points that have emerged from the individual Chapters, while noting some aspects of the way forward. The gap between practice and policy is revisited, while noting the challenge of diversity as a key European policy imperative – a challenge which ultimately makes us rethink received concepts of language and language community.

References

Appadurai, Arjun. 1996. *Modernity at large: Cultural dimensions of globalization*. Minneapolis: University of Minnesota Press.
Auger, Nathalie. 2014. Exploring the use of migrant languages to support learning in mainstream classrooms in France. In David Little, Constant Leung & Piet Van Avermaet

(eds.), *Managing diversity in education: Languages, policies, pedagogies*, 223–242. Bristol: Multilingual Matters.

Collins, James & Stef Slembrouck. 2015. Classifying migrants in the field of health: Sociolinguistic scale and neoliberal statecraft. In Christopher Stroud & Mastin Prinsloo (eds.), *Language, literacy and diversity. Moving words*, 16–33. London: Routledge.

Davis, Kathryn A. 2014. Engaged language policies and practices. *Language Policy* 13 (2). 83–100.

Derudder, Ben, Anneleen De Vos & Frank Witlox. 2012. Global city/world city. In Ben Derudder, Michael Hoyler, Peter Taylor & Frank Witlox (eds.), *International handbook of globalization and world cities*, 73–82. Cheltenham: Edward Edgar.

García, Ofelia & Li Wei. 2014. *Translanguaging: Language, bilingualism and education*. New York: Palgrave.

Heller, Monica. 1999. *Linguistic minorities and modernity: A sociolinguistic ethnography*. London: Longman.

Hélot, Christine & Andrea Young. 2005. The notion of diversity in language education: Policy and practice at primary level in France. *Language, Culture and Curriculum* 18. 242–257.

Herod, Andrew. 2011. *Scale*. London: Routledge.

Jernudd, Björn & Jiří Nekvapil. 2012. History of the field: A sketch. In Bernard Spolsky (ed.), *The Cambridge handbook of language policy*, 16–36. Cambridge: Cambridge University Press.

Rampton, Ben. 2012. Drilling down to the grain in superdiversity. *Working Papers in Urban Language & Literacies* 98. London: King's College.

Roels, Britt, Marie Seghers, Bert De Bisschop, Piet Van Avermaet, Mieke Van Herreweghe & Stef Slembrouck. 2015. Equal access to community interpreting in Flanders: A matter of self-reflexive decision-making? *The International Journal of Translation and Interpreting Research* 7 (3). 149–165.

Sassen, Saskia. 2001. *The global city: London, New York, Tokyo*. Princeton: Princeton University Press.

Shohamy, Elana. 2015. LL research as expanding language and language policy. *Linguistic Landscape* 1 (1/2). 152–171.

Sierens, Sven & Piet Van Avermaet. 2014. Language diversity in education: Evolving from multilingual education to functional multilingual learning. In David Little, Constant Leung & Piet Van Avermaet (eds.), *Managing diversity in education: Languages, policies, pedagogies*, 204–222. Bristol: Multilingual Matters.

Slembrouck, Stef, Piet Van Avermaet & Koen Van Gorp. 2018. Strategies of multilingualism in education for minority children. In Piet Van Avermaet, Stef Slembrouck, Koen Van Gorp, Sven Sierens & Katrijn Maryns (eds.), *The multilingual edge of education*, 9–40. London: Palgrave.

Van Avermaet, Piet. 2009. Fortress Europe? Language policy regimes for immigration and citizenship. In Gabrielle Hogan-Brun, Clare Mar-Molinero & Patrick Stevenson (eds.), *Discourses on language and integration*, 15–44. Amsterdam: John Benjamins.

Vertovec, Steven. 2007. Super-diversity and its implications. *Ethnic and Racial Studies* 30 (6). 1024–1054.

Part 1: **Tensions between language policies and language practices**

Rudi Janssens
1 Language policies versus language practices: A new language conflict?

Abstract: Although freedom of language use was guaranteed by the Constitution, language has always been a contested issue in Belgium. The current political model is based on the pacification of the conflicts between the two main language communities and it is the result of a quasi-continuous process of state reform that starts from official language use in public contexts as the core political cleavage. This resulted in a complex organisation of public and semi-public institutions. This pacification model reflects the political conditions before 1960. Since then, Brussels has become a city of migration. Nowadays half the population has an immigrant background. The changing composition of the population obviously has an impact on linguistic practices. Within all different domains of language use, Brussels is characterised by growing multilingualism. The question raises to what extent this situation affects the traditional structure of the pacification model that aims at regulating the contact situations between the two traditional languages. This Chapter is based on survey research. It explores the consequences of language use within a multilingual urban context. After a brief historical introduction, language use in the multilingual urban context of Brussels will be analysed within different domains. To conclude, the impact on the bilingual institutional setting will be discussed.

1 From freedom of language use to territorialism

Since its independence in 1830, language has always been a contested issue in Belgium, although freedom of language use was guaranteed by the Constitution. Historically, the Romance-Germanic language border (Van Durme 2002) divided the country into two parts: north of this border, in the current Flemish Region, the overall majority of the population spoke Dutch dialects, in the south different Walloon and Picardian dialects were used as local vernaculars. In both parts of the country, the political, economic, cultural and religious elite spoke French. The linguistic difference was at the same time a social difference. Especially in Flanders, where the diglossic situation was characterised by Germanic dialects as the low language-varieties, and French as the high variety, this situation caused tension. Soon after the independence, the use of French was gaining

Rudi Janssens, Vrije Universiteit Brussel, VUB-BRIO, Pleinlaan 5, Brussels, Belgium.

https://doi.org/10.1515/9781501503207-002

ground in the domain of justice and administration while only primary education was in the local language. In Brussels, where the majority spoke a Dutch dialect, these three domains were almost exclusively French. The concentration of political institutions, administrations and the economic and financial sector led to a rapidly increasing number of French speakers in Brussels, putting pressure on the Dutch speakers to switch to French in public and even in private life. Many Dutch speakers adopted French as a home language. The fact that their children were learning and speaking French was vital for Dutch-speaking parents striving for inter-generational upward social mobility.

The Flemish Movement, originally a literary and cultural movement aspiring to the standardisation of the Dutch language, gradually became more politically oriented. When the basis of the electoral system changed from a tax-based system to a multiple voting system (1893), the Dutch-speaking middle class increased their political influence. The Equality Law (1898), officially recognising both French and Dutch as official languages, was their first major success. It was the result of a political discussion that started with the death penalty of two labourers from Flemish descent who did not understand French and were convicted by a French-speaking court. The resulting full bilingualism on a national level collided with the fear of the French-speaking civil servants that they would also need to know Dutch to retain their position. In 1921, the resistance against bilingualism in Wallonia led to the introduction of the territoriality principle as the rationale behind language laws. These laws determined where Dutch was accepted as an official language. From 1932 onwards, the results of decennial language censuses decided on the language status of the municipalities. The overall majority of the municipalities were officially monolingual. When 30% of the population tended to speak another official language than the majority language of the region, they were given the right to use that language in their contacts with the local government. When the second language reached the 50% threshold, it became the official language of the municipality. As a result, the language border itself shifted.

In a context of confrontation between political representatives of both language groups, the importance of census data for both language groups transformed its use into a political referendum pro or against local bilingualism. The results were regularly contested by the language group that felt disadvantaged. The results were influenced by the fact that the local municipalities were responsible for the data collection process, resulting in a variable methodological approach which often depended on preferred outcomes. Especially the region around the capital was subject to a gradual, contested, expansion of the bilingual territory, a phenomenon known as the "Brussels oil stain". The turmoil over the 1947 language census culminated, after 15 years of political conflict, into the fixation of the language border in the 1960s. Since then, the language status of every municipality has been embedded in the Constitution. The rationale behind the language policy is the creation of monolingual municipalities. Around the language border, contact situations have inevitably resulted in the institutionalisation of two types of bilingualism: full bilingualism in the case of Brussels, and a type of unbalanced bilingualism in municipalities with one official language but facilities for the other language, including the possibility to use it in official communication and primary education.

2 The Belgian pacification model

The current political model is based on a pacification of the conflicts between the two main language communities. It is the result of a quasi-continuous process of state reform built on a conflict prevention design with guaranteed group representation that starts from official language use as the core political cleavage (Lijphart 1984). This resulted in a complex organisation of public and semi-public institutions. The Belgian nation state was gradually "stripped", and competences were transferred to sub-national and local authorities. Parallel to the development of the Belgian state structure, competences were also transferred to the European level, sometimes even contradicting the Belgian political pacification logic. The pacification model progressively became a multi-level approach.

The first article of the Constitution today states that Belgium is a federal state, composed of regions and communities (Figure 1). Since the fixation of the language border, six stages of state reform have resulted in a division of power over different entities. Every stage transferred more powers from the federal (national) level to the regions and the communities. If regions or communities have authority over one specific policy domain, they exercise their authority autonomously and cannot be overruled by the federal level. Disputes between the different entities can only be settled legally by the Constitutional Court or they are subject to the next round of political negotiations. The federal level is competent for national defence, justice, finance, social security, national health and domestic and foreign affairs, although parts of these domains have been transferred to the regions and communities. Communities are competent for issues related to language and culture (for instance cultural policy, education, health policy, social welfare, integration, etc.). There are three communities: a Flemish-, French- and German-speaking one. Next to the communities, regions are competent for territorial issues (economy, employment, environmental issues, energy, transport, geographical planning, nature conservation, etc.). They also exercise supervision over provinces and municipalities, the two local political entities. There

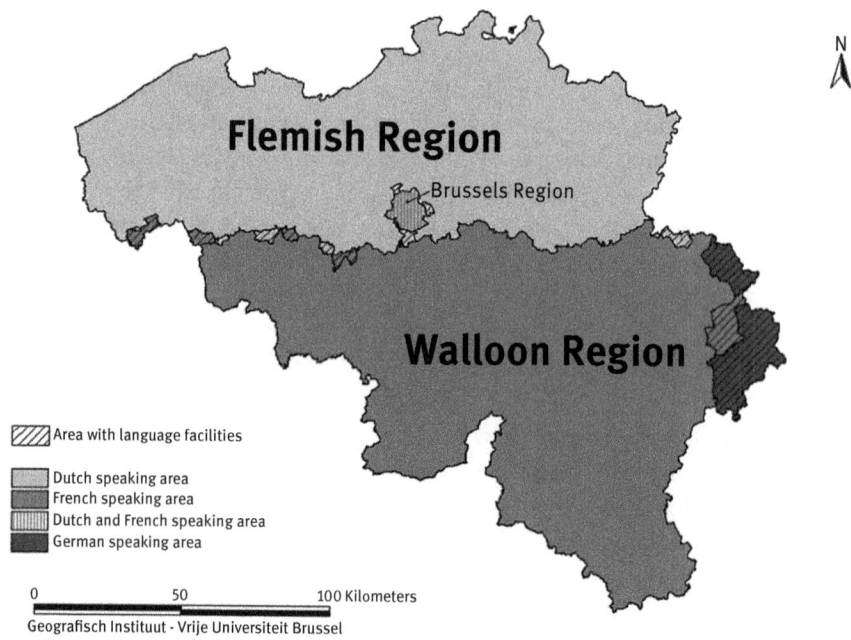

Figure 1: The Belgian multi-level political approach.

are three regions: the Flemish Region, the Walloon Region and the Brussels Capital Region. The federal level, the communities and the regions are each responsible for scientific research and international relations in their fields of competence. All entities and levels have their own elections, parliament, government and administration. To complete the picture, it is important to note a major imbalance in the ways the different entities have evolved as a result of different views held in the two main language communities: the Flemish Community and Region form one entity, the French Community was renamed in 2011 as the Walloon-Brussels Federation.

All these different bodies operate within a country with four different language areas: a Dutch-speaking, French-speaking, German-speaking and a bilingual (Dutch/French) one. There are three official languages, but there is no national language as an official language for the country as a whole. The official language of each municipality is registered in the Constitution. Apart from the federal government which is competent within all language areas, the Flemish Government is active within the Dutch-speaking language area; the Walloon Region and the Walloon-Brussels Federation are competent within the French-speaking area; within the German-speaking area the political power is exercised by the German-speaking Community and the Walloon Region; and finally, within the bilingual Brussels area, the Brussels Government and both the Flemish Government and the Walloon-Brussels Federation are competent. In the periphery of all three officially monolingual areas, municipalities with language facilities offer the possibility to use French in the Flemish-speaking area, Dutch and German in the French-speaking area and French in the German-speaking area. The main language contact area is the bilingual Brussels Capital Region. In the remainder of this Chapter I will concentrate on the language conflict in Brussels.

3 Brussels pacification by bilingualism

The Brussels Capital Region is the only officially bilingual area in Belgium. Due to the social status of French in the 19th and the first half of the 20th century, Brussels shifted from a city where the overall population spoke a Dutch dialect towards a region with French as the lingua franca. In the Belgian history of language struggles, Brussels has always been at the heart of the political discussion. The Frenchification of the Dutch-speaking population even led to the abolition of the language censuses and the start of a continuous process of state reform. Figure 2 illustrates the evolution of the results of the censuses for the current Brussels Capital Region. Only monolingual French and Dutch

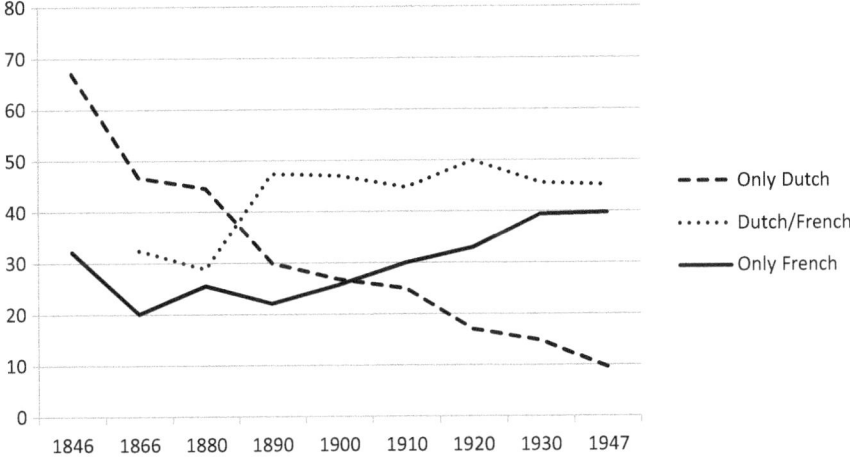

Figure 2: Percentage of the Brussels population per language group, based on the language censuses (Source: Belgian Law Gazette).

speakers and bilinguals were retained; the number of citizens speaking other languages or language combinations was negligible throughout the represented period of time.

Where in 1830 around 70% of the inhabitants of Brussels were monolingual Dutch speakers, one century later their number fell to less than 10%. But language use is not a zero-sum game. The steep decline in the number of monolingual Dutch speakers was primarily related to the growing number of bilinguals and not to a comparable increase of monolingual French speakers. Over a period of 100 years, the number of French speakers was situated between 20% and 40% of the population. The bilinguals had been the dominant group since 1900, although on the political level the discussion was focused on the Dutch-speaking versus the French-speaking community. Given the fairly stable proportion of French speakers, it was clear that most bilinguals originated from the Dutch-speaking group. At the beginning of the 1960s, the abolition of the language censuses, together with the fixation of the language border, had to prevent further Frenchification and the inherent expansion of the number of bilingual municipalities. To frame the complexity of the political solutions, one had to take into account that the majority of Belgium's population is Dutch-speaking, while within the borders of the Brussels Capital Region the majority is French-speaking. The linguistic pacification system is based on an equilibrium of checks and balances respecting both communities where they share common responsibilities. Different protection mechanisms on the national level often have a regional counterpart in Brussels.

Like the other regions, the Brussels Capital Region has its own elections, a parliament, and an administration. Of the 89 members of this parliament, 17 seats are reserved for Dutch-speaking representatives, 72 for French-speaking ones. In the voting booth, every voter first has to make a choice about the language of his preferred representatives. Once this choice has been made s/he can vote for the candidates on the different monolingual lists. All representatives together form the Brussels parliament that deals with regional issues. The executive power lies with the Government of the Brussels Capital Region that consists of one Minister-President and four Ministers, two of them French-speaking and two Dutch-speaking, added to which are three State Secretaries of which at least one is Dutch-speaking. The 17 representatives elected on the lists with Dutch-speaking candidates form the *Vlaamse Gemeenschapscommissie* (VGC, Flemish Community Commission). They deal with a number of specific community issues in cooperation with and under the supervision of the Flemish Government. A parallel structure is set up for the French-speaking representatives resulting in the French Community Commission. The powers of this commission depend on its agreements with the Walloon-Brussels Federation. This implies that two community commissions do not have the same competences, although together they form the Common Community Commission, which deals with the common aspects of health policy and assistance to persons (for instance, first aid) that affect both communities. To complete the picture, Brussels has 19 municipalities. The local councils do not work with separated seats for the two traditional language groups. At the level of local administration, both bilingual and monolingual lists with candidates are possible. However, if the local council appoints a Dutch-speaking alderman,[1] they receive extra financial support from the national government (Alen 1994).

Brussels is officially bilingual. Both Dutch and French have the same official status, regardless of the number of speakers. The linguistic composition of the population, as reflected in Figure 2, hardly permits linking an individual exclusively to one of the two prescribed "imagined communities" (Anderson [1983] 1991). The concept of "sub-nationality" does not exist, although theoretically, in the political discourse, every citizen is supposed to be a member of one language community. The institutionalisation of bilingualism "the Brussels way" is such that a Dutch or French speaker must be able to act as a monolingual in a bilingual city. In practice, every citizen always has the possibility to make the choice between the services of either language community. In the context of the administration, this implies that notwithstanding the fact that the administration related to the regional issues is bilingual, there are no bilingual forms. Instead, one has to make a choice between both languages. In education, one has the choice between two independent systems, with Dutch or French as the language of instruction. On every occasion, a citizen has a free choice between two options and a previous choice does not determine the next one: one can easily have an ID card in Dutch and a driving license in French, one can send one's daughter to a French-medium school and one's son to a Dutch-medium school and even switch afterwards. The Brussels concept of bilingualism can be perfectly illustrated by comparing the organisation of the educational system with those of other bi- or multilingual regions. In Luxembourg, with its three official languages, there is one school system for all pupils; during the curriculum the three languages are used as languages of instruction at school. Irrespective of linguistic background, the aim is to form trilingual Luxembourgian citizens. In the bilingual Canadian province of Québec, there are two educational systems organised by one Ministry of Education, one with English as the language of instruction restricted to Canadians from Anglo-Canadian descent, and the dominant system with French

---

[1] An alderman is a member of a municipal assembly chosen by the elected members themselves and responsible for certain policy areas in the municipality.

as the language of instruction for all others. The English-speaking Canadians have the right to pass on their Anglo-Canadian culture to the next generation, while other non-French speakers have to adapt to the local French-speaking majority, even if they use English as their home language. But also those who have the right to attend the English-medium system have access to the Francophone schools. In Brussels both official languages have an equal status. The relationship is not a hierarchical one as in the previous example. The idea is that both language groups can pass on their own culture and have control over their own system, but there is no clear membership criterion to decide to which communities one belongs. This openness is partly motivated by opportunism. Francophone politicians claimed that the choice for French-language education was the most logical one for Flemish parents, given the local dominance of French over Dutch. Flemish politicians appealed to the fact that only the Dutch-language education system could guarantee bilingualism for Francophone children.

Pacification in Brussels is not based on the traditional approach to power-sharing across all aspects of governance, but on the equal status of the two official languages, French and Dutch (O'Connor 2011). Segmental autonomy is given to the traditional language communities, but also to the region that has different responsibilities and exercises different powers. Dutch in Brussels is not threatened as a minority language, since all citizens can appeal to the services of the competent Flemish or Francophone authorities. This results in a multilevel political approach with a high degree of flexibility, but at the same time one that lacks the overarching accommodation to bridge the gap between these communities (Deschouwer 1999). While the various political actors within Brussels may "talk" to each other, the various public administrations and organisations do not, and operate within the status quo of the political design (O'Connor 2011).

4 From bilingual to multilingual Brussels

The pacification model dates from the political situation in the 1960s of the previous century. Since then, the composition of the population has changed radically. Labour migration, organised by the Belgian authorities, led to the presence of a Turkish and Moroccan immigrant community in Brussels, next to other Mediterranean nationalities that were already prominently present in the capital. Belgium's colonial past led to a strong African presence as well. As one of the main capitals of the EU and the seat of NATO headquarters, Brussels also hosts a lot of highly-skilled western immigrants, the so-called expats. With the events following the fall of the Berlin Wall, the enlargement of the EU and the right of EU citizens to move and reside freely within the territory of its member states, the nature of immigration has changed. The image of the immigrant, as a foreigner who comes to live and work in a new country, learning the local language and habits, and staying there for the rest of his/her life, has long been overtaken by an increasingly complex reality. Be that as it may, it is mostly conflicts in Africa and Asia and a worldwide economic crisis that have resulted in an influx of individual or groups of immigrants, which continue to dominate the public discussion and debate on migration.

Institutional, geopolitical and technological changes have enabled an increase in the magnitude and speed of the circulation of people, objects and information around the world. "Migration" is replaced by "mobility" (Urry 2000). An increasing proportion of people is likely to move around several times in their lifetime, in various directions and for various purposes, including study, and employment, but also retirement, leisure and tourism, added to which are family reunification, international marriages and other forms of "mobility" that do not necessarily correspond to the traditional image of migration. The decisions these people make almost unavoidably involve a language contact situation.

The last official figures of language use in Brussels, the census of 1947, predates the migration waves that started after the Second World War. Given the lack of reliable data, other types of statistics were used in order to assess the linguistic situation in the Belgian capital mainly based upon governmental data. By definition, they allow only two mutually exclusive options, and bilingualism or the presence of other languages than the official ones are excluded. In 1997, fifty years after the last language census, the Vrije Universiteit Brussel (VUB) began the preparations for the first *Language Barometer* (LB) study, the first scientific survey-study that attempted to arrive at a representative picture of the language situation in Brussels. Successive language barometer studies have strived to achieve the following objectives: to provide a representative picture of the language relationships in Brussels in all their complexities, to obtain a clear understanding of the dynamics generated by these language relationships, and to acquire an insight into the relationship between language and identity. They rely on 2500 face-to-face interviews of a representative sample of the adult Brussels population. To this end, a quota sample is selected from the National Population Register based on age, gender and municipality, selecting a respondent together with three alternatives from the same age group, sex and location in case the first respondent cannot or does not want to participate. This method ensures that the results are representative at the level of the Brussels Capital Region. In 2013, the results of the third survey were published (Janssens 2001, 2007, 2013).

Earlier census data made little difference between home language and language use. Given its lingua franca, Brussels was perceived as a French-speaking city. Dutch was the minority language and as such considered to be used within the confines of the speaker's own community. The Language Barometer Research took the "Fishmanian" approach to sociolinguistic analysis as a starting point: "Who speaks what language to whom and when?" (Fishman 1965).

Table 1 shows the evolution of the languages that are spoken "good to excellent" by the adult population of Brussels based on the three Language Barometer surveys (LB1 to LB3) 50 years later. These figures are based on self-reported knowledge.

Table 1: Languages spoken "good to excellent".

LB1 (2001)		LB2 (2007)		LB3 (2013)	
French	95.5%	French	95.6%	French	88.5%
Dutch	33.3%	English	35.4%	English	29.7%
English	33.3%	Dutch	28.3%	Dutch	23.1%
Arabic	10.1%	Spanish	7.4%	Arabic	17.9%
German	7.1%	Arabic	6.6%	Spanish	8.9%
Spanish	6.9%	Italian	5.7%	German	7.0%
Italian	4.7%	German	5.6%	Italian	5.2%
Turkish	3.3%	Turkish	1.4%	Turkish	4.5%

The top eight languages are the same across the three surveys. These are followed by the Berber languages (including Tamazight, Riffian and Kabyle), Portuguese, Russian, Lingala and Greek, which was ousted as the twelfth language by Polish in LB3. Fluctuations in German, Spanish, Italian and Turkish are limited over time and insignificant. On the other hand, the evolution of the four main languages is remarkable and worth noting in detail. Whereas in a comparison of LB1 and LB2 the differences related to French and English proficiency are insignificant, both are characterised by a statistically significant decrease in the most recent study. The decline in proficiency for Dutch develops with the same intensity (–5%), which means that English has now clearly become the second most known language in Brussels. The evolution in Arabic is even more striking: following a decline we now see a significant increase, which means that the language comfortably moves up to become Brussels' fourth language. The reasons for these evolutions are manifold, although we will not discuss them in detail in the context of this Chapter: not all people moving to Brussels know French or use it as a lingua franca; there is a high drop-out rate in education resulting in decreasing levels of proficiency in the second and third school language; linguistic diversity among speakers of varieties of Arabic goes hand-in-hand with a second and third generation considering the variety of language spoken locally among them as "Arabic" regardless of linguistic descent and proficiency. The same pattern can also be found for Turkish. For both Arabic and Turkish, the transnational link plays an important role. As far as the increasing number of German speakers is concerned, this is caused by the rising number of German nationals living in the city.

But the figures referring to self-reported knowledge are hard to compare since every language score hides a different reality. Table 2 is based on the number of adults that report to speak the language "good to excellent" and indicates where they learned the language first: at home (whether or not in combination with another language), within the Belgian educational system (as a language of instruction or via a separate language course) or elsewhere. The categories are not used cumulatively, e.g. those who have acquired the language as a home language are not included in the group of those who learned it at school.

Table 2: Language typology (LB3).

	Dutch	French	English	Arabic
Home language	48.9%	67.9%	5.8%	90.8%
Single language	22.4%	36.6%	4.0%	55.3%
Combination French/Dutch	26.3%	15.5%		32.0%
Other combination	0.2%	15.8%	1.8%	3.5%
Belgian education	41.8%	13.1%	60.0%	
Language of instruction	16.7%	8.4%		
Course	25.1%	4.7%		
Elsewhere	9.3%	19.0%	34.2%	9.2%

Of all those people speaking Dutch at a good or excellent level, not even half of them grew up in a family where Dutch is/was spoken. Dutch is no longer a language used within the Flemish minority community itself but a language of wider communication within the Brussels context, which is also illustrated by a growing number of non-Dutch speakers whose children attend Dutch-medium education. The fact that more than half of those speaking the language at home learned it in combination with another language is striking. Although the figures of the adults with French as a home language are higher, they show a similar evolution with a growing number of bilingual families with French as one of the home languages and a decline in the number of monolingual French-speaking households. English is clearly a language learned at school and is seldom spoken as a home language. What these three languages have in common is the potential to be used outside the traditional context of home language community. This in contrast to Arabic, which is almost exclusively learned at home and can merely be used with other Arabic speakers who learned the language at home as well. Given the variety of vernaculars labelled as "Arabic", this language might have a kind of lingua franca effect as well.

Home language refers to primary language acquisition that occurs within the family. Home language is not only essential in the context of language learning and language attitudes but also forms the basis for the political pacification model. This political logic leads to the question whether, in terms of linguistic background, this type of model is still tenable for the current sociolinguistic make-up of the population. Notwithstanding a few political disputes on Brussels' linguistic diversity, the dichotomy of two language communities continues to form the basis for the organisation of public services and for the political, cultural and social organisation of the region. However, this dichotomy is not really a true reflection of the population's linguistic knowledge. The group of traditional bilinguals that speak Dutch as well as French has always existed. These bilinguals form, despite all reservations regarding operationalisation and accuracy of the counts, the largest group of Brussels residents since the language census in 1890, accounting for 40%, and they continued to do so until the last census, in 1947. Bilingual families are therefore a constant feature in the Brussels context. Certainly, bilingual families are no exception in the current metropolitan context with its high migration figures, but bilingualism is no longer restricted to the combination of French and Dutch. Table 3 shows the evolution of home languages drawn on the basis of the official languages of the Brussels Capital Region. Since the combination of Dutch with another language than French occurs in less than 1% of cases among Brussels residents, it is not included as a separate category but incorporated in that of Dutch-speaking families. This means that the following five categories are retained: Brussels residents that grew up in a family that only speaks French, a family that only speaks Dutch, a traditional bilingual family speaking both French and Dutch at home, new bilingual people that grew up in a family that speaks French combined with a

Table 3: Home language of the family of origin.

Home language	LB1 (2001)	LB2 (2007)	LB3 (2013)
French	51.7%	56.4%	33.6%
Dutch	9.1%	6.8%	5.4%
Dutch/French	10.1%	8.7%	14.1%
French/Other language(s)	9.4%	11.4%	14.9%
Other language(s)	19.7%	16.7%	32.0%

language other than Dutch, and other language speakers who grew up in a family that did neither speak Dutch nor French.

The group of Brussels residents from monolingual French-speaking families is the largest, but whereas it represented over half of Brussels residents in the previous surveys, its share has currently fallen to one third. The group of Brussels residents that grew up in a family that does not speak any Dutch nor French is almost as great and it increases. Although, based on the evolution between LB1 and LB2, one could expect that higher numbers of the next generation of migrants would exchange the language of their parents' country of origin for French, this does not appear to be the case and they tend towards a more exclusive use of the immigrant languages. The number of Brussels residents from monolingual Dutch-speaking families continues to fall, though the difference with LB2 is not significant. The decrease is less pronounced than could be expected based on the basis of LB1 and LB2. In contrast, there is a significant increase in the number of traditional bilingual families. The number of citizens from new bilingual families also rises significantly and represents almost 15% of Brussels' residents. The immigrant languages' stronger position also reflects this trend. These languages compete, in family terms, with French rather than Dutch. Migrant families are faced with the choice of either retaining their own language within the family or adopting French as the second family language. To provide a clearer picture of this evolution and to enable a glimpse into the future, Table 4 shows the distribution of the home languages of the family of origin of the youngest generation.

Among young people, traditional monolingual families based on one of the official languages only account for one third of the population, given the 2013 results. It appears that the official languages are mainly spoken in families that combine them with another language, and this not only applies to Dutch but also to French. For the youngest age category, bilingual families are as natural

Table 4: Home language of the family of origin (18–24 years old).

Home language	LB1 (2001)	LB2 (2007)	LB3 (2013)
French	49.6%	53.7%	28.5%
Dutch	2.0%	0.7%	4.1%
Dutch/French	5.0%	4.4%	13.7%
French/Other language(s)	26.2%	30.9%	32.3%
Other language(s)	17.2%	10.3%	21.3%

as French-speaking or Dutch-speaking families in the past. The basis of the political model continues to narrow, especially if we take the expected influx of citizens from abroad into account (Deboosere et al. 2009).

The changing composition of the population obviously has an impact on linguistic practices. As Louckx (1982) already stated in his study on the Dutch speakers moving to Brussels in the 1960s, the linguistic composition of the family is the best predictor of language use and the least susceptible to change. In the current complicated linguistic situation of Brussels, this is still the case. Regardless of the linguistic background of the parents, they want to pass on their native tongue to the next generation. Whereas partners from a different linguistic background might opt for one family language, once they have children the number of bilingual families significantly increases. Even the choice of French as the single family language used between the partners does not prevent the intergenerational transmission of other languages.

But even in conversations with more distant relations that are traditionally considered as much more susceptible to change, the use of different languages becomes more and more the norm. Tables 5 and 6 illustrate the evolution of language use with neighbours and on the work floor. The categorisation is based on the three main "contact languages", those languages that can be used in a broader context and are taught at school and are therefore useful in different language domains and with the majority of the citizens. Note that in the following tables, the category "French" refers to all those who exclusively use French in the situation described or French in combination with another language (with the exception of Dutch and English), just as it is the case for the other categories.

Whereas the figures of the first LB survey indicate the dominance of French in conversations with neighbours with the combination French/Dutch as the most evident alternative, this situation has obviously changed. The exclusive use of French diminished by 30%, and the vast increase of the use of English,

Table 5: Language use in the neighbourhood.

Home language	LB1 (2001)	LB2 (2007)	LB3 (2013)
French	82.9%	87.5%	61.8%
Dutch	1.5%	1.0%	0.7%
English	0.3%	0.5%	0.6%
French/Dutch	11.5%	8.2%	11.6%
French/English	1.5%	2.2%	5.9%
French/Dutch/English	0.8%	0.4%	18.3%
Other language(s)	1.5%	0.4%	1.2%

Table 6: Language use in the professional context.

Home language	LB1 (2001)	LB2 (2007)	LB3 (2013)
French	73.3%	40.7%	32.2%
Dutch	4.3%	0.6%	1.7%
English	4.8%	2.3%	1.7%
French/Dutch	10.6%	25.0%	16.7%
French/English	2.4%	10.3%	17.0%
Dutch/English	0.3%	0.3%	–
French/Dutch/English	3.5%	20.3%	30.7%
Other language(s)	0.8%	0.5%	0.2%

not only in conversations with neighbours but in all public language domains, is highly significant. In 2001 combining languages in the neighbourhood was rather rare. Only 14.8% did, almost all by combining both official languages. In 2013, more than one third of the citizens of Brussels use different languages within their neighbourhoods. Combining languages in public is not uncommon. The public language of Brussels before the first migration wave was "Brussels", a Dutch dialect gradually Frenchified. Multilingual cities tend to develop a local lingua franca, a language based on the general lingua franca but with a strong influence of the dominant migrant community in the neighbourhood. Even in cities with a prestigious strong international language as its lingua franca this evolution can be found. Language contact in a multilingual environment does not lead to a shift towards the lingua franca but rather to the use of different languages and languaging (Swain 2006; see also Van Mensel 2014).

Another important evolution is the use of English. When asking the respondents of the surveys about their own proficiency, English usually comes second. Nevertheless, although the language is omnipresent as a second lingua franca, in the linguistic landscape of the city, in industry etc., in previous surveys (Janssens 2001, 2007) almost nobody mentioned the use of the language in daily conversations. But unlike in the preceding surveys, now English is effectively used in conversations within the different language domains, even in official communication with front-desk civil servants. Most people claim they use English part of the time, although only to a limited extent (Janssens 2013).

Language use at work is indicative for this evolution. Table 6 presents an overview of the contact languages and language combinations spoken in the workplace by those respondents working in Brussels. In this context both the use of English and the fact of combining languages became more prominent. Regardless of the language, monolingual work environments are becoming more rare; French is still spoken in about one-third of the companies as the only language of conversation in the workplace where twelve years ago this was still the case in three-quarters of the jobs. Trilingualism is not merely a job requirement but the languages are actually used as well. Half of the employed use Dutch or English in their work-related activities.

5 Implications of multilingualism for the pacification model

The "mobility"-approach (see Urry 2000) refers to the complex process of temporary and permanent migration, where most countries are both the origin and the destination for people moving within a global, or at least European, context. Mobility also involves linguistically mixed neighbourhoods and language contact as a potential source of misunderstanding and conflict. Moreover, language is not only a means of communication, but also an identity marker and a key to social cohesion. The concept of social cohesion refers to a set of ideas that problematises differences between immigrants and natives and seeks, via governmental policies, to solve such problems by fostering "shared values" and "common identities" (Bartram, Poros, and Monforte 2014: 137). Social inclusion, however, does not go that far. This concept as it is used here refers to the feeling of belonging to a group sharing some language features that make them identifiable as a group. Inclusion is the opposite of exclusion, it is the possibility of that group to participate to a greater or lesser extent in the social, political, economic and/or cultural life of a country, a region or a municipality (Grin et al. 2014). Mobility and inclusion therefore emerge as two key dimensions of the challenges multilingual European societies are confronted with, including Brussels. On the one hand, the fact that people are not restricted in their spatial movement to study and work is considered as positive, on the other hand, a society strives for a maximum of inclusion. One can expect that the more mobile people are, the less inclusive a society is, and vice versa. The challenge is to find a balance that maximises both mobility and inclusion. Brussels' pacification model is such a balanced system of laws and institutions establishing inclusion in a society characterised by two language groups. It does not imply the use of a common language but is based on a particular form of bilingualism. Mobility and multilingualism caused by migration and mobility undoubtedly affects this balance. Within the different domains of language use, Brussels is characterised by a growing multilingualism. The question raises to what extent this situation affects the traditional structures of the pacification model that aims at regulating the contact situations between French speakers and Dutch speakers but does not leave room for other language speakers, unless they perceive themselves as a member of one of the two traditional groups.

Due to the political system of segmental autonomy (see infra, the Belgian pacification model), language communities have their own areas of competence, such as education, but also integration policy. Whereas this might look obvious for Flanders and Wallonia, for Brussels this implies that both the Flemish Community and the Walloon-Brussels Federation are responsible for the local integration policy, and this results in two independent policies. In reality, it means that all non-EU citizens can choose to participate in either policy, although they are not obliged to make a choice between the two; they are free to use facilities such as language lessons and employment counselling offered by these communities and the regional authorities. While in the past individual bilinguals were ignored as a category, nowadays other language speakers are in a similar position and are expected to become a member of one of the two traditional "imagined" language communities, notwithstanding their language competences.

Whereas one expects adults to take the initiative to make use of the possibilities offered by the communities, children can rely on education as a direct link between migrant families and traditional language communities, at least if they do not attend European or private schools in and around Brussels. Community control over the educational system, and the possibility to pass the language and culture to the next generation, are two of the pillars of the pacification process.

Figure 3 illustrates the remarkable evolution of the background of the pupils in the Dutch-medium school system. Unfortunately, comparable figures for French-medium education are lacking. The Dutch-medium education system has always attracted French-speaking pupils, especially when a growing number of children of immigrants entered the French-medium system from the 1970s onwards. This resulted in the early 1990s in a situation with an almost equal proportion of pupils from a monolingual Dutch-, French- or traditional bilingual speaking background. Almost 17% spoke one or more other languages at home. In the following 20 years, the number of Dutch-speaking children was halved. The number of pupils from traditional bilingual and French-speaking families increased by 50%, while the category of children raised in families speaking other languages tripled. Nowadays, approximately 37% have Dutch as a home language, and not even 10% of the pupils come from a monolingual Dutch-speaking family. However, the pedagogical approach and the educational objectives are grafted on a classroom with Dutch-speaking students.

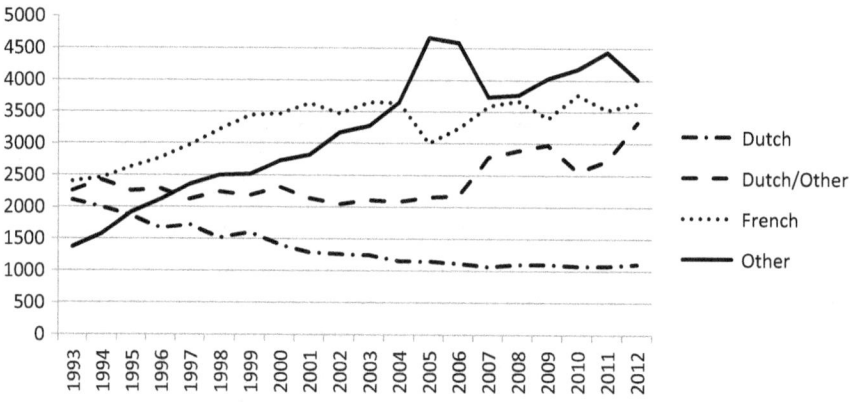

Figure 3: Language background of pupils in Dutch-medium schools (Source: VGC).

Apart from the pedagogical problems of dealing with an educational system based on Dutch as the home language while only a minority of the children speak that language at home, the link between the communities and their educational institutions is subject to heated political debate. Given the demographic boom and the fact that the majority of these children do not grow up in a monolingual Dutch-speaking family, the following question is raised about the target population of Dutch-medium education: to what extent should the Flemish Community, as a minority, contribute to the education of non-Dutch-speaking pupils in Brussels? On the one hand, respect for free choice means that anyone who prefers Dutch-medium education should be able to attend a Dutch-medium school. On the other hand, the Dutch-medium schools in Brussels pursue the same goals as the schools in Flanders with an overall majority of Dutch-speaking children in a dominant Dutch-speaking environment. This discussion resulted in a political compromise. An enrolment procedure was developed with priority rules for Dutch-speaking pupils. This policy provoked some protest among non-Dutch-speaking families, on the one hand, and Dutch speakers, on the other, as both experienced they could not enrol their children in their preferred school. As a result, the freedom of education, another fundamental right enshrined in the Belgian Constitution, can no longer be guaranteed.

But the main underlying question is the sustainability of the current pacification model based on two imagined communities (see Benedict 1991) that no longer reflect the actual nature of the population. Should social inclusion be based on a Brussels community as a whole rather than on the current conceptualisation based on two language communities currently representing a minority of the population? One can argue that a shared history or religion are not necessary conditions for social inclusion. Yet, common values and language or languages play an equally important role in an urban society. In Brussels, cohesion is traditionally shaped by the institutionalisation of the two traditional language communities, with transversal links to the Brussels Capital Region as a political entity. Whereas the problem in the 1960s was how to deal with bilinguals, the current question is how to link the present-day multilingual population to political structure. In other words, do Brussels citizens identify with one of the two traditional language communities providing (partial) social inclusion or not? In order to shed some light on this issue, the Language Barometer Research Programme uses the notion of "identification" as an alternative for the vague and ubiquitous concept of "identity". In the analysis, identification refers to the relation between the person and a concept in which they recognise themselves or want to identify with. It does not mean that this is the predominant factor of his or her personality or that it might not be subject to change. The importance of identification does not lay in the categorisation of citizens as such, but primarily in the extent that it influences language-related behaviour and attitudes. For that purpose, the respondents in the LB-surveys of 2007 and 2013 were asked to make a choice between several alternatives based on language, geographic entity, ethnicity and nationality.

The most popular concepts the respondents identify with refer to the local context, independent of language community. More than 55% of all respondents identify with Brussels, almost 37% with the local municipality. Both figures are significantly higher for LB3 than for LB2. Significantly lower, but still important, are more general concepts which are equally independent of the linguistic categories: 40% of the respondents see themselves as Belgians, around 15% as Europeans. The least popular concepts are those linked to a specific language community. In both surveys, almost 20% see themselves as Francophones. Within the group of Dutch speakers, there is a remarkable shift. Where in 2007 4% of the respondents considered themselves as Flemings and less than 1% as Dutch speakers, in the recent survey 4% of the respondents see themselves as Dutch speakers and only 2% as Flemish. Within the first group, apart from the people with Dutch as a family language, some second-generation immigrants are found who never spoke Dutch as a family language but who attended Dutch-medium schools. This group sees itself as part of the Dutch-speaking community but reject the label "Fleming" that is frequently used as a synonym for extreme right politics or as a symbol of "too much" Flemish involvement in Brussels. Among all respondents 30% identify with a concept related to one of the traditional language communities. So, who are the Flemings and Francophones of Brussels? Are they the ones who learned the language at home and are considered to be a member of one of the traditional communities, or do they identify with community-related concepts? In both cases, more than half of the population does not fit the traditional categories.

Nevertheless, the differences according to identification are most striking when we look at language-related choices. One can take the elections as the fundamental link between the citizens and the political system. The political logic is best illustrated by the electronic voting procedure to appoint members of parliament. First, a citizen has to make a choice between voting for French-speaking or Dutch-speaking political candidates before they can make an ideological choice. Identification, irrespective of the personal interpretation and motivation on which it is based, plays a crucial role in this voting behaviour. Identification with being a Dutch speaker or Fleming, for some two opposing positions, both result in a significantly higher score for a Dutch-language list. Identification as a French speaker or Walloon, together with the impact of the media and linguistic proficiency, is important in the preference for a French-language list. But the majority of voters from monolingual Dutch- or French-speaking families prefer bilingual lists.

The home language, often considered as the basis for political choice, is far more important in the choice for a Dutch-language list than for a French-language one. In this respect, the political representation of the Dutch minority group remains important in a dominant French-speaking environment. But in total, not more than 30% of the population in Brussels prefer to be represented by monolingual lists. Education loses ground as the main socialiser when it comes to political identification and it is partly replaced by the media in determining citizens' political orientations. The link between home language and the political system still remains, but the citizens who exclusively speak Dutch or French at home have become a minority themselves. As a result, identification with the current political model decreases.

6 Towards a new pacification model?

The pacification of the traditional language contact situation in Brussels is the result of hard-fought agreement between the two traditional language communities. Current language contact and the challenges that it raises put new dimensions in the foreground. The few examples cited above provide some insight on the current language situation and how people deal with sociolinguistic diversity. The use of one dominant lingua franca does not contradict a growing linguistic diversity and the use of different languages within the same language domain. This attitude illustrates the linguistic dimensions of the super-diverse nature of Brussels society.

Linguistic diversity is not only a sociolinguistic concept but also a political one. Multilingualism contrasts with the principles of self-rule for community based aspects in the Brussels model. Bilingualism in Brussels, as described in the introductory part of this Chapter, is synonymous with a dual system of monolingualism. The shift towards multilingualism, currently also challenged by the observed reality of "languaging" (Swain 2006), is far from evident and it presupposes a radical change in the way of thinking about language, administration and education, and last but not least the concepts of integration and inclusion.

The political and social model of Brussels is the result of a historical confrontation between two languages. In the 1960s, this model was the most appropriate answer. It respected the identity of both language communities and the reality of social life in the capital region. As such, it is often studied as a laboratory of language contact. This reality has changed. If identification is the driving force behind the social, and as a result of that, also behind the political order, then the current model in Brussels is untenable. Language practices not only determine language policy but impact society as a whole. The shift towards multilingualism is far from evident and it presupposes the need for radical change in the way of thinking about language, administration and education, and last but not least for how we understand integration and inclusion.

References

Alen, André. 1994. Het Belgische federalisme [Belgian federalism]. In André Alen, Jean Beaufays & Frank Delmartino (eds.), *Federalisme: Staatkundig, politiek en economisch* [Federalism: Statemanship, political and economic], 135–185. Antwerpen: Maklu.

Anderson, Benedict. [1983] 1991. *Imagined communities: Reflections on the origin and spread of nationalism*, 2nd edn. London: Verso.

Bartram, David, Maritsa Poros & Pierre Monforte. 2014. *Key concepts in migration*. London: Sage.

Deboosere, Patrick, Thierry Eggerickx, Etienne Van Hecke & Benjamin Wayens. 2009. The population of Brussels: A demographic overview. *Brussels Studies*. http://journals.open edition.org/brussels/891 (accessed 28 May 2019).

Deschouwer, Kris. 1999. From consociation to federation: How the Belgian parties won. In Kurt Richard Luther & Kris Deschouwer (eds.), *Party elites in divided societies: Political parties in consociational democracy*. ECPR Studies in European Political Science. London: Routledge.

Fishman, Joshua. 1965. Who speaks what language to whom and when? *La Linguistique* 2. 67–88.

Grin, François, László Marácz, Nike Pokorn & Peter Kraus. 2014. *Mobility and inclusion in multilingual Europe: A position paper on the MIME project*. Version presented at the MIME Kick-Off Conference, University of Geneva, 31 March. https://www.mime-project.org/resources/MIME-POSITIONPAPER-V4.pdf (accessed 28 May 2019).

Janssens, Rudi. 2001. Taalgebruik in Brussel: Taalverhoudingen, taalverschuivingen en taalidentiteit in een meertalige stad [Language use in Brussels: Language relations, language shifts and language identity in a multilingual city]. *Brusselse Thema's* [Brussels Themes] 8. Brussels: VUBPRESS.

Janssens, Rudi. 2007. *Van Brussel gesproken: Taalgebruik, taalverschuivingen en taalidentiteit in het Brussels Hoofdstedelijk Gewest.* [Speaking of Brussels: Language use, language shifts and language identity in the Brussels-Capital Region]. Brussels: VUBPRESS.

Janssens, Rudi. 2013. *Meertaligheid als cement van de stedelijke samenleving: Een analyse van de Brusselse taalsituatie op basis van Taalbarometer 3* [Multilingualism as the cement of urban society: An analysis of the Brussels language situation based on Taalbarometer 3]. Brussels: VUBPRESS.

Lijphart, Arend. 1984. *Democracies: Patterns of majoritarian and consensus government in twenty-one countries*. New Haven: Yale University Press.

Louckx, Fred. 1982. Vlamingen tussen Vlaanderen en Wallonië: Taalaanvaardings- en taalontwijkingsprocessen in een meertalige situatie bekeken vanuit de sociologische literatuur over etnische en raciale verhoudingen [Flemings between Flanders and Wallonia: Processes of language acceptance and language avoidance in a multilingual situation viewed from the sociological literature on ethnic and racial relations]. *Taal en Sociale Integratie* [Language and Social Integration] 5. Brussels: VUBPRESS.

O'Connor, Karl. 2011. *Sustaining power-sharing: The bureaucracy, the bureaucrat and conflict management*. Exeter: University of Exeter doctoral dissertation.

Swain, Merrill. 2006. Languaging, agency and collaboration in advanced language proficiency. In Heidi Byrnes (ed.), *Advanced language learning: The contribution of Halliday and Vygotsky*, 95–108. London: Continuum.

Urry, John. 2000. *Sociology beyond societies: Mobilities for the twenty-first century*. New York & London: Routledge.
Van Durme, Luc. 2002. Genesis and evolution of the Romance-Germanic language border in Europe. In Jeanine Treffers-Dalle & Roland Willemyns (eds.), *Language contact at the Romance-Germanic language border*, 9–21. Clevedon: Multilingual Matters.
Van Mensel, Luk. 2014. *Language labels, language practices: A multiple case study of parents with children enrolled in Dutch-medium education in Brussels*. Namur: University of Namur doctoral dissertation.

Paola Catenaccio and Giuliana Garzone
2 Multilingualism and immigration in the educational system: The case of Italian schools

Abstract: This Chapter focuses on multilingualism and immigrant languages in Italy, and reports on a preliminary research on educational policies and practices in a small sample of schools with a significant presence of pupils with limited Italian proficiency due to their history of recent immigration.

After an overview of different forms of multilingualism in the EU with special regard to non-national languages, the discussion considers Italy's policies implemented over time towards regional and minority languages and, later, immigrant languages. Special consideration is given to mediation activities, which are currently the staple of measures aimed at favouring the integration of immigrant students while helping them preserve their native languages.

Against this background, the study describes and discusses a survey we conducted in selected primary, junior high and high schools in the Greater Milan area (Lombardy) with a view to identifying teachers' attitudes and expectations in respect of the perceived challenges posed by a multilingual/multicultural class population, and to assess the way in which such perceived challenges are addressed, or it is believed they should be addressed, by the teachers interviewed. The informants selected were teachers and heads of schools participating in a project set up by the University of Milan for the training of language mediators specialised in pedagogical assistance. Emerging practices are investigated against the background of existing policies – both at national and at supranational level – designed to protect and promote local minority and heritage languages, which turn out to be ill-equipped when they deal with immigrant languages.

1 Introduction

This Chapter reports on some preliminary research on educational policies and practices in a small sample of Italian schools with a significant presence of

---
Paola Catenaccio, Università degli Studi di Milano, Università degli Studi di Milano, Piazza Indro Montanelli 1, Sesto San Giovanni (MI), Italy.
Giuliana Garzone, IULM International University of Languages and Media, via Carlo Bo 1, Milan, Italy.

https://doi.org/10.1515/9781501503207-003

students with limited Italian proficiency due to their history of recent immigration. A survey was conducted in selected primary, junior high and high schools in the Greater Milan area in the Italian region of Lombardy, an area with an increasingly diverse school population. The aim was to identify teachers' attitudes and expectations in respect of the perceived challenges posed by a multilingual/multicultural class population, and to assess the way in which such perceived challenges are addressed, or it is believed they should be addressed, by the interviewed teachers. The informants selected were teachers and heads of schools participating in a project set up by the University of Milan for the training of language mediators specialised in pedagogical assistance. Emerging practices are investigated against the background of existing policies – both at national and at supranational level – designed to protect and promote local minority and heritage languages, but ill-equipped to deal with immigrant languages.

In order to provide a comprehensive overview of the contextual factors influencing the development of local policies and practices, the first part of this Chapter sets out to examine EU policies regarding regional and minority (R/M) languages and immigrant languages, focusing in particular on the way in which they converge with and/or are integrated into the overall linguistic policy of the European Union, with its traditional emphasis on multilingualism and multiculturalism. It also attempts to assess their impact on the linguistic policies implemented in Italy, a country where immigration has a fairly new but rapidly consolidating history. Consideration is given to the actions taken, both at EU and at national level, to extend the scope of policies about regional and minority (R/M) languages to cover the linguistic rights of immigrant communities, with the attendant duty to provide educational means to favour linguistic integration into the host country. The current situation in Italy is used as a case study to illustrate these broader issues and the consequences of institutional choices (or lack thereof) to address changing demographics and cultural conditions.

After a short overview of different forms of multilingualism in the EU[1] with special regard to non-national languages, the discussion will consider Italy's policies towards regional and minority languages and those aimed at immigrant languages. The latter will be discussed in detail, looking at developments over time and current challenges, and focusing on mediation activities which are at present the staple of measures aimed at favouring the integration of immigrant students while at the same time helping them preserve their native languages.

---

[1] Among forms of multilingualism also cases of "political bilingualism", such as that of Belgium (amongst others), are included.

1.1 Forms of multilingualism in Europe

The issue of multilingualism has been widely debated since the inception of the EU and has always figured amongst its declared priorities, as may be expected in a supranational organisation embracing twenty-eight countries and as many as twenty-four official languages.

In the course of the decades, there have been frequent engaging declarations on multilingualism, and rules and policies have been introduced in various forms to support "a multilingual Europe"; however, recent reports on multilingualism in Europe betray a degree of dissatisfaction with its current state, especially in light of the fact that a coherent legally binding EU policy on language and multilingualism is still missing both at continental and memberstate level (Nic Shuibhne 2004; Krzyżanowski and Wodak 2011: 116; Moore 2011). The very definition of "European multilingualism" is inevitably subject to multiple interpretations and challenges, enmeshed as it is in a number of concepts – e.g. "European identity", "integration", "inclusion" – which are rather vague and have been negotiated and re-negotiated in the course of the institutions' history as many times as there have been accessions, giving rise to bipolar notions such as European vs. non-European, official vs. non-official languages, national vs. minority languages, which are basically centred on the idea of inclusion and exclusion (Wodak 2008; Krzyżanowski 2010).

The picture is extremely complex, and repeated calls for a stronger promotion of multilingualism among European citizens has yielded only partial results, with a significant persistence of deeply ingrained forms of hegemonic multilingualism, i.e. situations where preference is given, both in learning and in usage, to a restricted number of more widely spoken languages (English, French, German and, less prominently, Spanish and Italian), while the others are learnt much less, if hardly at all, outside their country/geographical area of origin.

This complexity is heightened by the presence, besides national languages, of several other lesser spoken languages which go under the umbrella term of "minority languages". In the European context the expression "minority languages" is vague and is now variously interpreted as referring to languages other than the twenty-four official ones used in different areas of the Union, including non-territorial languages (e.g. Romani), but also the languages of more or less recent, mostly economic, immigration (see Gogolin 2002). The latter, however, do not appear to enjoy the same degree of protection as national minority languages. For instance, the *European Parliament resolution on the protection of minorities and anti-discrimination policies in an enlarged Europe,* clearly states that it is "necessary to draw a clear distinction between (national) minorities, immigrants and asylum seekers" (European Parliament 2005: 407), but does so for the purpose of identifying "national minorities" which are entitled to protection, excluding all others.

Even for national minority languages, at any rate, rights are far from being fully established. Despite their reiteration in a number of successive documents (e.g. *Framework Convention for the Protection of National Minorities* 1995, *Charter of Fundamental Rights of the European Union* 2000/2009, *Treaty of Lisbon* 2007/2009) aimed at redressing a situation where there is no "system of adequate minority protection nor a EU level language policy and planning for regional and minority languages" (Romaine 2013: 126), such a system is not yet really in place.

Against this background, immigrant languages fare even worse. Even the broadest interpretation of EU provisions for the protection of minority languages does not include the languages of immigrants, however numerous their speakers may be. This issue does receive some thought in EU documents, but only occasionally and hardly systematically. For instance, the *European Commission (EC) Green Paper on Migration and Mobility* (Commission of the European Communities 2008) emphasised the critical importance of children from immigration backgrounds learning the host language as early as possible while retaining the heritage language and culture of the country of origin (Extra and Yağmur 2012). The problem is also considered in the most recent institutional document in this domain, the *Policy Recommendations for the Promotion of Multilingualism in the European Union by the Civil Society Platform on Multilingualism* (Commission of the European Communities 2011), which declares in its opening paragraphs:

> All languages that are in regular use by a community, whether territorial or Diaspora, are important and should be included in language policy; not just the official working languages of the European Union. This includes among others less-widely used languages, languages of immigrant communities, minority languages. This will help guarantee Europe's cultural diversity as well as the basic human rights of all citizens.
> (Commission of the European Communities 2011: 6)

In the text, consideration is given to "lesser used languages", "regional and minority languages" and "immigrant languages", but no specific indications on how to develop suitable policies are provided.

As regards specifically immigrant languages, the Platform adopts the same approach as the Green Paper (Commission of the European Communities 2008), recognising the need "for clear and fair language policies for immigrant languages so that immigrants are helped to integrate by learning the languages of their host societies, and that they are also able to transmit their mother tongues within the family should they wish to do so" (Commission of the European

Communities 2011: 32). At the same time, it affirms the impossibility to teach all immigrant languages in schools. Overall, the Platform, as well as most EU documents, reports and declarations, tends to attach by far prevalent attention to overall linguistic integration and to autochthonous regional and minority languages, overlooking immigrant languages. There is therefore an evident policy gap which is left to individual member states to fill in the ways they see fit, and which may overlap – but also conflict – with the provisions, if any, which are in place for national minority languages.

2 Minority languages in Italy

Italy has a relatively long tradition of protection of national linguistic minorities, the principle being enshrined in the Italian Constitution, whose article Art. 6 states: "The Republic safeguards linguistic minorities by means of appropriate measures". These measures have been implemented in Italy for those minority languages that are national languages in other neighbouring European countries (French in Valle d'Aosta, German in Trentino and South Tyrol, Slovene in Friuli Venezia Giulia).[2]

In 1999 an Act of Parliament (*Legge n. 482, Norme in materia di tutela delle minoranze linguistiche storiche*, [Provisions for the protection of historical linguistic minority groups], Parlamento Italiano 1999) was passed to reinforce the protection contained in the Constitution in conformity with the principles laid out by "European and international institutions" (Art. 2). The new law was introduced at a time when the spread of standard Italian had determined a decline in the use both of dialects and of the languages of the historical minority groups (Barni 2008: 218; cf. De Mauro 1994), which were therefore in danger of being progressively abandoned.

The protection accorded by the 1999 Statute (which was granted not without debate on eligible languages; see Telmon 2006: 61; Maraschio and Robustelli 2011: 77; also Pellegrini 1977: 18–19) regarded twelve "historical" languages and cultures: Albanian, Catalan, German, Greek, Slovene, Croatian, French, Franco-Provençal, Friulian, Ladin, Occitan and Sardinian languages and cultures.

This attention for regional and minority languages, however little spoken, is not matched by similar efforts invested in the protection/preservation of

---

[2] The special protection accorded to these languages already in the late 1940s and early 1950s right after the enactment of the Italian Constitution was admittedly connected with the desire to avoid separatist sentiments in the border areas.

immigrant languages and immigrants' linguistic integration, in a context where today, on the Italian scene, immigrant languages "often have a more prominent appearance than R/M languages but enjoy less recognition, protection and/or promotion" (Extra and Yağmur 2012). Differently from regional and minority languages, speakers of immigrant languages cannot count on dedicated teaching, and only to some extent on extraordinary public funding, despite the fact that they have become in many ways much more prominent than national minority languages. This has resulted in new minority languages being more socially relevant and at the same time less institutionally recognised than traditional minority languages. Significantly for the purposes of this study, while national minority languages continue to benefit from policies which guarantee that they are taught in schools (amongst others), no similar provisions are in place for immigrant minority languages, whose presence and daily use in Italy has grown exponentially over the last few decades.

2.1 Immigrant population in Italy

Starting from the last two decades of the twentieth century, Italy has become a host country to growing numbers of immigrants. The immigration pattern has been roughly the same as with many countries of recent immigration, with young male adults often arriving first, and families following at a later stage.

On 31 December 2014, at the time of the research reported in this Chapter, there were 5,014,437 foreign nationals resident in Italy, amounting to 8.2% of the country's population. These figures include 75,067 children born in Italy to foreign nationals (14.9% of total births in Italy), but exclude all unregistered immigrants. The distribution of foreign born population is largely uneven in Italy: almost 89% of immigrants live in the northern and central parts of the country (the most economically developed areas), while only 11% live in the southern half of the peninsula (ISTAT 2015).

With the progressive rise in immigrant resident population, there has been a parallel increase in the number of students of immigrant background (both in primary and secondary education), whose presence in Italian schools has grown progressively (data are taken from Ongini and Santagati 2013). More specifically, between 2002 and 2012 there was a four-fold increase in the foreign student population (primary and secondary education), while over the same period the overall foreign population trebled. In the school year 2016/2017 non-Italian students in Italian schools amounted to around 826,000, and accounted for 9.4% of the overall student population (MIUR – Ufficio di Statistica 2018: 8).

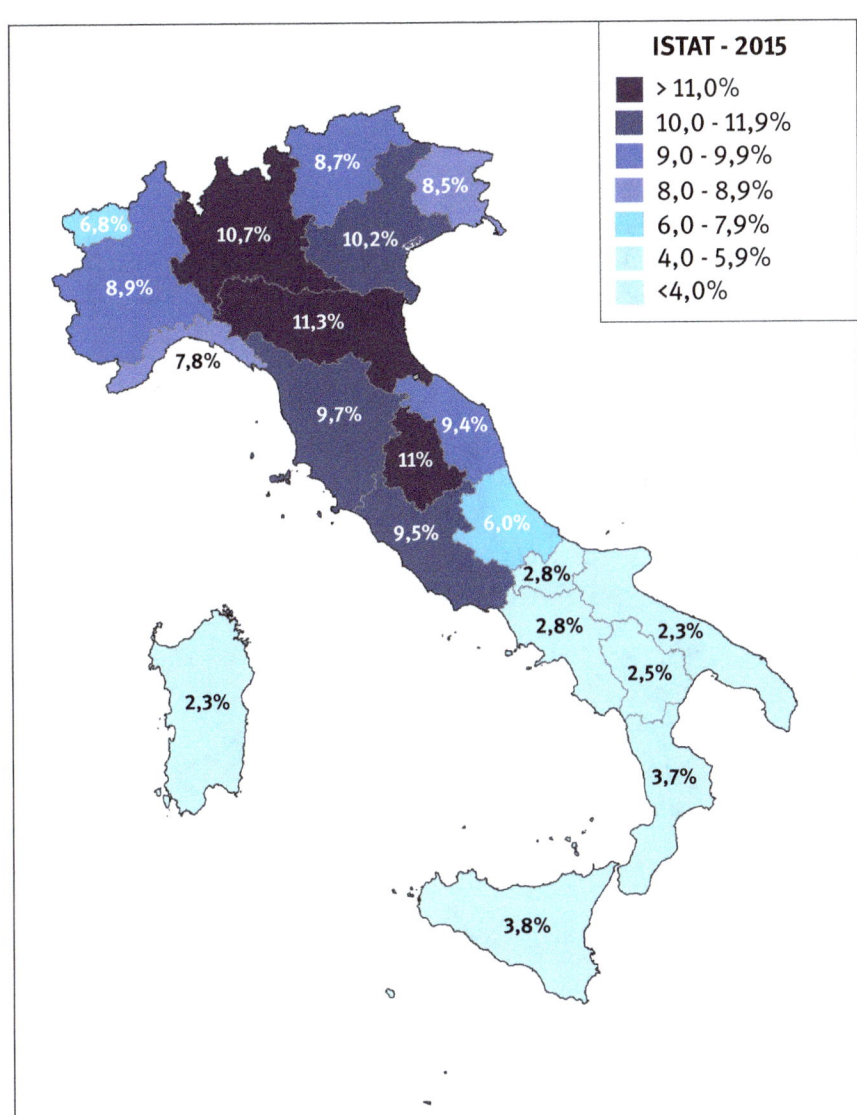

Figure 1: Foreign residents as a percentage of the regional population, data from latest Italian national census, 2011. www.istat.it (accessed on 18 January 2016).

As with overall immigration rates, the incidence of non Italian students is higher in the northern regions, and is especially high in Lombardy, where the number of foreign students tops 100,000, accounting for more than 20% of the total student population (see Figure 2 below).

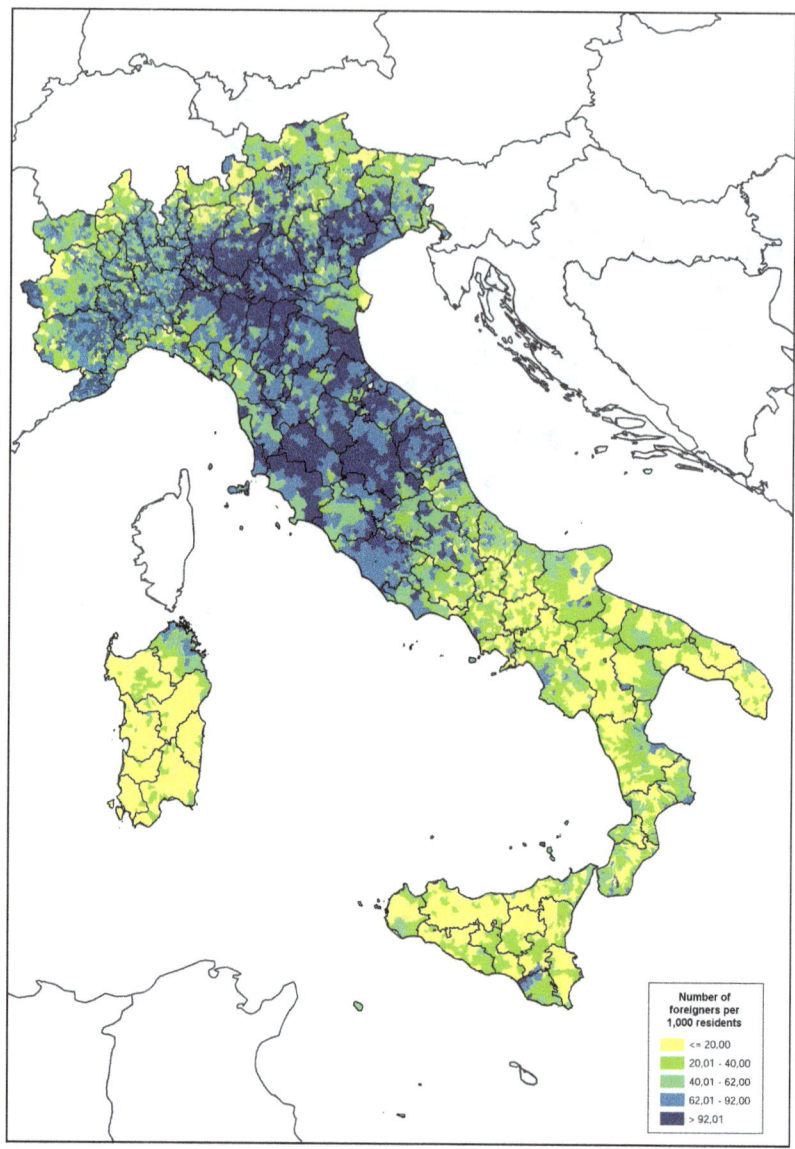

Figure 2: Percentage of non-Italian students over the total number of foreigners per 1,000 residents.[3]

---

[3] MIUR – Ufficio di Statistica (2014: 5).

Over 60% of Italian provinces (urban districts)[4] have at least one school where Italian students are now a minority. Considering that the overall number of schools in Italy tops 55,000, schools attended by a majority of students with an immigrant background remain an exception; even so, they are part of an emerging social phenomenon which cannot and should not be ignored. Of the immigrant groups present in the schools, Romanians are the largest group (19.2%), with Moroccans and Albanians vying for second place (13.6% and 12.4% respectively; MIUR – Ufficio di Statistica 2018: 29). Numerous other nationalities are represented, some of them displaying very localised concentrations (for instance, Chinese students concentrate in some Tuscan cities and in Milan).

In terms of distribution across age ranges, the presence of non-Italian students is highest in primary schools[5] (the first level of compulsory education) and decreases in more advanced education.

For what concerns higher-level secondary education (post-middle school and the first national assessment, which is administered to all students aged 14), the educational pathways of students with an immigrant background appear to be considerably more limited than those of their Italian counterparts. Faced with multiple high school options (for the first time in their educational career: up to middle schools all students study the same subjects in preparation for the first national assessment), students of immigrant background tend to converge (whether by choice or obeying more or less explicit teacher and/or family pressures) towards vocational courses rather than choosing longer and more challenging careers leading to high-school degrees granting access to university or higher paid occupations.[6] This represents an additional problem: on the one hand, students of immigrant background may not have access to the educational opportunities they deserve; and on the other, they often end up being over-represented in some schools, leading to the development of enclaves which may limit opportunities for meaningful integration with their peers and in society at large.

---

[4] There are 107 urban districts in Italy, 80 of which are provinces proper, with the remaining ones being metropolitan cities (14), town consortia (6), and autonomous provinces (2). Urban districts are administrative entities which are also in charge of education.

[5] http://demo.istat.it/ (accessed on 28 February 2014).

[6] In Italy, students are free to choose the high school they want to go to. In the last year of junior high school activities are carried out to help them identify the secondary school that is most suitable for them. At the end of such activities teachers also issue an official educational career advice, which students are under no obligation to follow. Of course, in addition to aspirations, there are many factors that contribute to students' choice, e.g. school performance, economic conditions, family orientation, cultural background, personal tastes and aspirations, etc.

2.2 Multilingualism and multiculturalism in Italian schools: Recent policy updates

The growing presence of school-age children and teenagers of immigrant background is having an increasing impact on the Italian school system. This phenomenon, albeit with its local peculiarities, is in line with similar developments in many countries around the world, where multilingual and multicultural classrooms are rapidly becoming the norm. While multilingualism and multiculturalism should not be conflated, they often co-occur, and more prominently so in environments which welcome recently immigrated children, such as schools. It is widely recognised that teachers' attitudes towards multiculturalism are crucial if culturally aware instruction is to be provided (Aragona-Young and Sawyer 2018). This is certainly a crucial aspect of contemporary education, and one which should be given greater consideration than it currently receives in many environments. However, for many in-service teachers the primary issue in the management of multilingual and multicultural classes is one of language competence, where by "language" is typically meant the official language of instruction, which, in most cases, is the mainstream variety of the country's official language.

Proficiency in the language of the host country remains a priority goal in education programmes targeted at children of immigrant origin. However, multilingual competences have started to receive greater attention of late, and the role of heritage languages in education has been the object of growing academic interest over the last few decades (see Trifonas and Aravossitas 2018). Academic attitudes towards heritage language instruction and multilingual classes have certainly changed over the decades. Back in 2000, Cummins highlighted the fact that bilingual children were "in the crossfire" in educational systems which all too often saw bilingualism as something to be eradicated; he argued for a transformative pedagogy capable of effectively challenging the roots of inequality (Cummins 2000). The call for the development of pedagogical methods and policies suited to "bridging the global and the local" (Gorter, Zenotz, and Cenoz 2014) has since gained momentum, but continues to prove difficult to implement (Liddicoat and Taylor-Leech 2015).

Italy is a latecomer to the debate, owing to its relatively recent immigration history. Only in the last couple of decades has the school population of immigrant background started to become sizeable, and to require that specific strategies be devised and implemented to favour the educational success of its members. The issue has been addressed first and foremost as one of integration. In 2006 the Ministry of Education, University and Research issued a new

Ministerial Memorandum entitled *Linee guida per l'accoglienza e l'integrazione degli alunni stranieri* [Guidelines for the reception and integration of foreign pupils] (MIUR 2006). In 2007 additional guidelines were issued entitled *La via italiana per la scuola interculturale e l'integrazione degli alunni stranieri* [The Italian way for an intercultural school and the integration of foreign students] (MIUR 2007), which highlighted intercultural education as the "integrating background" (i.e. a guiding principle or foundation) necessary in an increasingly plural society. No further documents outlining education-related policies were published in the following years, and the development and implementation of strategies of integration was left by and large to the initiative of individual schools.[7] It was not until 2014 that the Ministry of Education, University and Research issued a new set of guidelines entitled *Linee guida per l'accoglienza e l'integrazione di alunni stranieri* [Guidelines for the reception and integration of foreign students] (MIUR 2014). Announced on the European Commission website at the time of their publication (February 2014) as "the result of a long process of collecting and processing data and experiences",[8] at the time of writing the guidelines represent the latest and most up-to-date policy document issued by the Italian government on the topic.

In the 2014 document there is a clear attempt to foster an education culture where multilingualism and multiculturalism are seen as an asset and not only as a problem. International studies, experiences and instances of best practices are taken as a starting point for introducing policies which are more attentive to the needs of foreign students.

While the attainment of proficiency in Italian remains a key objective (cf. section 6 of the Guidelines), the document draws a distinction between different levels and types of linguistic competence. In particular, the Guidelines distinguish between Italian L2 for communication on the one hand, and Italian L2 as a medium to acquire discipline-specific contents (MIUR 2014: 16), emphasising that while the acquisition of the former is usually completed in a few months, for the latter several years may be needed and, more importantly, the involvement of the entire teacher team is required (with each and every teacher acting also as a facilitator). Moreover, the importance of peer interaction with

---

[7] Italy appears to have been lagging behind, compared to other contemporary democracies, on the topic of integration policies. According to the Multiculturalism Policy Index (http://www.queensu.ca/mcp/, accessed 15 October 2015), Italy scores very low, indicating a weak commitment to integration policy implementation.
[8] http://ec.europa.eu/ewsi/en/resources/detail.cfm?ID_ITEMS=40217 (accessed 12 March 2014).

Italian students is emphasised, thus taking a firm position against proposals advanced in the past of enrolling non-Italian students in "bridging classes" aimed exclusively at teaching them Italian.[9]

The Guidelines identify three separate phases in the development of linguistic competences:

- An initial stage, in which Italian is learnt for the purposes of communicating with peers and teachers. Specific instruction in Italian L2 is provided, more intensive at the beginning and gradually decreasing over the following months.
- A "bridging phase", where students must develop academic competences in the L2. This phase is defined in the guidelines as the "most delicate" one. The entire teaching team is involved, as students must consolidate their linguistic competences while acquiring discipline-specific contents.
- In the third stage the language issue remains in the background, but is no longer defined as a "problem". The strategies deployed by teachers to convey discipline specific contents will still entail elements of simplification and "facilitation", but they will no longer be specifically aimed at foreign students, focusing, instead, on mediating the inevitable heterogeneity of the class as a whole; under these circumstances, "il loro punto di vista diverso su un tema geografico, storico, economico, ecc., e la loro capacità metalinguistica, che nel frattempo ha avuto modo di allenarsi e che si è affinata, potranno essere potenti occasioni per introdurre uno sguardo interculturale" [their (of students with an immigrant background) different points of view on issues relating to geography, history, the economy etc., and the metalinguistic competences they will have meanwhile been able to develop and improve, will become powerful opportunities for the introduction of an intercultural perspective – our translation] (MIUR 2014: 18).

The activities to be implemented in order to achieve this latter objective are presented as a form of "pedagogical and didactic craftsmanship" ('artigianato pedagogico e didattico', MIUR 2014: 18), an expression which suitably describes the inevitable uniqueness of each and every situation.

Parallel to a more carefully orchestrated articulation of language teaching/learning objectives, greater attention to the multiple languages spoken by pupils

---

[9] A bill was introduced in 2008 to establish "bridging classes" for newly arrived immigrant students, but after a heated debate it was dropped. The issue is occasionally raised again locally, but so far it has not been brought back to Parliament for further discussion.

is also recommended, albeit without giving specific direction on how this could be done in practice. The guidelines insist that visibility should be given to all languages represented in any given school, explicitly following, in this, the recommendations contained in the 2010 *Guide for the development and implementation of curricula for plurilingual and intercultural education* (Beacco et al. 2010) issued by the Council of Europe (CoE), which is often quoted in the Italian guidelines. More specifically, the guidelines quote the Council of Europe document when referring to the universal right to quality education in the service, amongst other things, of the construction of individual and collective identities within a framework of greater social cohesion: "plurilingual and intercultural education realises the universal right to quality education, covering: acquisition of competences, knowledge, dispositions and attitudes, diversity of learning experiences, and construction of individual and collective cultural identities. Its aim is to make teaching more effective, and increase the contribution it makes, both to school success for the most vulnerable learners, and to social cohesion" (Beacco et al. 2010: 7).

In addition, the guidelines also quote the Council of Europe's wording when claiming that "to accommodate plurilingual and intercultural education, existing curricula may have to be modified substantially – but without abandoning the aims of the previous curriculum" (Beacco et al. 2010: 8), thereby emphasising continuity, as opposed to "revolution" in the school system. Thus, amongst the encouraged actions is the development of materials to be used in the reception phase of foreign students (multilingual information brochures and multimedia messages), but also the use of bilingual entry tests aimed at ascertaining the competences effectively achieved during their previous school career. A greater focus on academic language skills is also encouraged, as well as activities aimed at promoting multilingual language awareness (identification of loanwords, bilingual narratives, etc.). Besides these, the introduction in the curriculum of non-EU languages is also encouraged, with the establishment of courses aimed both at students having those languages as their mother tongues, and at Italian students.

The advice of the guidelines also covers final performance evaluation. In Italy, students undergo two national assessments: one at age 14, compulsory for all students, at the end of the junior high school, and one at the end of secondary education, which is taken only by those students who have opted for a full five-year course (shorter courses are also available in vocational schools).

For the first national assessment, the guidelines state that those pupils whose language competences are too limited to enable them to communicate effectively in Italian may be aided by teachers who speak their language, or by language mediators. Moreover, the guidelines envisage the possibility that foreign students may be given the opportunity to be taught certain subjects in their language of origin, in which case those subjects will be tested in the language used for their teaching.

For what concerns the national assessment at the end of secondary school, the guidelines insist that additional courses aimed at native language maintenance and consolidation carry specific credits[10] to be considered in the final assessment. Similarly, the inclusion of a language- and culture-specific perspective in students' projects should be given suitable weight.

Indirectly linked to the first national assessment is the topic of access to higher education after completing junior high, which is singled out for special attention in the guidelines. As highlighted above, after the first-level national assessment foreign students often tend to enrol in vocational education courses. This has led to a progressive "educational segregation" which the guidelines insist should be avoided at all costs. Among the causes of this trend, the sociocultural expectations of immigrant families obviously play a role. However, a component of bias on the part of teachers is also likely to be present, and should be the object of specific action. In particular, the guidelines lament the fact that foreign students, upon arrival, are frequently enrolled in lower classes than those they should be in and, in the following years, are often made to repeat the same school year. The guidelines warn that this is not only detrimental in terms of motivation and self-esteem, but may well be due to too much importance being given to linguistic factors which are not tackled suitably. Thus, students of immigrant background are first assessed on the basis of competences they cannot have (knowledge of Italian), and then held back by their failure to develop specific competences in Italian language academic skills. A greater focus on the development of academic Italian is therefore greatly encouraged.

The guidelines seem to be inspired by a genuine desire to favour both the social integration and the academic success of students of immigrant background. However, they do so in very general terms, and without providing practical indications as to how this could be achieved. They are, in other words, highly aspirational, but fall short of suggesting institutional pathways for the achievement of the ambitious goals set forth in the document.

---

10 These credits would contribute to the total amount of credits that secondary school pupils need to obtain in order to be admitted to the final exam.

3 Multilingualism and limited language proficiency in Milanese schools: Assessing needs and expectations

In the previous section we have provided a brief description of the principles set forth in the official documents. In order to find empirical evidence of how these principles are implemented in actual teaching practice, we took advantage of the relationship established with some schools in the Milan area thanks to a pilot project conducted by the University of Milan in collaboration with schools located in high-immigrant-density areas, and carried out a survey-based study of pedagogical policies. Before going on to discuss survey results, a brief description of the project is in order.

The project aims to devise ways of offering support to schools struggling to provide for the needs of pupils with limited language skills. The request for assistance came from the schools themselves, thus indicating that language proficiency and cultural issues were perceived as a question that went beyond the competence of teaching staff and required specialist intervention, primarily by involving language mediation experts. As a first step in the project, identifying teachers' perceptions and expectations was crucial, as the intervention of language mediation experts was to be included in classroom activities and they would be ultimately responsible for the successful integration of these interventions in the didactic process. As a result, it was essential that the involvement of the language mediators should first be negotiated with teachers, taking account of (and possibly constructively challenging) their expectations. The project envisaged an adaptive framework of classroom interventions, subject to progressive adjustments in response to dialogue with different stakeholders. The first stage of the project, when the survey was carried out, involved teachers, while consultation of pupils, families and mediators was planned for a further phase.

The project, launched in 2005 by the University of Milan in collaboration with the Regional School Office for Lombardy, aimed to encourage cooperation between the university and local schools by setting up work placement projects thanks to which university students would contribute to school activities focused on language development and cultural integration aimed at pupils of immigrant background. The students involved were enrolled in an undergraduate programme in Language Mediation and Intercultural Communication, majoring in two languages chosen amongst English, French, German, Spanish, Russian, Arabic, Chinese, Japanese and Hindi, and the relevant cultures. Some of them were foreign students (mainly speakers of Romanian, Albanian and Arabic). In

2013, 36 placements where arranged within the programme framework. The greatest majority of placements (30 out of 36) was in *istituti comprensivi*, i.e. institutions comprising all levels of education from pre-school to junior high school, up to age 14. Five placements were arranged in three separate high schools, one of them being a tech high school whose offer includes vocational courses, and one placement was in a pre-school.

Of the *istituti comprensivi* involved, two accounted for over a third of all placements. Both of them are located in Sesto San Giovanni, a town on the northern Milan border with a growing presence of immigrant families, and have been relying for some years now on university students for assistance with the language needs of their pupils. In most cases language mediation and facilitation needs were requested by the schools for schoolchildren of immigrant origin attending primary school (aged 6–10), though in some cases middle school students were also involved.

The data on which the analysis is based were collected by means of interviews, and were later critically analysed against the dual background, on the one hand, of the ministerial guidelines and, on the other, of the actual conditions under which teachers operate, with all the implications of the latter for the pupils involved.

As regards the interviews, preference was given to the semi-structured form, a type of interview often chosen in qualitative research in the social sciences in which, typically, "the researcher has a list of questions of series of topics they want to cover in the interview, an interview guide, but there is flexibility in how and when the questions are put and how the interviewee can respond" (Edwards and Holland 2013: 29). This form was chosen because semi-structured interviews "allow much more space for interviewees to answer on their own terms than structured interviews, but do provide some structure for comparison across interviewees in a study by covering the same topics, even in some instances using the same questions" (Edwards and Holland 2013: 29).

Our "interview guide" included a set of questions aimed at eliciting data concerning existing protocols, practices and issues in the schools concerned, and the attitudes of teaching staff and head teachers towards the needs of pupils of immigrant origins. Attention was also specifically given to the role of linguistic and cultural mediators within educational institutions, which was of special interest for us on account of the ongoing project. The topics dealt with are the following:
- School details
    - Type of school, size (number of students, number of staff)
    - Incidence of immigrant-background students and their characteristics (country of origin, educational background)

    – Immigrant-background students' knowledge of Italian
    – Their cultural displacement / integration
- Admission to the school
    – Preliminary problems with bureaucracy (understanding procedures, filling in forms)
    – Assessment procedure on admission
    – Assignment to class
- Immigrant-background students' educational record
    – Progress in school career
    – Progress in the acquisition of Italian
    – Integration within the peer group
    – Information – if available – on the employment record after leaving school
- Problems and measures to counter them
    – Main difficulties encountered by / with immigrant-background students
    – Main measures taken to overcome difficulties
    – Role of language and culture mediators
    – Immigrant-background students' attitude towards: measures to assist them, initiatives to familiarise them with the Italian culture, initiatives to help them maintain contacts with their cultures of origin

All these points were touched upon in all of the interviews, although in each case more attention was given to the issues that the interviewee considered more important and relevant to the situation of the school where s/he was working. In some cases, the interviewer probed answers, trying to gather as many details as possible on information introduced by the interviewee.

Amongst the interviews that we carried out, we have selected two which represent quite well – in the light of all testimonies collected – the specific challenges faced by schools up to junior high on the one hand, and vocational schools on the other. They are summarised and commented upon in sections 3.1 and 3.2, also taking account of the various elements that emerged in the other interviews which – for reasons of space – cannot be reported individually. Our own critical analysis and discussion follow in section 3.3.

3.1 Primary and junior high school

In this section, we outline the situation in primary and junior high schools relying in particular on the elements that emerged in the interview with the headmaster of a comprehensive school, which we consider to be especially representative as it comprises pre-school, primary and junior high school. Of the same institution, located in Sesto San Giovanni, we also interviewed the teacher in charge of the reception and integration of foreign and immigrant-background students in the junior high. All the general information relied on in the exposition (statistical data, procedures, narratives) was also provided by the head teacher and his staff.

The incidence of non-Italian students on the total pupil population of the school (which amounts to almost 600 children) is around 17%. The majority of them were born in Italy, or moved to Italy at a very young age. The interviewees agreed that for these students Italian is effectively a native or quasi-native language, and that they therefore require minimal intervention on the part of the institution.

Radically different is the situation of those students who arrive in Italy at an older age, i.e. above 11, having already been enrolled in school in their countries of origin. Leaving aside problems arising from the traumatic experiences many of them have undergone, the first obstacle they encounter when entering the Italian education system is their lack of language skills. Some of them arrive with no knowledge of Italian at all, making it especially difficult for teachers to communicate with them and for them to interact with both teachers and peers. These difficulties are compounded with a more general sense of displacement which often results in relational difficulties and a tendency to prefer isolation.

The first contact with immigrant students and their families is at enrolment. Foreign language versions of the enrolment form are available at the school, and are especially useful for users of languages such as Chinese and Arabic. Immediately after enrolment, students are assessed for their language skills (more rarely for their competences in other subjects, primarily maths). This often results in them being assigned to a class lower than the one they should belong to by virtue of their age. When students are borderline between primary and junior high school, preference is given to their enrolment in the last year of primary school, so as to enable them to acquire suitable language skills before they enter further, more linguistically demanding stages of education.

The interviewees confirmed that it is therefore quite frequent for foreign students to be slightly delayed at entry level; they also stressed, however, that these students do not tend to accumulate any further delay in later years. The school policy discourages repetition, in the conviction that motivation and self-esteem are to be safeguarded. This was a point our informants insisted on. However, they also pointed out that such a choice has a potential downside, as by the time these students of immigrant background leave junior high school they may not have had enough time to acquire the same competences as their Italian counterparts. In turn, this is likely to have an impact on their future education, as their actual competences are only partly suitable for higher-level studies. While not being categorical about the inadequacy of such competences, and admitting that in some cases the language gap had been filled by the time these students left junior high school, the informants were pessimistic about the general achievability of competences in Italian suited to the type of study required in most high schools. In particular, students of immigrant background who were born or moved to Italy at a very young age usually have a better chance of doing well at school than students who arrived in Italy later in their childhood. The informants also emphasised the fact that the students with an immigrant background who are not hindered by linguistic deficit are well-positioned to do well because they, and especially their families, often are highly motivated and eager to succeed. Cases of students obtaining top marks in the national assessment exam (*esame di maturità*) are increasingly frequent, as are those of students that enrol in high schools with a view to having access to tertiary education. The local high school has been registering a growing number of foreign students' enrolments (as high as 30% of the total immigrant student population), and the trend is likely to continue in the future.

The interviewees self-reported a strong commitment, which they extended to the school as a whole, to the integration of immigrant-background students. The headmaster insisted on the initiatives undertaken to help newly arrived students overcome their difficulties. Chief among these, he claimed, are the language barriers which impede the pupils' interaction with their peers and with the teachers. In order to overcome these barriers, the school offered work placements to university students enrolled in language mediation courses, but also explored all avenues to enlist the help of professional language mediators. In 2013–2014, when this study was conducted, the school had the opportunity to use the services of two language mediators provided by a local cooperative and paid with European funds. The experience was precious for teachers and students alike. Having the opportunity to communicate through an interpreter enabled the pupils involved (one from China and one from Ukraine) to successfully tackle the first challenging weeks. Gradually the support was withdrawn (due to limited funding), but in the meantime the students had been able to overcome their initial difficulties.

The two language mediators hired (both of them native speakers of the languages concerned) were also enlisted as facilitators in activities targeted at the whole class and aimed at fostering awareness of and interest for the new students' countries and cultures of origins. According to the informants, these activities were much appreciated by both Italian and immigrant students; in particular, the latter appeared to have benefited from the status assigned to their culture and language by virtue of it being given pride of place in the classroom.

While the narrative of success prevailed in the first part of the interview, the two informants also highlighted some unexpected difficulties. When describing a set of cultural awareness raising initiatives where students of immigrant background were due to be given prominent roles, they reported ambivalent attitudes. Immigrant students were often reluctant to become involved in such activities, declining to participate. This reluctance extended also to individual projects, which they rarely choose to conduct on topics related to their countries of origin.

The informants lamented the students' unwillingness to display their cultural background and heritage, but at the same time also appeared to view unfavourably the attempts on the part of the students' families to maintain the bond with the country of origin by promoting literacy in the heritage language. Some children – most notably those coming from North African countries – receive additional formal schooling in their language of origin: many of them, the informants reported, go to Arab schools over the weekend, where they not only learn to read and write but also complete the regular school curriculum of their countries of origin. Italian teachers, however, have mixed feelings about this, as they believe it interferes with the students' performance at the Italian school, especially where writing is concerned, due to the different conventions used. While this belief does not appear to have been tested against the children's performance, it seems to be fairly ingrained in the respondents: they did not report openly discouraging the practice, but they did appear to feel rather strongly against it, repeatedly suggesting that it is detrimental to the students' performance in the Italian school.

Insistently over the interview, the informants raised the issue of Italian language proficiency. While not discounting the students' chances to achieve a competence high enough to enable successful integration in society, and reasonable academic success at school, they often lamented the lack of institutionalised linguistic support and confirmed the importance of the assistance of interpreters/facilitators during and beyond the reception phase. They therefore highlighted the need for specialised interpreters with a good knowledge of school syllabi and objectives, as well as with an ability to empathically relate to both students and families. The importance of language mediation was highlighted throughout the interview, and while it was understood that in time the need for such mediation would gradually decrease, the presence of specialised personnel capable of bridging the language gap was advocated as a necessary means to improve the chances of academic success of students of immigrant background.

3.2 Secondary schools

The second interview we present provides insights into the linguistic situation at secondary school level.

The headmaster we interviewed directs a vocational high school with specialisms in business and enterprise, and in tourism. Relying on data sourced from the Ministry of Education, University and Research, he answered our first question illustrating the distinctive characteristics of vocational high schools (*scuole professionali*) in the Italian educational system. These schools accounted for 13.6% of all new high school students in 2015, a relatively small percentage compared to high schools leading to tertiary education (*licei*), which accounted for 54.4%, and technical high schools (*istituti tecnici*), which covered the remaining 32% (MIUR – Ufficio di statistica, 2015: 16). In the Italian system, all types of high school, if attended for a full 5-year course, award certificates which grant access to university, at least in theory. De facto, however, while 80% of students attending a *liceo* will then go to university, the percentage drops to 30% for students of *istituti tecnici* and is as low as 10% for those coming from a *professionale*. The disparity in aspirational potential across the three types of school is visible from the very outset, at the time of enrolment: the majority of the students who achieve a pass grade in the national examination at age 14 enrol in a professional school (44.1% of all students graduating with a pass grade), while 90% of those who graduate with a top mark enrol in a *liceo*. The statistics of the Ministry of Education show that on average students of immigrant background rank below their Italian counterparts in the national examination. While the difference is not dramatic, according to our interviewee it is enough to account, statistically, for their over-representation in vocational schools compared to the other types of high school.

The Istituto Polo Morignoni is one such vocational school. It comprises two schools set in two different areas of the city both with a high percentage of immigrant population, and offers regular upper secondary five-year courses leading to the *esame di maturità* (the national assessment exam, equivalent to the A levels) granting access to higher education, as well as 3- and 4-year vocational courses providing mainly practical training for work. It has about 1,000 pupils, 66% of whom are of immigrant background; 20% of them were born in other countries and migrated to Italy during their lifetime. The most numerous nationalities are Chinese, various South American countries (mainly Peruvians and Ecuadorians), Filipinos and East Europeans (Romanians, Albanians, Russians, Ukrainians), and fewer students from a number of other countries, African and Asian.

According to the headmaster, students who were born in Italy from immigrant parents are fairly fluent in Italian. Many of them, however, do not fully master academic Italian. For students who came to Italy more recently after some schooling in their countries of origin, the use of Italian is a challenge, even more so for newly arrived teenagers who in some cases only know the Italian they have studied on their own while preparing for immigration for family reunification. In a number of cases – the informant reported – language problems are compounded by recent trauma. In 2013–2014, out of the 120 students that enrolled in the first class, 15 had just arrived in the country by immigrant boats. For these students, participating in school activities could be very challenging due to their linguistic isolation, particularly when their mother tongue was shared with no other students in the class. It is in cases like this, lamented the head teacher, that the need for language mediators is most notable. Not being able to count on the help of specialists to overcome the language barrier puts additional pressure on both the school and the students.

A special committee has been set up in the school to take care of assigning students to classes and providing assistance in all cases that are deemed to require it. Second-generation students are mainly assigned to classes on the basis of their age, but in some cases those who have an inadequate command of Italian are assigned to a lower class. This policy is adopted in the conviction that being exposed to less challenging academic contents may enable students to develop their confidence while they learn Italian. To the same end, formal academic assessment is postponed for these students until the end of the first school year they attend. This grace period sometimes extends until the end of the second year. This practice aims to prevent students from dropping out. In terms of academic performance, our informant reported that the overall results of students of immigrant background are very uneven, with motivation as the crucial factor determining academic performance. Inadequate command of Italian, sometimes amounting to total lack of knowledge, can be obviated in a relatively short time if the student is keen on learning and works hard. Occasionally there have been cases of students starting out with no knowledge of the language that have passed their final exam with flying colours. According to the headmaster, this confirms that in line of principle there are no impediments to the academic success of students from an immigrant background. He insisted on this point, which challenges the widespread narrative, common in some circles, that students with an immigrant background are destined to be underachievers.

In order to enhance the students' chances of academic success, the school provides linguistic support for enrolled pupils who do not speak Italian at all or are limited users of the language, in the form of extra-curricular courses of 60 hours which are only partially financed by the local authorities (Provincia di Milano) and partly generously offered pro bono by teachers of Italian. This type of language instruction, however, is only delivered to students who are deemed by the school committee to be especially needy. For all the others, even when Italian (especially academic Italian) does remain a challenge for them, no extra tuition is available. Some help is offered by their teachers of Italian, but this is done in the course of regular classes, often to the detriment – the informant laments – of disciplinary instruction.

While the concern for adequate command of Italian is prevalent in the headmaster's narrative, he also mentioned, somewhat surprisingly for us, the importance for students of immigrant background to preserve their heritage languages. Such preservation might be difficult for unaccompanied minors, who do not have a strong social network to rely on. In the past, there were some mediators for the most widely represented languages to offer help with Italian and provide assistance in the preservation of the pupils' mother tongues. They also had the task of translating the most important documents, memoranda, routine communications, into the foreign languages for the students and their families. Our informant expressed regret for the fact that the presence of mediators had been discontinued for budgetary reasons, but was hopeful, at the same time, that the *Mediatori a scuola* [Language mediators in schools] project could provide the opportunity to re-introduce some of these support services.

Referring to the role of language and culture mediators at school, he mentioned that their collaboration would also be useful to introduce activities aimed at intercultural awareness-raising as he considered such activities essential in the diverse social setting of this kind of school in order to foster a sense of community and collaboration among learners who come from so many different backgrounds. He also reported that consistent efforts are made to start a dialogue going, with ad hoc activities aimed at intercultural acquaintance, some of which are planned within the Italian, History and Geography lessons (*Lettere*) with role plays and discussions, while others are more formally organised outside curricular hours, the most interesting being a film club, i.e. the showing of movies from the pupils' different countries of origin, chosen by the students themselves, followed by a moderated discussion. However, the lack of specialised staff with adequate competences, also of a linguistic kind, was perceived by the informant as a shortcoming which to some extent compromised the efforts being made.

The topic of language mediation was raised again with reference to the need to foster a truly multicultural approach, and the importance of preserving the students' heritage languages was mentioned time and again. The headmaster re-iterated that the school would be more than willing to offer curricular teaching in the languages of origin, but this is not possible, first of all because there are so many different languages. And even if some of the languages were selected for teaching, no funding is available to hire teachers. Something, he argued, could be done using mediators instead of teachers. This, of course, would require that the mediators hired should be highly qualified, having been trained in ad hoc university courses.

While our informant's observations were based on his experience of the problems in the educational institution he was responsible for, he did suggest that his was by no means an isolated experience. He referred to informal networks of head teachers who share experiences and attempt to find common solutions. His narrative pointed to the conclusion that multilingualism and multiculturalism are widespread in some areas of Italy, and in particular in the large urban areas. In comparison with the information gathered from lower high school informants, it appeared that high schools could count on a lesser degree of institutional support from governmental or local bodies. The formal provision of support to limited users of Italian is felt to be inadequate, so much is left to the educational staff's initiative and generosity. This applies to all immigrant languages, also those that are included amongst the languages of the Union (e.g. Romanian, Bulgarian, Slovene, etc.).

3.3 Discussion

The interviews with teaching staff and headmasters provide illuminating insights into their views and attitudes towards students of immigrant background. One aspect which emerged clearly from the interviews is their educational staff's dedication to the students in their care. The social integration and academic success of these students is a key priority which is pursued with relentless energy despite what they frequently refer to as a dramatic shortage of resources and a degree of indifference on the part of the institutions.

At all levels of education, linguistic and cultural integration are actively pursued by all those involved in the didactic process (teaching staff, head teachers). The acquisition of language proficiency in Italian is perceived as a key priority, and indeed as the deciding factor for academic success and beyond. This emerged especially when talking about junior high school students: our informants explicitly mentioned lack of suitable competences in academic Italian (as opposed to conversational Italian) as the single most significant factor in limiting students' choices of high school, which is generally believed to be a good predictor of socio-economic success. Indeed, from the interviews we gathered that students' proficiency in Italian weighs heavily in the career advice that teachers are prepared to give them. On more than one occasion the high school teachers interviewed said that the school would routinely issue students with advice to enrol in schools which are perceived to be less challenging, such as vocational courses. The informants did acknowledge that at least some of these students had a high potential for academic success, but feared that language difficulties would result in frustration and eventually dropout. Students who had been issued career advice for *liceo* – the kind of high school leading to tertiary education – were mentioned as rare exceptions. Teachers were very proud of them, hopeful and to an extent fairly confident that such cases would increase, but viewed them as rather extraordinary.

It is probably because of the importance attributed to language proficiency for future academic success that our junior high school informants were especially keen to enlist the help of language mediators and facilitators for the purposes of Italian literacy improvement. While showing genuine interest in and commitment to accepting and even promoting immigrant students' cultural backgrounds, they were much more reluctant to accept what might be defined as their language rights. Indeed, families' attempt to foster literacy in the heritage language were seen as in competition with the achievement of academic success in the Italian school, and in particular as detrimental to the development of academic Italian skills. This suggests an ambivalent attitude towards the acceptance of diversity: while cultural diversity is welcomed, linguistic diversity is often framed as a problem. The fact that junior high school is the stage in education where the future education path of students is decided may play a role: teachers feel responsible for equipping students of immigrant background with the tools required to successfully face the challenges posed by high schools. One aspect that struck us as relevant is that the schools did not appear to have any protocols in place to liaise with the later levels of education. While the passage from primary school to junior high school is carefully orchestrated in Italy (thanks to fact that in the vast majority of cases local primary and junior high schools share the same head teacher), there seems to be an abrupt break between junior high and high school which goes to the detriment of students of immigrant background.

This scenario accounts for the view our primary and junior high informants had of language mediators: they essentially saw them as tools to establish meaningful relationships with children with limited Italian, and later as helpers in the attainment of language proficiency. While far from forfeiting their responsibilities as teachers, our informants repeatedly declared that they lacked expert staff. This suggests that they tend to separate language learning from the acquisition of disciplinary competences. To an extent, this is in line with the ministerial guidelines, which envisages dedicated language instruction in the first stage of the students' school attendance. But lack of resources often prevents the evolution envisaged by the guidelines.

The interview with the high school headmaster painted a picture that had both points of contact and of divergence with the ones emerging from the interviews with primary and high school informants. He made a clear distinction between students of immigrant background who had arrived in Italy early in their childhood, and students of recent immigration. This distinction was also made by the primary and junior high respondents; but at high school level it appeared to be of greater concern, and to have a greater impact on the approach taken by the school in managing diversity. Longtime residents' command of Italian is adequate to social interaction, but it is often unsuitable for academic tasks, and therefore would require specific action. On the other hand, for students of recent immigration the language barrier causes a serious hindrance, needing the help of trained mediators to ensure gradual integration and progressive participation. Vis-à-vis this complex picture, the school's approach to teaching and especially assessment, in particular for students of recent immigration, appear to be a very nurturing one, with assessment delayed until the students are ready to face it with reasonable chances of success.

A substantial difference that emerged between lower level schools and high school was the attitude towards heritage languages. While primary and junior high school informants seemed to be ambivalent towards heritage language (and especially literacy) skills, the high school headmaster expressed a strong conviction that such skills had to be preserved and supported. This meant subscribing to a dual perspective on language competences – the perceived need to help students improve academic Italian skills and at the same time to encourage heritage language maintenance as part of their identity building, a task which faces various hurdles, first and foremost the of lack of resources – most notably in the form of specialised language mediators.

The difference in approach between informants working respectively in lower level and in high schools may be due, at least partly, to the different stages of identity building characterising pupils in the two different contexts. Identity issues may be of greater importance in young adults as opposed to children, although we had no means to test whether the informants' opinions on this point was due to pre-existing beliefs or observation of students' behaviour.

Our survey was conducted with a view to identifying the attitudes of teaching staff and head teachers in different grades of school towards children/young adults of immigrant background, and their perceived needs of such children and young adults, with a view to coordinating the intervention of language and culture mediators in the schools. Our finding suggested that in all cases head teachers were fairly confident that they could organise cultural integration activities, but they felt they needed the help of mediators to bridge the language gap, both for the purposes of social integration and – more prominently – in order to foster language skills in the language of the host country, with special regard to academic language skills. In high school, a pro-active approach language maintenance was also viewed favourably.

While having many points in common, the attitudes we detected suggest slightly different conceptualisations of the preferred form of integration on the part of our informants. At primary / junior high school level our informants seemed to advocate a form of acculturation of immigrant children closer to the assimilation end in Berry's acculturation theory (1997), i.e. one in which children identify primarily with the host culture (even though acceptance of their different cultural background is emphasised). At high school level, the approach seemed to favour what Berry (1997: 10) calls "integration", which involves simultaneous identification with the culture of origin and the host culture.

The practices enacted to foster the preferred forms of integration in the two levels of education investigated match, ideally at least, the progressive steps envisaged by the guidelines issued by the Ministry of Education in 2014. At high school level, they also embrace the valorisation of the heritage language promoted by the official documents – again, at least in theoretical terms. It does not appear, however, that the adoption of such practices started after the publication of the guidelines; rather, they seem to have developed independently, and on the basis of the schools' practical experience.

All informants confirmed that schools are ill-equipped to deal with the needs of students of immigrant origin. They also clearly stated that they view the expert intervention of language mediators as key to the successful pursuit of both social integration/identity building and academic achievement goals. While they did not appear to be concerned about the need to raise intercultural awareness among the teachers (which was taken for granted), they worried about the language gap, and prioritised it over other types of concerns.

4 Conclusions

This research is a first step in the process of designing suitable strategies to help students of immigrant background to fully develop their potential. Its findings are only preliminary, as they are based exclusively on views and perceptions of service providers, i.e. teaching staff and head teachers, but not on those of other key stakeholders – crucially, the students and their families. This is of course an issue which will have to be addressed in the future. Greater involvement of all stakeholders is fundamental for the devising of practices which meet the expectations of all the parties involved. It is important that language mediators are also considered because these professionals are on the frontline of school integration. In our project, interviews with these stakeholders were planned for a later stage, as it was felt that asking students and their families for their opinions might give more useful results if they could be asked to evaluate existing practices. Similarly, it was deemed more useful to interview language mediators once they had had some practical experience of the way in which their professional skills could be best put to use.

The involvement of all stakeholders in the finding of solutions for the increasingly acute problem of assisting and integrating immigrant background students into the education system is a crucial problem also for the country itself. Italy's relatively recent history of immigration means that the active participation of stakeholders' groups is only starting to be promoted, primarily because in many cases they still lack sufficient political weight. Hopefully this will change in the near future, and give way to practices emerging from the negotiation of perceived needs on the part of all parties involved.

This study also has other implications. In particular, it exposes the gap in national legislation regarding the protection of minority rights, first and foremost minority languages. As highlighted from the outset, the Italian legislation does feature specific provisions regarding national minority languages. Law 482/1999, which was long overdue, contains measures aimed at maintaining them in good health and offering regular compulsory and/or optional teaching in those languages in public schools. The introduction of this statute can be seen a sign of good will, in spite of the polemics regarding the choice of the languages to be protected.

But in the state of evolution that already characterised the linguistic situation at the turn of the millennium, with a constant increase in the number of speakers of other languages and in the number of other languages spoken due to immigration, the measures laid down in Law 482/1999 seem largely inadequate. Passed at a time when migration flows were already changing the Italian linguistic scenario profoundly, that Statute was looking backward rather than forward. Not only did it exclude the so-called "diffuse languages" like Romani, but also ignored the immigrant languages that were already spreading in Italian society, and have continued to spread ever since.

As a result of this shortsighted policy, today in Italy there are urgent linguistic needs that are catered for neither in the school system nor in any other institutional contexts. In the school system this shortcoming is felt in a particularly acute manner – as the results of this preliminary investigation confirm, broadly matching the findings of existing reports on the impact of immigration-led changing demographics on the school system.

In primary and junior high schools the integration of foreign students is a burning issue. Our research suggests that the schools analysed invest plenty of energies in devising – often under conditions of what has been aptly termed "craftsmanship" – ways to help their students integrate both socially and academically. These activities, however, are clearly underfunded, and too often rely on the initiative of the individual school, frequently in combination with other partners on the territory. Nonetheless, they have been instrumental in setting up forms of academic support from which young students from immigrant background have clearly benefited. On the basis of more general information gathered from teachers and head teachers in the course of the interviews, there are reasons to believe that the findings reflect widespread situations and policies, at least in the Milan area.

As regards upper secondary and vocational schools, although in some areas of Italy, and in particular in the large urban areas, at this educational level there is a high degree of multilingualism entailing a whole range of important pedagogical issues, institutions seem to be much less keen to help than in the lower levels of schooling. Linguistic assistance to non-Italian students and the promotion of multilingualism are grossly underfunded, if funded at all, and much is left to the good will of the teaching staff and the head teacher.

It is evident that multilingualism in Italy is a much more massive phenomenon than is officially acknowledged in legislation. It is to be hoped that catering to newly emerged linguistic needs and assisting speakers of "other" languages within the school system will be put at the top of relevant institutions' agenda, although it seems clear that for the time being possible solutions can be found on a local level, while ad hoc legislative measures are unlikely to be introduced any time in the foreseeable future. In the meantime the grand principles set forth in the official documents would largely remain a dead letter or wishful thinking, were it not for the initiative and the proactive efforts of individuals working in schools, who really care for the future of the students that are entrusted to them.

References

Aragona-Young, Emily & Brook E. Sawyer. 2018. Elementary teachers' beliefs about multicultural education practices. *Teachers and Teaching* 24 (5). 465–486.

Barni, Monica. 2008. Mapping immigrant languages in Italy. In Monica Barni & Guus Extra (eds.), *Mapping linguistic diversity in multicultural contexts*, 217–242. Berlin: Mouton De Gruyter.

Beacco, Jean-Claude, Michael Byram, Marisa Cavalli, Daniel Coste, Mirjam Egli Cuenat, Francis Goullier & Johanna Panthier. 2010. *Guide for the development and implementation of curricula for plurilingual and intercultural education*. Strasbourg: Council of Europe, Directorate of Education and Languages.

Berry, Jon W. 1997. Immigration, acculturation, and adaptation. *Applied Psychology* 46. 5–34.
Commission of the European Communities. 2008. *Green paper. Migration & mobility: Challenges and opportunities for EU education systems*. {SEC(2008) 2173}. http://eur-lex.europa.eu/LexUriServ/LexUriServ.do?uri=COM:2008:0423:FIN:EN:PDF (accessed 28 May 2019).
Commission of the European Communities. 2011. *Civil society platform on multilingualism: Policy recommendations for the promotion of multilingualism in the European Union by the Civil Society Platform*. http://ec.europa.eu/languages/information/documents/report-civil-society_en.pdf (accessed 28 May 2019).
Cummins, James. 2000. *Language, power, and pedagogy*. Bristol: Multilingual Matters.
De Mauro, Tullio. 1994. *Come parlano gli italiani*. Firenze: La Nuova Italia.
Edwards, Rosalind & Janet Holland. 2013. *What is qualitative interviewing?* London: Bloomsbury Academic.
European Parliament. 2005. *European Parliament resolution on the protection of minorities and anti-discrimination policies in an enlarged Europe* (2005/2008(INI)). http://eur-lex.europa.eu/LexUriServ/LexUriServ.do?uri=OJ:C:2006:124E:0405:0415:EN:PDF (accessed 28 May 2019).
Extra, Guus & Kutlay Yağmur. 2012. *Language rich Europe: Trends in policies and practices for multilingualism in Europe*. Cambridge: Cambridge University Press.
Gogolin, Ingrid. 2002. *Linguistic diversity and new minorities in Europe. Guide for the development of language education policies in Europe: From linguistic diversity to plurilingual education*. Strasbourg: Council of Europe, Language Policy Division, Directorate of School, Out-of-School and Higher Education, DGIV.
Gorter, Durk, Victoria Zenotz & Jasone Cenoz (eds.). 2014. Minority languages and multilingual education: Bridging the local and the global. Dordrecht, Heidelberg, New York & London: Springer.
ISTAT. 2015. *Bilancio demografico nazionale. Anno 2014*. https://www.istat.it/it/files/2015/06/Bilanciodemografico.pdf?title=Bilancio+demografico+nazionale+-+15%2Fgiu%2F2015+-+Testo+integrale.pdf (accessed 28 May 2019).
Krzyżanowski, Michał. 2010. *The discursive construction of European identities: A multilevel approach to discourse and identity in the transforming European Union*. Frankfurt am Main, Berlin, Bern, Bruxelles, New York, Oxford & Wien: Peter Lang.
Krzyżanowski, Michał & Ruth Wodak. 2011. Political strategies and language policies: The European Union Lisbon strategy and its implication for the EU's language and multilingualism policy. *Language Policy* 10 (2). 115–136.
Liddicoat, Anthony J. & Kerry Taylor-Leech. 2015. Multilingual education: The role of language ideologies and attitudes, *Current Issues in Language Planning* 16 (1–2). 1–7.
Maraschio, Nicoletta & Cecilia Robustelli. 2011. Minoranze linguistiche: La situazione in Italia. In Gerhard Stickel (ed.), *National, regional and minority languages in Europe*, 73–80. Frankfurt am Main, Berlin, Bern, Bruxelles, New York, Oxford & Wien: Peter Lang.
MIUR. 2006. *Linee guida per l'accoglienza e l'integrazione degli alunni stranieri*. C.M. n. 24, 1 March 2006. Roma: Ministero dell'Istruzione, Università e Ricerca. https://archivio.pubblica.istruzione.it/normativa/2006/cm24_06.shtml (accessed 28 May 2019).
MIUR. 2007. *La via italiana per la scuola interculturale e l'integrazione degli alunni stranieri*. Roma: Ministero dell'Istruzione, Università e Ricerca. https://archivio.pubblica.istruzione.it/news/2007/allegati/pubblicazione_intercultura.pdf (accessed 28 May 2019).

MIUR. 2014. *Linee guida per l'accoglienza e l'integrazione degli alunni stranieri*. Roma: Ministero dell'Istruzione, Università e Ricerca. http://www.istruzione.it/allegati/2014/linee_guida_integrazione_alunni_stranieri.pdf (accessed 28 May 2019).
MIUR – Ufficio di Statistica. 2014. *Gli alunni stranieri nel sistema scolastico italiano a.s. 2013/2014*. http://www.istruzione.it/allegati/2014/Notiziario_Stranieri_13_14.pdf (accessed 28 May 2019).
MIUR – Ufficio di statistica. 2015. Focus "Esiti dell'esame di Stato e degli scrutini nella scuola secondaria di I grado" A.S. 2014/2015. http://www.istruzione.it/allegati/2015/Focus%20scrutini%20I%20grado%20a.s.%202014-15.pdf (accessed 28 May 2019).
MIUR – Ufficio di statistica. 2018. Gli alunni con cittadinanza non italiana A.S. 2016/2017. https://www.miur.gov.it/documents/20182/0/FOCUS+16-17_Studenti+non+italiani/be4e2dc4-d81d-4621-9e5a-848f1f8609b3?version=1.0 (accessed 28 May 2019).
Moore, Robert. 2011. Standardisation, diversity and enlightenment in the contemporary crisis of EU language policy. *Working Papers in Urban Language and Literacy* 74. London: King's College.
Nic Shuibhne, Niamh. 2004. Does the draft EU constitution contain a language policy? Paper presented at the II Mercator International Symposium, Europe 2004: A new framework for all languages? http://www.ciemen.org/mercator/pdf/simp-shuibhne.pdf (accessed 4 March 2014).
Ongini, Vinicio & Mariagrazia Santagati. 2013. Alunni con cittadinanza non italiana. Approfondimenti ed analisi. *Quaderni ISMU* 1. Milano: Fondazione ISMU.
Parlamento Italiano. 1999. *Legge 15 dicembre 1999, n. 482. Norme in materia di tutela delle minoranze linguistiche storiche*. http://www.camera.it/parlam/leggi/99482l.htm (accessed 28 May 2019).
Pellegrini, Giovanni Battista. 1977. *Carta dei dialetti d'Italia*. Pisa: Pacini.
Romaine, Suzanne. 2013. Politics and policies of promoting multilingualism in the European Union. *Language Policy* 12. 115–137.
Telmon, Tullio. 2006. La sociolinguistica e le leggi di tutela delle minoranze linguistiche. *LIDI-Lingue e idiomi d'Italia* I (1). 38–52.
Trifonas, Peter Pericles & Themistoklis Aravossitas. 2018. Heritage and language: Cultural diversity and education. In Peter Pericles Trifonas & Themistoklis Aravossitas (eds.), *Handbook of research and practice in heritage language education*, 3–26. Dordrecht, Heidelberg, New York, London: Springer.
Wodak, Ruth. 2008. "Communicating Europe": Analyzing, interpreting, and understanding multilingualism and the discursive construction of transnational identities. *Studies in Greek linguistics: Proceedings of the annual meeting of the Department of Linguistics, School of Philology, Aristotle University of Thessaloniki. 28 edn., 21–22 April 2007*, 57–88. Thessaloniki: University of Thessaloniki.

Part 2: **Responses to multilingual challenges in the field of societal practices**

Stef Slembrouck
3 Rescaling the problem of language difference: Some observations for policy and practice of language support in an era of globalisation

Abstract: This Chapter addresses the relevance of TimeSpace-scale analysis and scaled decision-making for understanding and shaping the distribution and allocation of linguistic strategies and resources when forms of language support are organisationally and interactionally made available in institutional and professional contexts of service provision. Contemporary conditions of immigration-affected multilingualism have put in the foreground questions of language, activity and space, in ways which challenge more traditional frameworks which view multilingualism exclusively as properties of individual speakers and of communities of speakers of the same language (entities defined by ethnicity and/or nationality). An alternative framework puts equal emphasis on the organisational and interactionally-manifest distribution of linguistic resources in and across particular spaces and activities, as well as on how enacted strategies depend on the context-sensitive affordances of particular spaces and activities. At the same time, it is demonstrated how sociolinguistic scales interact with language ideological assumptions about language, community membership, institutional identity and instrumental reliability. The Chapter builds further on the results of two empirical studies conducted in the Flemish-Belgian context of heightened (sub)urban multilingualism following successive immigration waves since the 1960s. Taken together, the two studies provide strong evidence for the interpretative relevance of "scale", as an explicit and reflexive "tool" when engaging with contexts where policy has to demonstrate flexibility and context-sensitivity. "Rescaling" thus provides a purposeful metaphor for formulating directions for multilingual capacity building. The Chapter concludes with a discussion of a set of "scaled" policy recommendations.

Stef Slembrouck, University of Ghent, Department of Linguistics, Faculty of Arts and Philosophy, Blandijnberg 2, Ghent, Belgium.

https://doi.org/10.1515/9781501503207-004

1 Introduction

One can begin this Chapter with a somewhat provocative question: Why might one hesitate to continue to treat interpreting as a separate field of study? I must add here straight away that the answer to this question is not a matter of professional or disciplinary autonomy. I do not wish to doubt whether interpreting counts as a separate vocation with very specific professional requirements and its study as a legitimate area of linguistic enquiry. Answering the question is more a matter of how one responds to the complex communicative demands that have emerged as a result of the spread of globalisation-affected multilingualism and the unprecedented rise in the salience of situated language difference which has accompanied it. As a matter of fact, the point about situating "interpreting studies" today is arguably mirrored in that of locating "professional discourse studies". Until 1990, it was quite possible to study the interaction between professionals or institutional service providers and clients from within a monolingual paradigm. Since then, multilingualism and its range of possible manifestations have become part of the picture, cross-nationally, to an extent that today it is quasi impossible to claim representativeness in, say, a study of doctor-patient interaction in most urban contexts without embracing the mix of monolingual and multilingual practices characteristic of it. Note how "language difference" has come to play an important role in both types. It has been highlighted for apparently "monolingual encounters" in research which focuses on health care encounters with patients who have limited knowledge and use of the locally dominant language (Roberts, Sarangi, and Moss 2004; Roberts et al. 2005). Similarly, community interpreting[1] has in recent decades witnessed an unprecedented spread across institutional domains and settings, as one way to attend to the requirements of a multilingual context in which professional and client do not share the same first language. Yet, in one and the same breath one must add here that professional interpreting counts as only one in a range of possible responses which may serve to bridge a language gap, for instance in medical consultations. Other possibilities include: patients who attempt their best in the locally dominant language (already mentioned), doctors who code-switch into the patient's home language, doctors and patients who resort to the use of a common lingua franca, the presence of a close friend, neighbour or relative who interprets on behalf of the client, etc. Within this set

---

[1] To avoid misunderstandings, note that "community interpreting" here does not refer to "interpreting provided from within the community", but instead "a specific segment of professional interpreting which serves community purposes". It is sometimes referred to as "social interpreting" and contrasts with "conference interpreting".

of possibilities, the triadic model (communication which involves a third party mediator) features commonly alongside the dyadic interaction model (only two participants), and it often alternates with it within the same institutional space (sometimes, within a single institutional encounter). Diversity in practices and approaches is not only the result of the occurrence of mixed client populations (e.g. patients with and without an immigrant background frequenting the same neighbourhood health clinic). More importantly, within the group of clients with other first languages than the locally dominant one, some strategies for bridging the language gap count as dyadic (e.g. lingua franca use), while other strategies count as triadic (e.g. reliance on an interpreter). For the discourse analysts of professional practice and for sociolinguists of multilingualism, interpreted interaction counts as one of the phenomena necessarily under consideration. And, similarly, for those who started out or situate themselves primarily in interpreting studies, it has become rather difficult to stay away from the pressing imperatives of a sociolinguistics of globalisation. Globalisation has deeply affected the interactional dynamics of institutional encounters between clients and the professionals or service providers who attend to their needs. Within the complex field of possibilities, interpreting counts as but one type of response to the challenges posed by multilingualism and language difference, and understanding its role, function and potential requires that it is being situated within a more encompassing understanding of the dynamics of contemporary multilingualism.

The mainstay of my Chapter is with the larger picture of the dynamics of choices when a language difference presents itself and a form of mediating support is invited to deal with it. The specific context which I will be addressing is that of heightened multilingualism as a result of the successive immigration waves which Flanders, and Belgium more generally, have experienced over the past 50 years – a set of developments which in many ways is not so very different from the experiences of neighbouring countries: organised labour migration in the early 1960s (Turkish, Maghrebi, and before that Italian), followed by waves of political and economic refugees from the 1990s onwards – post-Yugoslav wars, East to West/South to North migration within Europe, post-colonial migration, etc. In my Chapter I will report on two studies and I will be talking for the most part, though not exclusively, about health care.

A central concern in my analysis is the relevance of spatial analysis and the concept of "scale" for understanding the distribution and shaping of linguistic resources when forms of language accommodation and support are interactionally made available in situations of occupational and professional service provision. A scale-sensitive analysis of local, on-the-ground multilingualism accords with an "extroverted sense of place" (Massey 1994). Such a sense of place integrates our understanding of the local with that of the global. Massey (1994: 5) replaces the bounded notion of place with one of "articulated moments in networks of social relations and understandings". This is necessary because a large proportion of those relations, experiences and understandings are constructed on different scales. Theorists of scale have subsequently built on research on place by asking how change in any one place is affected by and affects change at different geographic scales (see Slembrouck and Vandenbroucke in press for an overview).

> "[S]cale theorists have sought to conceptualise how scales come into existence and articulate with one another and how events at a particular scale are shaped by their relationships with different scales. [...] Their important addition is stressing the need to consider how the fortunes of territories of a particular scale are shaped by the social construction of scale in co-evolution with globalization." (Sheppard 2002: 313, 314–315)

The presence of populations of diverse national and/or ethnic ancestry in a particular locality, and how this condition has affected the range of recorded uses of linguistic resources of diverse ancestry, provides one striking example of this.

2 Temporal and spatial scales in the multilingual dynamics of urban spaces

Conditions of globalisation, including those of immigration-affected urban multilingualism, have put in the foreground questions of language, activity and space, in ways which have challenged more traditional conceptualisations of multilingualism which one-sidedly viewed multilingualism as a property of the individual speaker and of geographically-bounded communities of speakers of the same language (entities typically defined by ethnicity and/or nationality). As argued elsewhere, multilingualism is not exclusively what individuals have or lack; it is just as much about what the environment, as a structured determination and interactional emergence, enables and disables them to deploy (Blommaert, Collins, and Slembrouck 2005a: 213). An alternative to the more traditional view therefore emphasises the organisational and interactionally-manifest distribution of linguistic resources in and across particular spaces and activities. For each site and activity, the specific distribution of languages and (remedial) interactional strategies can be thought in terms of:
1. a set of available languages and language varieties, which is hierarchically-organised – both in terms of frequency of occurrence and in terms of participant preferences; such a hierarchically-organised set of choices often evolves over time.

It can also be thought of as:
2. a process and dynamics of decision-making which informs language choice and strategy of communication at the moment of speaking, with choices such as "adjust to the visiting interlocutor's language", "resort to the locally-dominant language", "opt for the use of a lingua franca", "call upon a multilingual employee", "involve an informal interpreter", "organise a phone interpreter", etc.

Such an alternative view advances a scaled perspective on urban multilingualism – looking outward from the site and centre of interaction into the neighbourhood and beyond. Note that the point here is not to deny nor erase the relevance of a community perspective from the picture (e.g. the relevance of the concept of a "local Turkish community")[2]; it is rather that one examines first of all how specific urban spaces of activity are affected by and transformed in the course of the successive globalisation waves which result in encounters with differently-scaled linguistic resources, because diverse groups of institutional clients of transnational ancestry assert their presence in the catchment area of an institutional site. The mobilisation of resources through which a particular locality responds to the forms of language difference which present themselves is itself a scaled phenomenon.

In the proposed view, the language user can be thought of as a subject who inhabits particular spatial trajectories and, as part of these trajectories, s/he engages in specific encounters which come with specific language choices (for instance, Turkish when buying bread, Albanian when speaking to a next-door neighbour, French at the Moroccan grocery store, Dutch at the gate of the local primary school, etc.). Such a view is based on the idea that neighbourhoods count as polycentric units (Blommaert, Collins, and Slembrouck 2005b), in the sense that the institutional sites which typically occur in a neighbourhood space (primary school, health clinic, church, mosque, etc.) to varying degrees both reflect and normatively influence the distribution and use of specific linguistic resources, as can be "heard" and "read" in the centres themselves and in the urban spaces which surround them.

A spatialised perspective on urban multilingualism thus prioritises that, while an individual client may possess skills for languages x, y and z, the actual use of any of these depends on the multilingual affordances of particular

---

[2] The question of "language community" is one that, following two decades of research which has stressed unprecedented linguistic diversity, needs to be re-examined and possibly re-thought (Rampton 2010).

spaces and activities in these spaces. And while it is true that the specific make-up of such a local multilingual regime is in obvious ways a reflection of its population of users, it cannot be concluded that there is a one-on-one mapping of person-based repertoire and spatially-configured use. Indeed, a newcomer may find herself "without a language" to use. Therefore, the relevance of spatio-temporally located multilingual regimes cannot be explained away on the basis of a simple survey of person-based characteristics (counting speakers and their languages). The multilingual urban unit of analysis is organised both "a-personally" and "interpersonally": it has a configuration before the language user enters, but it is also interactionally asserted, maintained and transformed in the course of language use. The dynamics of language choice during interaction is as much pre-set by expectations of place and activity (specific linguistic resources are habitually attached to these) as it is the outcome of negotiation on the basis of the individual repertoires of the interactants. In that sense, local regimes of language are hierarchical constructs and, while their application in real-time interaction is subject to various forms of human agency, the constructs present themselves as a mixture of, on the one hand, more durable and relatively permanent dispositions and, on the other hand, emerging "inscriptions" in the multilingual urban landscape. As an aspect of social structure, this begs explanation in its own right: users inhabit spaces, they are subjected to their regimes, but they also produce an effect on these regimes. Some languages have a long-standing presence in an institutional site; the use of other languages may emerge and be there for some time and disappear again; yet other languages are not used at all, even though they form part of some individual clients' repertoires, etc.

For each institutional site, therefore, one can list the languages that typically occur, and situate their distribution spatiotemporally. The emphasis on time/space scale(s) for understanding transnational and globalisation-affected processes of distribution and socio-economic agency has been invited by a number of authors and theoretical commentators (e.g. Smith 1992; Swyngedouw 1997; Coe and Yeung 2001, etc.). Collins, Slembrouck and Baynham (2009) and Slembrouck and Vandenbroucke (in press) offer detailed discussions. Let me restrict myself here to the following key points about "scale". The notion of "scale" is central to geography as a discipline. While originally it was mostly a metric concept reflective of analytical size and degree of detail on the assumption of a taken-for-granted vertical hierarchy "from the body to the globe" (and activities that can be situated at a particular scale), recent decades, though, have witnessed a transformed, more constructivist perspective on the concept, as part of capturing the manifold, complex spatial and temporal dynamics of globalisation. Scales apply both vertically (e.g. a city district which becomes more international counts as "upscaling") and horizontally (e.g. a particular practice which has a particular geographic distribution). In addition, the stress has been on the interpretative construction of scale (cf. concepts of "up/downscaling", "rescaling"), how scales come into existence and are being maintained, and especially: how events at a particular scale are shaped in the context of things happening at other scales. For instance, the emerging Dutch of a recently arrived immigrant child in a local school which is seen by the teacher as that of a child who is coping well with new circumstances (= local scale, very recent) vs. the same Dutch being seen by the visiting school inspector as emblematic of a failing language integration policy (= national scale, around for longer). Thus highlighted is the social construction of scale, including the ways in which scale allocation itself is volatile, negotiated, reproduced, etc. in the course of social and economic activity and in a context of other, differently-scaled phenomena. This of course raises questions of situated agency and note in this particular respect the importance of the human (speaking) body as a scale in its own right (see Herod 2011: 59–89), indeed the point where the perspective of multilingualism as a characteristic of individuals meets with that of place and space. As Slembrouck and Vandenbroucke (in press) note, "while interpretative orientations to the complexities of time and space have been necessitated by the globalised era, it is the speaking and acting body, anchored in time and space, which must particularly invite the attention of anyone interested in processes of language use and communication".

The relevance of spatio-temporal scales is encouraged by the empirical questions that come to mind when one is charting the range of multilingual solutions which are deployed in a context of language difference between service supplier/institutional agent and client. Think of the neighbourhood health clinic as an example. Is proficiency in language x provided from within the centre, or is it introduced from the outside? When it is provided from within the health centre, is the provider the professional service supplier or one of the assistant staff – e.g. a receptionist? Is the linguistic resource widely and durably transmitted in the national context or is its provision less commonly available and does it therefore count as more one-off and locally-accomplished (e.g. compare the occurrence of French which features in every pupil's secondary school trajectory, with the example of the immigrant physician's Russian)? In the case of language support provided from outside the institution, is the resource higher ranked because the provider is professionally certified, with certification applying nationally, or is it informally provided by a neighbourhood-based relative or friend? When provided from the outside, how far and how long does the resource have to travel before it can enter into the arena of interaction? For instance, phone interpreting comes with a re-scaling of the geographic unit within which to locate a sought-after linguistic resource; the resource is also quasi-instantly available and geographic distance does not matter. In contrast with this, on site professional interpreting may, depending on the sought-after language resource's scarcity, result in networks being tested, support having to travel a distance and requiring an appointment which has to be made well ahead of the encounter itself. One further question may be whether local centres develop specific initiatives oriented to re-scaling often-needed resources, for instance by facilitating in-house access. For each of these questions, an analysis of scaled dimensions of time and space helps us complete the picture about the local language regime and its specific dynamics of decision-making in the area of language provisions.

3 The language regimes of two neighbourhood health centres in Ghent and the local solutions which they developed (2003–2004, 2008)

My first case study concerns a detailed set of initial descriptions which formed part of an ethnography of how two neighbourhood health centres in Ghent, around the turn of the century, responded to conditions of heightened multilingualism in the patient populations they serve. The fieldwork for this was conducted in 2003 and 2004.[3] The two studies in the health clinic formed part of a wider ethnographic project on various aspects of multilingualism in "immigrant neighbourhoods" situated on the so-called "19th century ring" around the Flemish/Belgian city of Ghent. The two neighbourhood health clinics (NHC, *wijkgezondheidscentra* in Dutch) were: NHC De Sleep (situated in De Muide, the northern part of the city) and NHC De Brugse Poort (which serves patient populations of the adjacent districts of Brugse Poort and Rabot, in the northwestern part of the city). Ghent is characterised by considerable diversity in the immigrant patient populations which inhabit these neighbourhoods and the health needs of these populations at the time were mainly, though not exclusively, served by the NHCs. In the case of NHC De Sleep, this resulted in a

---

3 In both cases, the research was funded through a research sabbatical at the Flemish Academic Centre of the Royal Academy of Sciences and the Arts (Brussels). The research fellows were: James Collins and Stef Slembrouck. Jan Blommaert was involved in the wider neighbourhood multilingualism project. The follow-up fieldwork in the NHCs in 2008 was done by Slembrouck.

fairly homogeneous patient population, while in the case of NHC De Brugse Poort the demographic picture was highly diverse.

Figures 1 and 2 below provide an overview of the evolving language hierarchies in the two neighbourhood health centres whose multilingual practices were studied. The general picture is one which the two centres have in common and locates individual language provision in terms of temporal and spatial proximity/distance. In addition to this, as can be seen on the separate figures, the two centres had each invested in a re-scaling of their supply for particular languages.

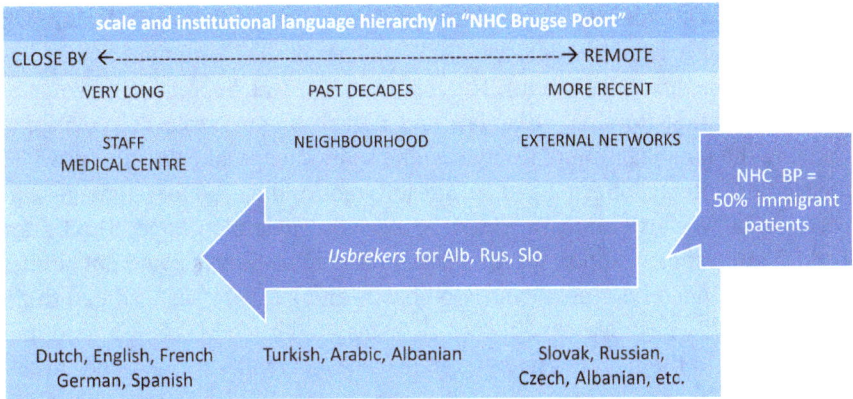

Figure 1: Institutional multilingual landscape. Scale and language hierarchy in NHC Brugse Poort.

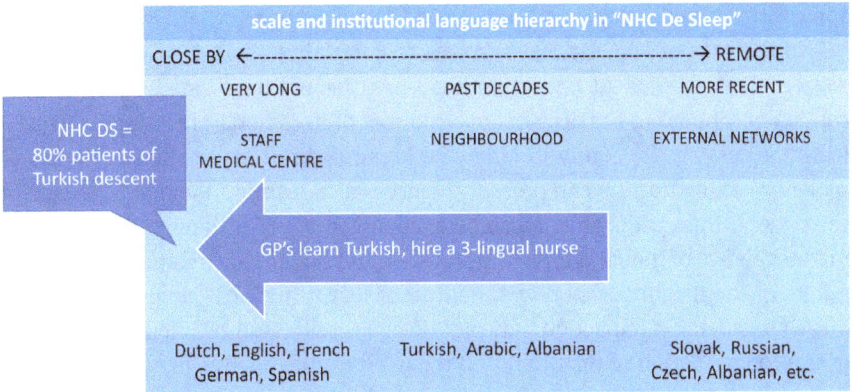

Figure 2: Institutional multilingual landscape. Scale and institutional language hierarchy in NHC De Sleep.

In the case of NHC Brugse Poort (with only about 50% patients of immigrant descent and a highly diverse and rather quickly evolving patient population), a turning point occurred – around the turn of the century – when the health clinic was facing shorter-term realities of often-needed resources for particular immigrant languages (e.g. Slovak, Russian, Albanian, etc.). These languages were less established in the neighbourhood. Compared to Turkish and Arabic, they occurred in smaller numbers but were nevertheless more frequently needed. This resulted in the centre's investment in the development of a written bilingual chart-flow instrument, in three languages, to support front-line medical consultations with patients in Slovak, Albanian and Russian. The instrument was called *IJsbrekers* ['ice-breakers'] (see Collins and Slembrouck 2006 for a more detailed description and analysis of the instrument and its impact on the medical interaction). The instrument, it was hoped, would contribute to relocating Russian, Albanian and Slovak on the scale of provisions, bringing the languages more firmly into the spatio-temporal "here-and-now" of the medical interaction itself and, as a result, reduce the need for language support which was externally-provided beyond the neighbourhood. Unlike for Turkish and Arabic, support for Albanian, Russian and Slovak could not be successfully provided on a neighbourhood basis, and some of this also had to do with the staff's negative experiences with neighbourhood-provided, informal interpreters. In the field interviews, references were made to "paid and unreliable translators for Albanian", as well as the impracticalities of professional interpreting which had to be arranged by appointment. Introducing *IJsbrekers* was therefore a matter of bringing the three "foreign" languages closer to the deictic centre, the "I-you-here-now" of speech in the neighbourhood health clinic. It was also perceived as a way to undo the attributed negative effects of some forms of neighbourhood-organised language support.

In the case of NHC De Sleep, it was reported that about 80% of its patients were of Turkish descent and three additional factors were listed which significantly contributed to the decision of a number of its general practitioners to start learning Turkish: (1) equity in language learning effort especially with younger patients – if the doctors can present themselves as learning the first language of the patient, then patients will also be encouraged to learn Dutch; (2) an increasing prevalence of diabetes type II, particularly among first-generation male immigrants in the neighbourhood who had never learnt the local language (diabetes has a considerable impact on patients' lifestyles and requires intensive coaching over a longer period of time); and (3) the need for the doctors to be able to communicate directly with recently-arrived newcomer spouses about family planning. As a result of the general practitioners' language learning efforts, Turkish as a linguistic resource was more fully brought into the here-and-now of the medical dyad. For some of the general practitioners in the centre, their linguistic repertoire now included Turkish, as an addition to the other languages they spoke: Dutch (the locally dominant language) and the linguae francae which one typically expects most GP's to speak in Flanders (English, French – and to a lesser extent: German and sometimes Spanish). In addition, a somewhat similar re-scaling move was accomplished for Arabic in the centre, when a trilingual professional nurse (Turkish, Arabic, Dutch) was hired specifically for a number of outreach functions, including the weekly diabetes consultations and follow-up home visits to young families in the neighbourhood.

3.1 A few comments on otherness and trust

The initial study of the two neighbourhood centres also brought home another major insight, one which invites us to consider the relevance of professional and other ideologies of language and communication. Linguistic ideologies can be defined as "systems of belief" and collectively- or individually-held ideas about the role, function and value of language (or a particular language) in a societal or situational context (Woolard 1998). Mertz (1996) specifically raises the question of linguistic ideologies which are tied to the use of specific text types and interaction forms in designated professional contexts. As noted in Collins and Slembrouck (2006: 263), enlisting a third party for purposes of language support is often perceived by professionals as a sacrifice in expert autonomy and a loss of control over the situation. Such a professional language ideology provides us with a variant of the more general preference for key participants in a communicative dyad to sort out the communicative problems posed by language difference without having to recruit support from outside the situation. An example here which illustrates this is that of the doctor who prefers lingua franca use – say, French – over reliance on a third-party interpreter for the patient's first language. Securing the directness, the one-on-one nature of the communication, is often considered to be more practical and more important than a less-than-optimal mastery and use of the linguistic code (in other words: rather struggle in French than bring in an interpreter for Lingala). Similarly, the nearness of the informal interpreter, and that her role can be construed as a role similar to that of a trusted friend or relative who accompanies the patient to the doctor's consultation equally underlines the strength of the nearness-pole when choices in favour of a particular linguistic strategy are situated on a spatio-temporal cline. These observations about "nearness" also underline the dimensions of trust and distrust (cf. we tend to trust what is close and near vs. we tend to distrust what comes from further afield). Within the ethnographic study, the experience with informal interpreters occurred as a mixed one. One doctor in a related set of interview data (De Maesschalck et al. 2010) anecdotally captured her positive experiences with informal interpreters by referring to an advice given to one of her patients: "next time again bring your niece", meaning: this solution has worked well and we should stay with it; it is handy to have your niece close-by to help out. This experience contrasts starkly with the negative depiction of unreliable/paid neighbourhood-provided translators for Albanian in NHC De Brugse Poort, or the general practitioners' decision at the NHC De Sleep to take lessons in Turkish so as to secure a more private, unmediated one-on-one interactional space in the contact with young, newcomer-spouses. The larger observation is therefore that considerations of trust and familiarity intersect with the scalar dynamics – e.g. what is near is more likely to be trustworthy, while at the same time: when what is nearer cannot be trusted or is not available, the challenge is either to accomplish nearness in some other way or to seek assistance from further away.

4 Insights from a cross-sectoral study (health, education and local authority) on the use of strategies of language support (2012–2013)

The second study is a more recent, larger-scale study of decision-making, use and effects in the provision of multilingual resources of language support, with particular reference to community interpreting and translation in Flanders (2012–2013).[4] This study was cross-sectoral and covered the domains of health, education and local authorities (including social welfare). It concentrated on three geographical areas: Ghent (an urban context, with a long-standing tradition of organised language support), South-West Flanders (a mixed urban/rural context, with more recent multilingual provisions) and Flemish Brabant (an urban/suburban context, in which language support is enacted against a background of historically-inherited, polarised bilingualism). For this study, orally conducted questionnaires were used with professional and occupational end users and with institutional clients. The results led to the formulation of a number of hypotheses which were subsequently substantiated through focus group

---

[4] This study was financed with an EIF-ESF-grant. The Principal Investigators were Stef Slembrouck, Piet Van Avermaet and Mieke Van Herreweghe; the researchers were Britt Roels, Marie Seghers, Bert De Bisschop.

sessions with various stakeholders. See Roels et al. (2015) for an overview and detailed discussion of the hypotheses.

Even though the professional end users in the survey unequivocally noted the advantages of professional community interpreters over informal ones, considerable variation was recorded – even arbitrariness – in the actual reliance on professional community interpreting. This was the case across domains and even within single organisations, with unequal treatment of clients as a result – for instance, when clients move between institutions and, in some cases, across successive contacts within the same organisational unit. At the same time, the survey affirmed the participant preference for direct communication, speaker autonomy and self-supportiveness noted in the earlier ethnographic enquiry. Very importantly, this preference was here noted as a characteristic of both the professional end user and the institutional client (the latter point had not been established in the previous ethnography). The institutional clients also demonstrated a strong awareness that the locally dominant language (Dutch) is important to them. Its use counts as a demonstration of integration and of the capacity to manage on their own. These findings are corroborated by studies elsewhere, e.g. Hadziabdic et al. (2009) in Sweden, where immigrants from former Yugoslavia report (in the health context) that the use of a community interpreter increases their sense of dependency.

As represented in Figure 3, the cross-sectoral survey provided further evidence of the relevance of the scale of relative distance/proximity noted earlier. The scale is now represented as one of decision-making in the reliance on a particular linguistic bridging strategy. As depicted in Figure 3, a general preference for solutions which are nearby or on-site can be noted (cf. what is practical, what is familiar, what is trustworthy and agrees with a perception of speaker autonomy). The scale has as its extreme points, at one end, "provided in-house by the main interlocutors" (and dyadic) and at the other end "arranged by appointment to travel from further afield" (and triadic). As we move from the pole of nearness on the left to that of distance on the right: first choice: the use of Dutch, the

	implicit logic of decision-making		
in-house DYADIC ←			by appointment → TRIADIC
INSIDE THE DYAD	STAFF MEDICAL CENTRE	NEIGHBOURHOOD	EXTERNAL NETWORKS
use of dominant language use of a lingua franca	rely on multilingual employee	rely on informal interpreter	rely on professional interpreter

Figure 3: Scale of decision-making. Implicit preferences in choice of strategy.

dominant language → next: reliance on a multilingual employee within the organisation → next: an informal interpreter → finally: a professional interpreter who is supplied external to the organisation. The use of a lingua franca can be both resourced by the service provider or a multilingual employee.

A second scale can be argued to be superimposed on the gradient in Figure 3 and it is likely to reinforce its effects. It marks the relative availability of the languages. In other words, the chances that a well-established language (e.g. French, English, German) will be available within the organisation itself are bigger than in the case of more recent minority languages (e.g. Turkish, Arabic, Russian, etc.). The relative "proximity/distance" of a language thus exists on at least three dimensions: (i) it is less/more likely to be the case that the professional is proficient in it; (ii) it is more/less likely to be the case that the professional will have learned the language and (iii) there are more/fewer institutionalised opportunities for learning the language.

Taking the picture as a whole, it would appear then that professional interpreting loses out, as this language bridging strategy appears to manifest itself as a kind of "last resort" choice, one which is in general avoided but is necessary and even inevitable in the context of specific language proficiencies which are more rare. Conclusion: the scalar dynamics of language provisions arguably underlines the prevalence of a curative (or: remedial) perception of community interpreting.

To complete the picture of the survey's results, it is important to note the relevance of a number of factors which influence the way in which the decision-making invites a particular positioning on the cline:

1. Cost factors negatively influence the choice to rely on a professional interpreter.
2. The end user's familiarity with the instrument of professional interpreting had a positive effect on its frequency of use. This finding underscores the importance of how familiarity interacts with an assessment of trust and how the trusted and the familiar are to be situated on the pole of nearness on the left of the scale. The survey noted that end users who are more familiar with professional community interpreting were more likely to continue to rely on the instrument in the future. More than the actual number of clients with other languages than Dutch, familiarity and previous experience of having worked with a professional interpreter increase the chances that a professional interpreter will be enlisted again in the future.
3. What the communication will be about plays an important role. The use of a professional interpreter is often accounted for as informed by the topic of the conversation. Factors which play a role include the complexity of the topic/information, its importance and consequentiality, alongside its

personal and sensitive nature. Clients, in particular, reported the need for professional interpreting when they have to talk about matters of critical health, residency permits, and their children's education. Note in this respect how, in the Flemish system, the decision to bring in a professional interpreter is the end user's prerogative. For the client it may be more difficult to influence decision-making in a particular direction. The professional end user may consult the client on this, but at the same time s/he is not under any obligation to actually do so.

4. The survey also made clear that we need to consider how the professional end user is positioned in the language ideological debate about the role and function of the dominant language. A narrowing of the concept of integration to "the civil obligation to learn the dominant language" tended to go together with increased reluctance to enlist a professional interpreter, while a view on integration in terms of "full participation in institutional procedures and processes" tended to go together with a more positive attitude towards externally-recruited professional interpreting. To some extent, this turned out to be domain-specific: voices which defended the need for interpreting on the basis of accessibility and who attributed integration effects to its use were more commonly found in the health sector, as compared to for instance the domains of education and local government.

5. Fifth, and, finally, there is the important role of the professional end-user's perceptions of the language proficiency of the individual client. This area may well be where we have to look for Achilles' heel. Can one rely on doctors, civil servants in local authorities, teachers in schools, psychiatrists, etc. to engage in an adequate and realistic assessment of the language needs of a client? The survey reported how the client's language proficiency in the dominant language is rarely assessed systematically or thoroughly, and decisions are often made on the basis of limited, coloured or ad hoc information which might be faulty.

5 A few observations and implications for policy and practice – each seeking to "re-scale" the problem of language difference

Spatio-temporal considerations of scale are not only useful when our efforts are directed at understanding the decision-making dynamics of multilingual provisions. They may also usefully underpin the development of multilingual policy.

In the final sections of the Chapter, I want to turn to a number of recommendations for practice. In each case, "scale" is at the heart of what is being suggested.

a. The application of a scalar logic suggests that decisions in the area of language support are not made at random, but instead they are subject to a complex set of interacting considerations which form a meaningful whole and which can be viewed as a kind of problem-solving scenario. One recommendation for policy here might therefore be: make explicit what is now often implicit, raise awareness about the strengths, weaknesses, pitfalls and implications of particular strategies and solutions, and transform an existing (often implicit) logic of decision-making into a more sophisticated instrument of informed (i.e. explicit) decision-making. One of the key weaknesses of an implicitly scalar logic is that it runs the risk of being ill-informed in the way it is applied in practice. In fact, the 2012–2013 survey revealed that professional end users' knowledge of the pros and cons of particular forms or strategies of language support varies considerably. There is also considerable variation when the professional end users answer the question when a move to the next step on the scale is justified (e.g. when not to opt for a lingua franca, even though you regularly do so with this particular client; e.g. when to insist that it is better not to rely on an informal interpreter for this particular conversation, even though the client has repeatedly brought along the same informal interpreter and this has tended to work well for most purposes so far, etc.). Far from advising against the use of externally-provided interpreters – be they professional or informal – an advocacy may prioritise reflexive decision-making and heightened awareness of the context-specificity of choices, their strengths and weaknesses. By being adequately explicit about the grounds on which to decide in favour or against the deployment of a particular strategy, one must heed the risks which accompany taken-for-granted solutions which are adopted routinely and across the board. The absence of an explicit instrument or protocol of decision-making in the context of multilingual mediation remains in all likelihood the most important insight reported in Roels et al. (2015). If anything, this points to the need for a policy which stimulates situated reflection and active awareness about choice and strategy, as well as balanced and nuanced decision-making.

b. Especially when it comes to assessing the proficiency of the client in the dominant language or in a lingua franca, the survey noted considerable variation and even outright subjectivity. The latter is a very difficult area. Can one expect a professional end user in a few minutes' time to arrive at a well-informed picture of the functional language proficiencies of a particular client? A possibility one could think of here is to insist pro-actively (more than "curatively") on the presence of a bilingual professional interpreter during the client's very first encounter at the institution. One obvious advantage is that this would provide an occasion to explain the institution's functioning, its procedures and protocols. On top of that, it would provide the possibility to achieve maximum clarity between professional and client about their language learning histories, about current proficiency levels, about client expectations, about a realistic and feasible action range for an instrument of language support in the case of this particular client and professional, etc. Could one therefore think of an assessment of the client's language repertoire and his/her language needs as part of the professional interpreter's brief during such a first encounter?

c. The scalar logic which underpins decision-making is premised on an ideologically-informed preference for the deictic "zero degree" of the interactional here-and-now (Baynham 2009), the interactional security, comfort and trustworthiness provided by the "I" talking directly to the "you" and sorting everything out between the two of them in the unfolding "here-and-now". While policy must at times counteract the negative effects of taken-for-granted ideologies, there is no *a priori* reason why policy cannot at times go with the direction of an ideology. One can draw a rather obvious conclusion from this: it is worth investing in the professional's own individual capacity to embody a particular form of language support by learning one of the minority languages. NHC De Sleep provides examples of how this has been done successfully in practice. The multilingual professional offers the advantage of being both proficient in the client's first language, while maintaining the advantage of unmediated face-to-face interaction between expert and client. However, one must add here immediately that the professional's relative proficiency in a foreign language should not be interpreted as a *carte blanche* decision to dispense at all times with the possibility of a professional interpreter for that language (see my point a. above). Much depends on the topic talked about, its relative critical consequentiality, the absence or presence of particular sensitivities or complexities, etc.

d. A fourth recommendation is undoubtedly that we underline the rescaling effects of efforts to invest in opportunities for building capacity in less commonly occurring (immigrant) languages. Our current educational system, and the opportunities of language learning which it provides, is a product of histories of geographical proximity, economic importance and collectively experienced cultural affinity. I am limiting myself here to the case of Flanders. The commonly taught foreign languages in secondary education are French and English, and to a lesser extent German, and lesser still Spanish (though growing in popularity). With the exception of French, the inclusion of particular foreign languages in the curriculum – also at higher education levels – is not at all motivated by the actual presence of numbers of speakers of these languages within the geographical territory of Flanders. Foreign language teaching appears to be organised first of all to the extra-territorial scale of the federal state as a whole and of foreign/neighbouring communities (i.e. locations where the language learned is spoken as a "first language"). We do not seem to talk about curricular inclusion which is warranted by the scale of diversity "inside Flanders". The point is both about which languages are on offer and how we orient to their anticipated uses. Granted a number of exceptions and more recent niche developments, the basic premise appears to be: "we learn a foreign language in order to travel, not in order to be able to talk to our neighbour". And, yet, a monitored increase in proficiency for particular languages could make a big difference, if it can be combined sensibly with particular professional destinations (doctors, teachers, etc.). Note that the trilingual general practitioner (Dutch-English-Russian) is not hampered in his/her career if the demand for Russian diminishes gradually in the longer term or disappears altogether, but s/he is likely to make a big difference in any kind of situation where command of, in this particular example: the Russian language, turns out to be a crucial prerequisite for adequate diagnosis and therapy. At the same time, we are not seeking large numbers: e.g., the provision of general practitioners who can do consultations in Russian can remain small-scale.

e. Finally, I have a few notes on the "re-scaling" efforts which were developed in-house by the two health centres in the first study. The *IJsbrekers* instrument which I discussed earlier provides an interesting point of departure here. As would be typical for a written instrument, the potential of a transfer to another context was within its scope. Indeed, about a year after its development the instrument was picked up by Médecins Sans Frontières and used in refugee camps. Somewhat ironically, however, the instrument's lifespan in the NHC De Brugse Poort itself was much shorter: *IJsbrekers* was used only occasionally, and sometimes more as a glossary than as an interaction-monitoring instrument; its shortcomings were noted in-house and it was cast aside and became an artifact of locally-enacted language policy which was shown to the researchers during their fieldwork to illustrate the local health clinic's commitment to addressing the challenges posed by a multilingual clientele. The two developments noted here illustrate two important dimensions which bear on the relative success of local bottom-up policy initiatives: on the one hand, there is the fate of a short life span, especially when the tool is not supported by higher level policy and matching resources to work towards a refinement of the original design, once its shortcomings have been noted. On the other hand, the written nature of the instrument enabled its successful transfer to another context of frontline global health care. In comparison with this, the general practitioners' efforts to learn Turkish in NHC De Sleep turned out to be a much more durable investment, even though its spatio-temporal scope remained inevitably tied to the locality of the health centre (as the resource, oral proficiency in Turkish, is literally tied to the practitioner who embodies it). The important question raised here is where the two can meet and how they may successfully reinforce one another: on the one hand, the value of context-sensitive solutions which originate in bottom-up perceptions of a problem situation and, on the other hand, what it takes to ensure that locally-accomplished success stories secure a durable lifespan beyond the confines of the local context in which they originate. In this respect, suggestions (a) and (c) above are situated more at the end of how local strength is "up-scaled": (a) strengthening self-awareness about locally deployed logics of decision making and how these interact with local contextual factors and (c) promoting individual choices to learn a language on the part of the end users, whereas suggestion (d) is more oriented more to the need to invest in higher-scale structural provisions of opportunities for learning specific languages which are applied top-down.

In brief conclusion, it would appear then that a scalar approach is useful not only from the point of view of describing and interpreting complex multilingual realities, but that it also comes with the potential of suggesting particular configurations oriented to successful communication strategies. One of the challenges in such an exercise continues to be that determining the relative weight of particular factors is not necessarily the same for each individual, language, interactional situation or communicative dyad.

References

Baynham, Mike J. 2009. "Just one day like today": Scale and the analysis of space/time orientation in narratives of displacement. In James Collins, Stef Slembrouck & Mike J. Baynham (eds.), *Globalization and language in contact: Scale, migration, and communicative practices*, 130–147. London: Continuum.

Blommaert, Jan, James Collins & Stef Slembrouck. 2005a. Spaces of multilingualism. *Language & Communication* 25. 197–216.

Blommaert, Jan, James Collins & Stef Slembrouck. 2005b. Polycentricity and interactional regimes in "global neighbourhoods". *Ethnography* 6 (2). 205–235.

Coe, Neil M. & Henry Wai-chung Yeung. 2001. Geographical perspectives on mapping globalization: An introduction to the JEG Special Issue "Mapping globalisation: Geographical perspectives on international trade and investment". *Journal of Economic Geography* 1. 367–380.

Collins, James & Stef Slembrouck. 2006. "You don't know what they translate": Language contact, institutional procedure and literacy practice in neighborhood health clinics in Urban Flanders. *Journal of Linguistic Anthropology* 16 (2). 249–268.

Collins, James, Stef Slembrouck & Mike J. Baynham. 2009. Introduction: Scale, migration and communicative practice. In James Collins, Stef Slembrouck & Mike J. Baynham (eds.),

Globalization and language in contact: Scale, migration, and communicative practices, 1–18. London: Continuum.

De Maesschalck, Stéphanie, Myriam Deveugele, Demi Krystallidou, Stef Slembrouck & Hildegard Vermeiren. 2010. Charting the larger map of practice: Multilingual health care in urban Flanders. Paper presented at the Sociolinguistics Symposium 18, Southampton, 1–4 September.

Hadziabdic, Emina, Kristiina Heikkilä, Björn Albin & Katarina Hjelm. 2009. Migrants' perceptions of using interpreters in health care. *International Nursing Review* 56 (4). 461–469.

Herod, Andrew. 2011. *Scale*. Oxford: Routledge.

Massey, Doreen. 1994. *Space, place, and gender*. Minneapolis: University of Minnesota Press.

Mertz, Elizabeth. 1996. Recontextualization as socialization: Text and pragmatics in the law school classroom. In Michael Silverstein & Greg Urban (eds.), *Natural histories of discourse*, 229–249. Chicago: University of Chicago Press.

Rampton, Ben. 2010. Speech Community. In: Jürgen Jaspers, Jan-Ola Östman and Jef Verschueren (eds.), *Handbook of Pragmatics Highlights*, 7, pp. 274–303.

Roberts, Celia, Becky Moss, Val Wass, Srikant Sarangi & Roger Jones. 2005. Misunderstandings: A qualitative study of primary care consultations in multilingual settings, and educational implications. *Medical Education* 39 (5). 465–475.

Roberts, Celia, Srikant Sarangi & Becky Moss. 2004. Presentation of self and symptoms in primary care consultations involving patients from non-English speaking backgrounds. *Communication and Medicine* 1 (2). 159–169.

Roels, Britt, Marie Seghers, Bert De Bisschop, Piet Van Avermaet, Mieke Van Herreweghe & Stef Slembrouck. 2015. Equal access to community interpreting in Flanders: A matter of self-reflective decision-making? *The International Journal of Translation & Interpreting Research* 7 (3). 149–65. http://www.trans-int.org/index.php/transint/article/view/366/219 (accessed 12 March 2018).

Sheppard, Eric. 2002. The spaces and times of globalization: Place, scale, networks and positionality. *Economic Geography* 78 (3). 307–330.

Slembrouck, Stef & Mieke Vandenbroucke. In press. Scale. In Karin Tusting (ed.), *The Routledge handbook of linguistic ethnography*, 70–83. London: Routledge.

Smith, Neil. 1992. Geography, difference and the politics of scale. In Joe Doherty, Elspeth Graham & Mo Malek (eds.), *Postmodernism and the social sciences*, 57–79. London: Macmillan.

Swyngedouw, Erik. 1997. Excluding the other: The production of scale and scaled politics. In Roger Lee & Jane Wills (eds.), *Geographies of economies*, 167–176. London: Arnold.

Woolard, Kathryn Ann. 1998. Introduction: Language ideology as a field of inquiry. In Bambi B. Schieffelin, Kathryn Ann Woolard & Paul V. Kroskrity (eds.), *Language ideologies: Practice and theory*, 3–27. Oxford: Oxford University Press.

Kathelijne Jordens, Kris Van den Branden and Koen Van Gorp
4 "Only dirty things!" Functions of mother tongue use in collaborative group work

Abstract: This study explores socio-cognitive functions of mother tongue use during group work of bilingual pupils (Turkish-Dutch) in two mainstream primary schools in Flanders (Belgium). In each school, a group of four children performed three different tasks, related to different subjects of the curriculum in order to explore functions of mother tongue use (i.e. Turkish). During task performance, both groups of four bilingual pupils were guided by the first author of this study instead of their regular teacher, in a separate classroom. Following school language policy, task instructions were given in one language only, Dutch, the prescribed medium of instruction at school. However, during task performance, the pupils were allowed to use whatever languages they chose. Our data showed that the mother tongue was used for a range of socio-cognitive functions, including content-related and management-related talk. The main findings of this study thus indicate that the mother tongue fulfills an important role for cognitive as well as for socio-affective purposes, even for bilingual pupils who are not used to drawing on their full linguistic repertoire during task performance. The results challenge the view, currently prevalent in Flemish education, that a submersion approach is the only viable option for bilingual pupils speaking a minority language.

1 Introduction

The body of research into the use of mother tongues other than the prescribed medium of instruction in classrooms is growing. Studies mostly address L1 use

---
Note: Institutional address of the first author at the time of writing this Chapter.

Kathelijne Jordens, Centre for Language and Education (KU Leuven), Blijde Inkomststraat 7, Leuven, Belgium.
Kris Van den Branden, Faculty of Arts/Centre for Language and Education (KU Leuven), Blijde-Inkomststraat 21, Leuven, Belgium.
Koen Van Gorp, Centre for Language Teaching Advancement, Michigan State University, 619 Red Cedar Road, B135 Wells Hall, East Lansing, MI 48824, United States; Centre for Language and Education (KU Leuven), Blijde Inkomststraat 7, Leuven, Belgium.

https://doi.org/10.1515/9781501503207-005

in L2 classes (e.g. Storch and Aldosari 2010; Moore 2013) as well as L1 use in immersion contexts (e.g. Swain and Lapkin 2000; Reyes 2004). Some studies were conducted in the context of mainstream education with a monolingual medium of instruction, where the mother tongue is "smuggled in" (Moodley 2007; Probyn 2009). Most of these studies provide strong indications that the use of the mother tongue fulfils a range of socio-cognitive functions during task performance and thus can be considered a resource for learning (Turnbull 2001; Macaro 2005; Hall and Cook 2012).

In Flanders (the northern part of Belgium), however, studies into the functions of mother tongue use in education are scarce. The reason is quite straightforward: mother tongue use in the classroom is highly contested. The prescribed medium of instruction in education is Dutch, the official language in Flemish institutions. The vast majority of schools adopt a strict Dutch-only policy in class and on the playground (Van den Branden, Van Gorp, and Verhelst 2007; Jaspers 2008). This monolingual approach is adopted in an attempt to diminish the achievement gap between native and non-native speakers of Dutch. There is a strong belief amongst school teams that excluding mother tongues other than the medium of instruction contributes to better skills in the majority language and thus to better learning through that language (Jaspaert and Ramaut 2000; Spotti 2008; Ağirdag 2010).

In addition, few Flemish teachers master any minority languages. They feel that tolerating mother tongues they do not understand might lead to loss of control (Berben, Van den Branden, and Van Gorp 2007; Sierens and Van Avermaet 2014). Particularly in the case of Turkish, teachers tend to believe that if Turkish were tolerated, it would be overused. Pupils of Turkish origin constitute a relatively large minority group in Flanders, and they have been shown to actively maintain their mother tongue and culture (Leman 1997; Yağmur 2009). Also, teachers tend to doubt the ability of bilingual children to explain complex matters in Turkish, as their proficiency in Turkish is believed to be too poor (Ağirdag, Jordens, and Van Houtte 2014). Moreover, Flemish teachers tend to believe that mother tongue use mostly serves off-task purposes (Sierens and Van Avermaet 2014).

The current study aims to investigate what particular use pupils make of their mother tongue during collaborative group work, when they are encouraged to do so in an otherwise monolingual school context.

2 Literature review: Studies into the use of mother tongues in classrooms with a different official medium of instruction

2.1 Use of L1 in L2 learning

The majority of studies into the functions of mother tongue during peer conversation are situated in the L2 classroom. Most of these studies focus on the role of L1 in L2 learning during collaborative group work.

Storch and Aldosari (2010) investigated functions of L1 (Arabic) in three different ESL-learning tasks performed in pairs by university students. The researchers distinguish five different functions: task management, discussing and generating ideas, and deliberations of grammar, vocabulary and mechanics. Their results show that the most occurring function of L1 was task management (45% of all L1 turns), followed by deliberations over vocabulary (26% of all L1 turns).

De Guerrero and Villamil (1994), working with university students with Spanish as L1 who were enrolled in an English as L2 course, report L1 use for on-task, about-task and off-task purposes during peer revision of written texts. They find that 84% of coded episodes was on-task, 10% about-task and 6% off-task.

In a similar vein, Moore (2013) describes L1 use (Japanese) in an L2 course (English) at university. L1 use during the preparation of two oral presentation tasks served three functions: content creation, procedural purposes and off-task purposes. He finds that over different stages in the preparation of the oral presentations, the primary focus of L1 use shifts from procedural purposes toward content creation. When describing L1 use as a percentage of each category of activity, he reports "an overall trend to use L1 more during procedural and off-task interaction" (Moore 2013: 246).

All these studies were conducted with adult participants in an L2 class at university. Focusing on younger learners, Eldridge (1996) reported on L1 use (of Turkish) of 11–13-year-olds in the ESL class of a mainstream secondary school in Turkey. He found that 77% instances of L1 use was oriented to classroom tasks and 16% concerned procedural matters; talk in the L1 about something else was rare. He concluded that "code-switching appears to be a natural and purposeful phenomenon which facilitates both communication and learning" (Eldridge 1996: 310).

In an immersion context, Swain and Lapkin (2000) focused on pupils aged 11–13 years performing two tasks in language class. They report three principal purposes of L1 use: moving the task along (subdivided in sequencing, retrieving semantic information and task management), focusing attention (on formal aspects) and interpersonal interaction (disagreement and off-task talk). Moving the task along occurred most frequently in their data. They conclude that "the L1 was used for a variety of constructive purposes in a consensus-building collaborative activity" (Swain and Lapkin 2000: 258).

2.2 Mother tongue use in content learning

Reyes (2004) compared the use of code-switching in a formal context (during a science task) and informal context (during lunch) also in an immersion programme. The participants were 7- and 10-year olds in an immersion programme, including Spanish and English. The science task consisted of a work sheet to be filled out, with questions in both English and Spanish. Reyes described twelve functions of code-switching between the two languages involved. Switching on-task occurred most for the purpose of clarifying an idea or message.

Benjamin (1996) investigated the use of the mother tongue (Spanish) by five children in grade five of an English-medium primary school in New Mexico throughout their school day. She distinguishes six functions of Spanish, the most important one being "getting work done". She reports that children speak Spanish a lot when assigned group work, but no percentages of L1 use per function were calculated.

In a post-colonial South African context, where English is dominant and functions as the official medium of instruction, Moodley (2007) focused on the use of Zulu by grade 9 learners (aged 14). The participants were EL2 learners immersed in EL1 classrooms by choice. He reports that the teacher "used the monolingual English mode when interacting with pupils" (Moodley 2007: 712). Two tasks, each performed by two different groups, were observed: a literature task (answering questions about a text) and oral work (discussing HIV-related topics). Six functions of the use of Zulu were reported in the groups composed of bilingual Zulu-English speaking children, amongst which: seeking clarification and providing explanations; and group management and influencing peer behaviour.

3 Situating the current study

All studies described above have in common that they report on socio-cognitive functions of mother tongue use in a context where another language is the preferred medium of instruction and interaction. In such a context, mother tongue use is to a greater or lesser extent contested, but still considered as a resource in class (Turnbull 2001; Macaro 2005). In the context of Flemish education, however, the vast majority of schools adopts a Dutch-only policy, strictly prohibiting the use of other mother tongues at school (Ağirdag 2010).

A second main difference between the studies described and the Flemish context concerns the linguistic repertoire of the teachers involved. Unlike the teachers in the studies described above, the vast majority of Flemish teachers do not understand the mother tongues of their pupils if the latter belong to a minority group. As a result, they associate mother tongue use with a lack of control, and strongly resist its use at school (Sierens and Van Avermaet 2014).

A local project carried out in the city of Ghent, aiming to circumvent the prevailing educational language policy, was the "home language project" (Ramaut et al. 2013), in which primary schools incorporated the use of Turkish by pupils as well as by some teachers. School teams were coached during several years to integrate the use of Turkish in classroom discourse. The researchers reported positive effects of the use of Turkish in the classroom on the pupils' socio-emotional well-being. In a recent follow-up study of the project, Rosiers (2015) found that, even several years after the project had finished, bilingual Turkish-Dutch pupils still used Turkish during group interaction in 40% of the turns spoken, mostly for on-task purposes.

Apparently, when mother tongue use is welcomed and some teachers share the linguistic repertoire of their bilingual pupils, the mother tongue can be used as an asset for learning. However, in the Flemish context, these conditions are hardly ever met. Therefore, in contrast with the "home language project", the current study aims to investigate the functions of mother tongue use, in a context in which the medium of instruction remains monolingual Dutch. For the purpose of the study, the pupils were invited to use their mother tongue, Turkish, during the performance of a number of tasks. As mother tongue use appears to play a role in both language learning and content learning, three different tasks were given to the pupils: a language-oriented task, a task related to science and a task related to biology/history. The current study is explorative in nature. An artificial setting had to be created in which pupils were encouraged to use their (shared) full linguistic repertoires, as they were not used to speaking Turkish overtly at school. As a result, chances were high that they would feel inhibited to do so, even if they secretly talked Turkish at school. So, it was hard to predict whether Turkish would be used at all: would the pupils refrain from using Turkish because they were not used to and/or wanted to comply with the Dutch-only rules, or would they take the opportunity to use Turkish in class? Also, it remained to be seen for what purposes Turkish would be used across the different tasks.

So, this explorative case study is guided by two research questions:
1. Which purposes does the use of Turkish serve during group work?
2. Does the use of Turkish serve different functions across different tasks?

4 Method

4.1 Setting

Data were collected in two Dutch-medium primary schools located in Limburg, a region with a high concentration of pupils with an immigrant background, of which the vast majority is from Turkish origin. In both schools (called "green" and "blue"), this was reflected in a school population with more than 50% pupils speaking a mother tongue other than Dutch (mostly Turkish). At the time of the data collection (2013–2014), both schools had a one-language-only policy, compelling pupils to use Dutch both in class and at the playground. Their resistance toward mother tongue use is illustrated by the fact that the two school teams agreed to cooperate with this study only under strict conditions, namely that the use of mother tongue (Turkish) would be restricted to the periods of data collection, during which a group of four pupils was pulled out of the regular classroom to work with the researcher. So, to meet the school teams' demands, "multilingual islands in the otherwise monolingual sea of the school" were created: while the prevailing monolingual school policy remained unchanged, the two groups of four pupils were encouraged to use Turkish during the activities the first author organised in a separate classroom for the purpose of data collection.

4.2 Participants

In each school, two girls and two boys (aged 9–12) participated in eight group work sessions, spread over 1.5 years (while they were in grades 4 and 5). They were chosen randomly out of the group of all children who had indicated in a questionnaire that they used Turkish at home with at least one of their parents. In introductory interviews, all eight of them acknowledged that overall, Turkish was used more than Dutch at home. Informed consent of the school team and the parents were obtained.

All participants were born in Belgium, except for Melisa (blue group), who moved to Belgium when she was three years old. Since the pupils had been attending a Flemish, Dutch-only school for about seven years at the start of data collection, they can be considered emergent bilinguals. They had a similar socio-economic background: their parents were either unskilled blue-collar workers or unemployed.

4.3 Tasks

To explore functions of turns containing Turkish during group work, three different tasks were used: a language-oriented task (story writing); a task related to science teaching (experimenting with bubbles in water); and a task related to biology/history (a discussion task, deciding on the most probable hypotheses for the extinction of dinosaurs).

The study focused on the kinds of tasks pupils typically perform at school (according to the official curriculum of Flemish primary education). All of the tasks were cognitively challenging, raising the chances that the pupils would use multiple codes to find a solution. Challenge was created by choosing content which was new to the pupils and by inviting them to work without the guidance of a teacher.

During the language-oriented task (called *kami*), the groups of four were asked to write a story, based on pictures of a *kamishibai* (storytelling theatre). They chose one out of three picture sets and were asked to write the story and prepare to narrate it to a class of preschool children (which they did the following week). They were explicitly told that they could choose whatever language or mix of languages to prepare and tell the story, as the activity was part of a project week on "multilingual reading aloud": for one week, all languages were allowed during storytelling time. The green group choose *De wiebelbillenboogie* (Guido Van Genechten), the blue group choose *Issun-Boshi* (Joji Tsubota). Interestingly, the green group chose to write the story in Dutch, whereas the blue group chose Turkish. They justified their choices by referring to their audience (a group of preschoolers) which for the green group consisted of mostly Dutch-speaking toddlers and in the blue group of mostly Turkish- and Dutch-speaking toddlers.

The biology/history task (called *dino*) adopted an information-gap format, eliciting peer discussion until they reached a consensus. The goal of the task was to find out which of four different texts contained the most plausible hypothesis for the extinction of dinosaurs. The four target pupils had to discuss the different options, reach a consensus and present their conclusion to the "multilingual camera".

During the science task (called *bubble*), scientific experiments were carried out, all about "bubbles". Pupils observed sparkling water, described what happened when raisins were dropped in sparkling water, and studied the effect of baking powder in still water. The pupils had to make notes about their observations and hypotheses, and present the experiments to the (multilingual) camera later on.

In line with Flemish educational practices, all the handouts with instructions and guiding questions were designed in Dutch only, as were the first author's oral instructions and scaffolding. This was quite genuine because the first author does not master Turkish, much like the vast majority of Flemish teachers. Pupils were instructed, however, to use the languages of their choice while performing the task. So, whereas the medium of interaction was potentially multilingual, the medium of instruction was monolingual Dutch.

4.4 Data collection

Both groups of four pupils carried out the tasks. Pupils were pulled out of their regular class. The first author took them to another classroom where the five people in total were sitting around a table. Two cameras were installed to have maximum coverage of the children's verbal and non-verbal behaviour. In a first phase, pupils were reassured that they were entirely free to choose whichever language they wanted to use during data collection. The first author made clear she had a very positive attitude towards all languages (including Turkish), encouraging the pupils to use Turkish and praising them for their extensive linguistic resources. They were also invited to teach her a few words or expressions in Turkish or talk about Turkish habits before each task performance. The cameras were introduced as being "multilingual", understanding whichever language the children would use, including Turkish. In a second phase, instructions were given in Dutch about the task to be performed. Additionally, they all went through an "agreement card" stating (1) they would work together; (2) they could only call for help when they were completely stuck; and (3) any language could be used throughout the activity. In the third phase, the actual task performance took place. During this phase, the first author was not sitting with them at the same table, but she was reading behind the teacher's desk. However, she was always present in the classroom. She did not interrupt their interaction, but when they asked for help she tried to coach them and only intervened when their noise disturbed the neighbouring class. As the pupils were not used to doing group work, they called for her help quite often. In most cases, they got stuck in their negotiation, not being able to settle disputes and disagreements. Consequently, in most cases her support took the shape of calming them down and offering them help to solve the task, by providing feedback and asking guiding questions.

4.5 Data analysis

All videotapes were transcribed verbatim. A native bilingual speaker (Turkish-Dutch) transcribed all utterances in Turkish and provided translations. For the analysis only the corpus of phase 3 (the task performance itself) was used.

The analysis was carried out in two steps: coding for language, then coding for function.

4.6 Coding for language

The smallest unit of analysis was the "conversational turn", defined as the utterance or sequences of utterances (words one speaker utters) until a speaker stops or is interrupted (Sacks, Schegloff, and Jefferson 1974).

In a first step, every turn in the transcript was coded as:
- Turkish only: all words in one turn were spoken in Turkish (including frequently used loanwords).
- Dutch only: all words in one turn were spoken in Dutch (including frequently used loanwords).
- Both Turkish and Dutch: at least one word was spoken in either Dutch or Turkish, the other words in the other language.
- Other: this miscellaneous category contained turns consisting of merely a name (e.g. "Ali!") or a one-word exclamation (e.g. "Ooh!") or turns with at least one word spoken in another language than Dutch or Turkish (e.g. "Shit! *Dat gaat niet!*" [This doesn't work!] in which "Shit!" is uttered in English and the rest of the turn in Dutch). Each of these subcategories accounted for about 1% of the data.
- Unintelligible (code x): none of the transcribers could understand the whole turn.

For each transcript the number of turns in each of these categories was counted. The analysis revealed that Turkish was used in all task performances, but to a different extent. Table 1 summarises the language choices per task.

4.7 Coding for function

In a second step, all turns coded "Turkish-only" or "Both Turkish and Dutch" were coded for functions. This coding process was carried out in three phases.

Table 1: Percentage of turns in Dutch, Turkish, both, and other for each task.

Task	Green group (percentage)					Blue group (percentage)				
	Dutch	Turkish	Both	Other	Code x	Dutch	Turkish	Both	Other	Code x
Kami	93.13	1.28	1.28	2.72	1.59	45.00	34.99	9.74	1.80	8.47
Dino	80.48	8.55	3.01	4.94	3.02	67.20	16.93	4.02	4.87	6.98
Bubble	82.12	9.08	3.46	3.03	2.31	66.27	16.48	6.79	3.07	7.39

Firstly, in an open coding phase, categories of functions occurring in the data were identified (as opposed to drawing on a priori categories). An explorative content analysis was conducted, based on the principles of grounded theory (Glaser and Strauss 1967). This first inductive coding phase resulted in a tree with 47 different categories.

Secondly, axial coding was conducted, organising categories and subcategories obtained in the previous phase. Thus, a coding tree was obtained, consisting of four main categories, each subdivided in subcategories. This new data-based coding tree was then compared to typologies of mother tongue functions in existing frameworks (e.g. Swain and Lapkin 2000; Moore 2013; Reyes 2004) to make adjustments and additions. The comparison facilitated the identification of the categories which were most relevant to the functions of mother tongue use. Triangulation of data from the multiple sources provided a comprehensive view of mother tongue functions in an L2 context, by verifying and cross-validating our own coding with existing studies (Gort 2012).

Thirdly, the preliminary taxonomy thus obtained was used for selective coding, which was carried out with a research assistant. The preliminary taxonomy to the dino task as performed by the green group together was applied, discussing every single code, to make sure our interpretations converged. Then, the research assistant and the first author each coded one task performance separately, to check interrater reliability. The writing task performance of the blue group was chosen for this coding phase as it contained by far the most turns including Turkish. It was agreed on 85% of the turns coded. Consensus was found for all turns through extensive discussion, which was also the base for final adaptations to the coding tree. Finally, the research assistant coded all task performances, and the coding was checked by the first author. The research assistant was encouraged to take notes in case of doubt and to make suggestions for improvement. All dubious cases were discussed and resolved.

In the case of a turn containing Dutch and Turkish, the focus was on the function of the Turkish part. If one turn consisted of two utterances containing

Turkish, each with a different function, both functions were incorporated in the coding. For example, a turn like *Böyle yaz: küçük çin çocugu* ('Write like this: little Chinese child') was coded "urging" (the first part) as well as "content creation" (the second part).

To make sense of the exact meaning of the turn to be coded, adjacent turns in Dutch as well as the descriptions of what happened were examined. In case of doubt, video-recordings were looked at again. About 2% of turns was coded "x" because it was not clear to either the first author or the research assistant which functions would be appropriate, not even after consulting the context.

By going through the three phases described above, the final coding tree presented in Appendix 1 was obtained. It contains four main categories, each subdivided in subcategories: (I) content-related use of the L1; (II) management-related use of the L1; (III) L1 discussion of off-task interpersonal relations; and (IV) research-related use of the L1. Appendix 1 renders a detailed listing of all different functions emerging from the analysis of our corpus, with a description of each category and examples from our data. The main categories are briefly described here.

I. Content-related

The category "Turkish for content-related talk" was composed of three subcategories: "formulating ideas", "negotiation", and "presenting the task product". "Formulating ideas" was the code used for making proposals (in the case of the storyline in the writing task), or for formulating new arguments and hypotheses (in the case of the science tasks). A turn containing Turkish was coded as "negotiating" when pupils were discussing the exact meaning of a concept or when they formulated questions and answers about the content of tasks. When something they had written was read out loud to elaborate on that particular passage, it was coded "negotiation" as well. "Presenting the product" was a separate subcategory, only occurring in the story-writing task, when pupils read the story to the camera at the end of the performance. This was the only task in which this category was relevant. Reading outcomes of task performance out loud in Turkish did not occur in any of the other performances. While pupils were asked to present the product of every task performance to the "multilingual camera" in whatever languages they wanted, they always did so exclusively in Dutch.

II. Management-related

Within the category of management-related talk, eight subcategories were distinguished. "Establishing roles" was used to indicate that pupils were deciding on who would do what during task performance. "Meta comments" were evaluating comments on the performance itself, or on the language to be used. "Urging" was used when pupils encouraged each other to move on with the task. "Planning" and "checking" were categories used for discussing practical matters, looking forward and looking back respectively. A subcategory "material" was added for coding turns about using the task-related materials. The subcategory "climate" included turns in which pupils were annoyed with each other, calling each other names sometimes, and also included the turns in which conflict situations were repaired. The eighth subcategory was "joking on-task". We found it striking that many of the jokes were task-related. Therefore, we chose to code "joking" as either on-task or off-task.

III. Interpersonal relations

The subcategory occurring most frequently within interpersonal talk was "chitchat", or talking about issues that were not related to the task. Five more subcategories were distinguished within "interpersonal relations": "joking off-task", "quarrelling", "playing", "singing" and "swearing". All of these involved off-task talk, but they occurred less frequently then "chitchatting".

IV. Commenting on the research situation

This category is distinct from the previous ones in being directly associated with our study. It includes pupils' comments about the first author (her clothes, or whether she really did not understand Turkish) and about the research-related materials (mostly the cameras). This category also includes use of Turkish for teaching the first author Turkish words, as well as comments about the fact that one of her project leaders is a professor of Turkish origin, who the pupils admire very much.

5 Results

A table summarising the percentages of mother tongue use in each category for each task and each group is attached in Appendix 2. Here, an overview of the distribution of the four categories across tasks and groups is provided, based on Figure 1. The focus then shifts to some striking findings concerning the subcategories.

Considering all tasks, the category "management-related" occurred most frequently (42%), followed by the category "interpersonal" (27%). The category "content-related" accounted for 21%, while "comments on the research situation" only for 8%. This distribution is quite similar across the different tasks, irrespective of the proportion of turns containing Turkish.

4 "Only dirty things!" Functions of mother tongue — 103

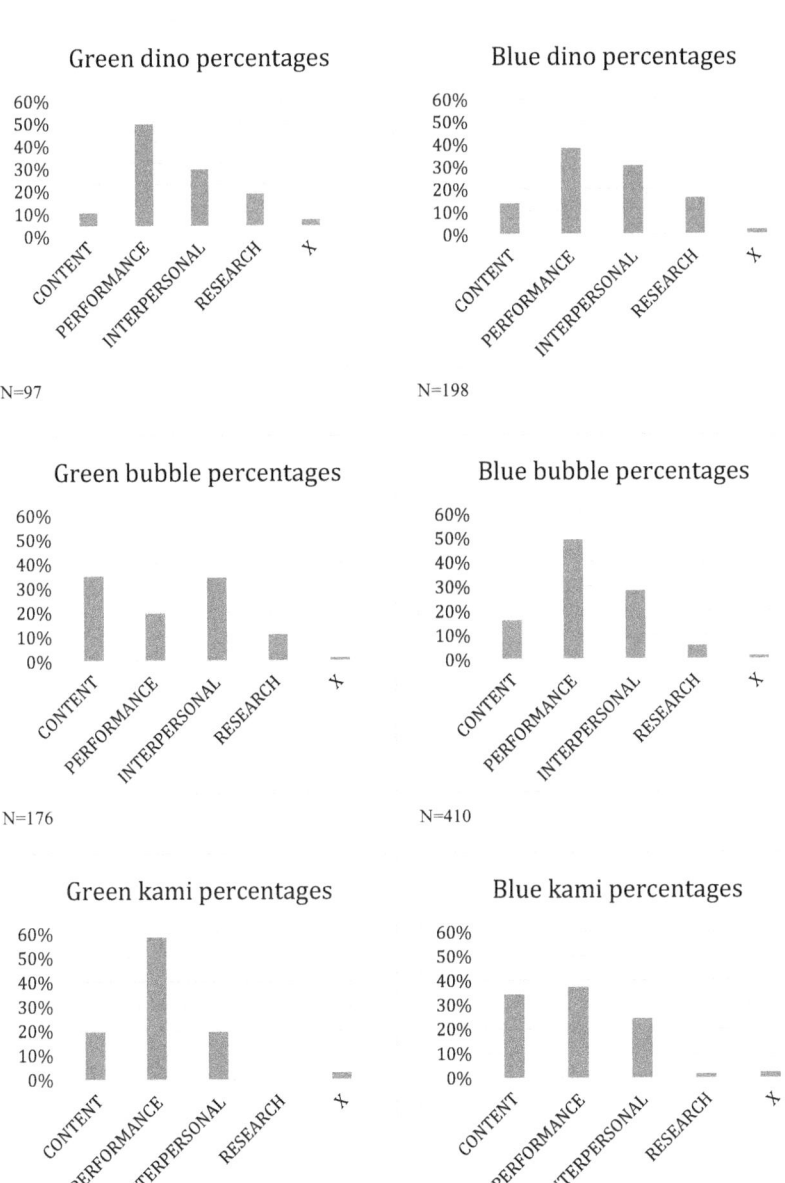

Figure 1: Percentage of turns containing Turkish per main category for every task performance of both groups.

The category "content" was represented in every task performance. It was rather low for the dino task in both groups (6% in the green group and 14% in the blue group), possibly because this was the first task the groups performed and thus the first time they were allowed to use Turkish. Maximum percentages of mother tongue use for content-related talk were found in the blue group performing the story writing task (34%) and the green group performing the bubble task (35%). This high percentage in the story writing by the blue group had to do with their choice to write their story in Turkish. Consequently, formulating ideas for the story and negotiating about the content happened for a substantial part in Turkish. In the bubble task performed by the green group, the rather high use of Turkish for content-related talk, was probably triggered by one particular discussion. Pupils started discussing in Turkish why the bubbles moved through the water and what would happen next. Once the discussion started in Turkish, the pupils seemed inclined to continue discussing content matter in Turkish. Also, pupils knew the Turkish equivalents for some of the words used in this task, for example *asit* (the Turkish equivalent for 'bubbles') and *kuru üzüm* ('raisin') and they continued using the Turkish terms throughout the task performance.

In five out of six task performances, the category "management-related" was the largest one. Only in the green group performing the bubble task this percentage was lower than the percentage of "content-related" and "interpersonal". The percentage of management-related talk in Turkish stood out in the green story writing task (58%). However, as the group chose to write the story in Dutch, only 36 turns contained Turkish, which calls for caution in the interpretation of proportions. Within those 36 turns, they used Turkish mostly for management-related talk, for example when evaluating the quality of their writing (8/36 or 22%), and when establishing roles (7/36 or 19%). It is noteworthy that across all task performances joking occurred more often as part of performance-related talk (up to 7% and 8% in the dino tasks for green and blue respectively) than during off-task talk.

L1 use to maintain interpersonal relationships was observed in every task. Minimum values for this category (19% or 7/36 in the green group and 24% or 130/534 in the blue group) were reported during the performance of the story writing task. During the performance of this task, indeed, both groups were enthusiastically involved in the story writing, which might have resulted in less off-task chitchat, playing and joking. During the performance of the other tasks, about one third of the turns containing Turkish was coded as "interpersonal relationships" (between 27% and 34%).

Comments on the research situation amounted to 15% (green) and 16% (blue) of mother tongue use during the dino task, which was more than for the other tasks. This may be explained both by the fact that the dino task was the first task they performed and by the fact that the pupils were not yet accustomed to the cameras and me.

For the sake of completeness, category "X" (turns containing Turkish that were not coded for a specific function) is reported in Figure 1 as well. Its maximum value was 3% (in green-dino).

6 Discussion

The pupils in this explorative multiple case study used their mother tongue (Turkish) during task performances for a whole range of socio-cognitive functions. Four main categories of purposes were distinguished in our data: "task-related", "management-related", "interpersonal relations" and "commenting on the research situation". Both the blue and the green group showed use of their mother tongue for all these purposes. These results are in line with findings reported in the literature, despite the different context in which this study was carried out: here, the pupils were allowed for the first time to use their mother tongue in an otherwise Dutch-only school environment. Apparently, when pupils are invited to use their mother tongue by exception, they do so quite naturally for a range of socio-cognitive purposes.

Three categories contained the majority of turns in Turkish: "task-related", "management-related" and "interpersonal relations". These findings are in line with the findings of De Guerrero and Villamil (1994) who reported mother tongue use for on-task, about-task and off-task talk, and with Moore (2013) who reported three similar functions: content creation, procedural purposes and off-task purposes. In the current study, it was a deliberate choice not to label the category "interpersonal relations" as off-task, though the option was taken into conisderation. Turns in this category were strictly speaking off-task, but in many instances they were linked with what happened before or afterwards on-task. For example, during the performance of the dino task in the green group, a quarrel arose between Ozan and the rest of the group. Ozan left for a few minutes, and the three others discussed in Turkish how they could make it up to him as it was his birthday. As soon as Ozan came back, the dispute was settled and the task performance could go on. Also, in both groups the pupils deviated from the task performance and chatted in Turkish, creating a pleasant atmosphere. Afterwards, this seemed to result in fruitful cooperation on-task. Apparently, the more sociable the off-task talk was, the more the pupils seemed to be prepared to cooperate afterwards.

In the current study, a fourth category was added, containing comments on the research situation (e.g. the camera or the research team). Swain and Lapkin (2000) categorise the use of the tape recorder under "task management". However, for our study, it was very clear that a distinction had to be made between "management-related" talk (what can be considered everyday school talk, like establishing roles or talking about materials like pens and paper) on the one hand, and research-related talk (for example talk about being recorded or the presence of the researcher) on the other hand. The pupils' comments on the research situation point to a certain consciousness of being observed as described by Labov's (1972) observer's paradox. However, only a small percentage (max 8%) of turns containing Turkish was categorised as "comments on the research". Most of the time the children seemed to act very naturally. Moreover, a considerable amount of their chats was clearly not meant to be overheard by the camera or by the first author, indicating that they often forgot they were being recorded. Taking this into account, the vast majority of the data seems to be reflecting natural classroom behaviour.

According to our data, the majority of turns containing Turkish served purposes related to the task content and performance. This is in line with results reported by De Guerrero and Villamil (1994), Eldridge (1996), Swain and Lapkin (2000), and Storch and Aldosari (2010). Comparing percentages of turns in each category would be inaccurate because of different definitions, frameworks and contexts, but the running thread seems to be that mother tongue use occurs mainly for on- and about-task purposes, and only to a lesser extent for off-task purposes.

This finding contradicts the belief, currently omnipresent in the Flemish educational system, that mother tongue use would more readily serve off-task purposes (Ağirdag, Jordens, and Van Houtte 2014). The results of the studies were quite surprising, especially in the blue group. While the first author and the research assistant were working with the pupils and watching the video-recordings afterwards, the pupils of the blue group gave them the impression that they were very playful and off-task very often. But the analyses carried out showed that the pupils were often on-task, albeit in a playful way. For example, while writing of the story, the pupils chose their own names for the characters in the story. One of the characters was a monster, so the discussion about which name to choose was quite vivid. In a similar vein, one of the girls in the blue group was often urging the others to cooperate in the task performance, getting angry at them and thereby giving the impression that she was quarrelling off-task. In fact, she was organising the task performance, trying to get her peers on-task.

This observation does not only have pedagogical consequences (cf. infra), but is also noteworthy with respect to the functional analysis of classroom discourse. Some of the turns belonged very clearly to one particular category. Others, however, could have been assigned to more than one category. For the quantitative analysis, the category which fitted most was counted, but often two or more functions were appropriate. For example, when establishing roles in consecutive turns, one of the boys in the blue groups asked one of the girls: "Are you the teacher, or what?". The turn was coded as establishing roles (also based on what was said just before), but it could have been coded as "joking related to task performance" as well. So while quantifying discourse can be very valuable and provide insight in different purposes of mother tongue use and the distribution across tasks, interpreting the discourse should be done with caution, taking into account that turns are often multifunctional (Ferguson 2009). Therefore, a purely quantitative analysis might overlook important layers of meaning, implications and implicit messages in the communication.

Another observation is that the distribution of functions might differ between children in the same group. For example, there was quite some swearing going on in the blue group, but a closer look revealed that it was one particular boy uttering all the turns coded "swearing". Also, this boy was more playful than his peers and gave the false impression that the whole group went off-task very often. Van den Branden and Van Gorp (2000) make a similar observation when reporting on the use of CLIM (Cooperative Learning In Multicultural Groups) during which roles were established in discussion exercises. Individual characters seemed to play a specific role in the group interaction, which had a considerable impact on the functioning of the group as a whole.

Not only the characteristics of individual pupils determine the course of the task performance. The exact unfolding of a task performance depends on many factors. As Berben, Van den Branden and Van Gorp (2007: 61) state: "Tasks on paper are not blueprints for uniform and highly predictable action". The actual task performance depends on who is involved, in which temper pupils are that day, whether they have had a quarrel just before and so on. Another aspect influencing language choices in task performance is whether certain words are known in their mother tongue. This is illustrated by the green group when they were talking about *asit* ('sparkling'). If the group had not known this particular word in Turkish, the discourse would have unfolded quite differently.

The fact that language choices become highly unpredictable, might enhance teachers' feeling that they "lose control" when tolerating mother tongue use in class. Indeed, as we experienced ourselves, it is a bit unsettling not to be able to understand the pupils, which sometimes leads to misinterpretations of what pupils say and do. Above, we gave some examples of pupils communicating jokingly or playfully on-task. In the data, instances can be found where the first author hushed them and even interrupted them in an attempt to get them back on-task, while in fact, they already were.

By way of conclusion, three misconceptions about mother tongue use in the classroom can be refuted. Firstly, the idea that "they will speak Turkish all the time" (as the teacher of the blue group claimed) seems to be an overstatement. Pupils spoke Turkish in maximum one third of the turns. Secondly, the assumption that their use of Turkish would be mainly off-task was not corroborated by the data collected. Thirdly, the idea that the pupils' proficiency in Turkish would not allow them to discuss subject matter seems unjustified. Pupils were perfectly able to interact in a mix of Turkish and Dutch during task performance, and to finding meaningful solutions to the complex problems they were exposed to. Moreover, they were able to present their results in Dutch only, the prescribed medium of interaction.

An obvious pedagogical consequence is that it is worth reconsidering Dutch-only rules in the Flemish classroom. Pupils were able to perform tasks, using Dutch and Turkish as one medium of interaction. Using their full linguistic repertoire did not undermine task performance; on the contrary, it seemed to facilitate it, as pupils drew on Turkish for organising their task performance, discussing content-related matters, and maintaining personal relationships. Even the pupils in this study, who were allowed to use Turkish openly for the first time, seemed to get some benefit. As for the teacher, this study shows that trust is a key factor: the majority of what pupils said in Turkish was content- and management-related, even though they were perfectly aware that the first author could not understand them. "Trusting them", however, is not a synonym for "just letting them be". If the first author left them work on their own for too long, they tended to drift away from task performance, or started calling for her help. So while trusting them when they speak Turkish is crucial, they still need the teacher to monitor their progress and to offer scaffolding and interactional support when necessary. This study shows that when the bilingual pupils are trusted and experience the active involvement of the teacher, they are able to carry out very complex tasks.

7 Conclusion

Socio-cognitive functions of mother tongue use in classrooms in different contexts have been reported in the literature. However, in these studies, mother tongue use as a medium of interaction in class was accepted and the teacher was able to speak or at least understand all languages used in class. This study was carried out in schools with an explicit Dutch-only policy, where teachers were not able to speak nor understand the mother tongue of the pupils. As a result, teachers and school teams were not inclined to tolerate mother tongue use in class, because of their beliefs that "it would be spoken too much" and/or "it would mostly serve off-task purposes" (Ağirdag, Jordens, and Van Houtte 2014). The aim of this study was to explore which functions mother tongue use served in peer-peer conversations during collaborative group work, when exceptionally tolerated as a means of communication.

The main findings of this study are in line with those of previous studies, in that the mother tongue was used for a range of socio-cognitive functions, including content-related and management-related talk. This implies that the results contradict Flemish teachers' perceptions that mother tongue use in class does not contribute to learning processes. As Swain and Lapkin (2000: 268–269) state: "To insist that no use be made of the L1 in carrying out tasks that are both linguistically and cognitively complex is to deny the use of an important cognitive tool". The data presented in this study showed that the mother tongue fulfils an important role for cognitive as well as for socio-affective purposes, even for bilingual pupils who were not used to drawing on their full linguistic repertoire during task performance.

One of the pupils confided to the first author: "They [the teachers] think we can only talk about dumb things in Turkish. In their opinion, Turkish is a dirty language". This study vividly illustrates that this belief is unjustified.

Acknowledgements: The authors would like to thank research assistant Annelies Jehoul for her meticulous help in coding the data. This work was supported by the Agency for Innovation by Science and Technology (IWT), Flanders (Belgium) under Grant 110008 (Valorising Linguistic Diversity in Multiple Contexts of Primary Education "Validiv").

References

Ağirdag, Orhan. 2010. Exploring bilingualism in a monolingual school system: Insights from Turkish and native students from Belgian schools. *British Journal of Sociology of Education* 31 (3). 307–321.

Ağirdag, Orhan, Kathelijne Jordens & Mieke Van Houtte. 2014. Speaking Turkish in Belgian schools: Teacher beliefs versus effective consequences. *Bilig – Journal of Social Sciences of the Turkish World* 70. 7–28.

Benjamin, Rebecca. 1996. The functions of Spanish in the school lives of Mexicano bilingual children. *Bilingual Research Journal* 20 (1). 135–164.

Berben, Martien, Kris Van den Branden & Koen Van Gorp. 2007. "We'll see what happens": Tasks on paper and tasks in a multilingual classroom. In Kris Van den Branden, Koen Van

Gorp & Machteld Verhelst (eds.), *Tasks in action: Task-based language education from a classroom-based perspective*, 32–67. Cambridge: Cambridge Scholars Publishing.

De Guerrero, Maria C.M. & Olga S. Villamil. 1994. Social-cognitive dimensions of interaction in L2 peer revision. *Modern Language Journal* 78 (4). 484–496.

Eldridge, John. 1996. Code-switching in a Turkish secondary school. *ELT Journal* 50 (4). 303–311.

Ferguson, Gibson. 2009. What next? Towards an agenda for classroom codeswitching research. *International Journal of Bilingual Education and Bilingualism* 12 (2). 231–241.

Glaser, Barney G. & Anselm Strauss. 1967. *The discovery of grounded theory: Strategies for qualitative research*. Chicago: Aldine.

Gort, Mileidis. 2012. Code-switching patterns in the writing-related talk of young emergent bilinguals. *Journal of Literacy Research* 44 (1). 45–75.

Hall, Graham & Guy Cook. 2012. Own-language use in language teaching and learning. *Language Teaching* 45 (3). 271–308.

Jaspaert, Koen & Griet Ramaut. 2000. "Don't use English words in Dutch": Portrait of a multilingual classroom in Flanders. In Georgii Khruslov & Sjaak Kroon (eds.), *The challenge of multilingualism to standard language teaching: Cases from Flanders, England, the Netherlands, Germany and Russia*, 10–18. Moscow: INPO.

Jaspers, Jürgen. 2008. Problematizing ethnolects: Naming linguistic practices in an Antwerp secondary school. *International Journal of Bilingualism* 12 (1–2). 85–103.

Labov, William. 1972. *Sociolingustic patterns*. Philadelphia: University of Pennsylvania.

Leman, Johan. 1997. School as a socialising and corrective force in inter-ethnic urban relations. *Journal of Multilingual and Multicultural Development* 18 (2). 125–134.

Macaro, Ernesto. 2005. Codeswitching in the L2 classroom: A communication and learning strategy. In Enric Llurda (ed.), *Non-native language teachers: Perceptions, challenges, and contributions to the profession*, 63–84. Boston: Springer.

Moodley, Visvaganthie. 2007. Codeswitching in the multilingual English first language classroom. *International Journal of Bilingual Education and Bilingualism* 10 (6). 707–722.

Moore, Paul J. 2013. An emergent perspective on the use of the first language in the English-as-a-Foreign-Language classroom. *The Modern Language Journal* 97 (1). 239–253.

Probyn, Margie. 2009. "Smuggling the vernacular into the classroom": Conflicts and tensions in classroom codeswitching in township/rural schools in South Africa. *International Journal of Bilingual Education and Bilingualism* 12 (2). 123–136.

Ramaut, Griet, Sven Sierens, Katrien Bultynck, Piet Van Avermaet, Stef Slembrouck, Koen Van Gorp & Machteld Verhelst. 2013. *Evaluatieonderzoek van het project 'Thuistaal in onderwijs' (2009–2012) Eindrapport* [Evaluation research of the 'Home language in education' project (2009–2012) Final report]. Ghent and Leuven: Universiteit Gent en Universiteit Leuven.

Reyes, Iliana. 2004. Functions of code switching in schoolchildren's conversations. *Bilingual Research Journal* 28 (1). 77–98.

Rosiers, Kirsten. 2015. Translanguaging om te leren? Een interactie-analyse in een Gentse superdiverse klas [Translanguaging to learn? An interaction analysis in a Ghent super-diverse class]. Paper presented at ORD 2015, Leiden, 17–19 June.

Sacks, Harvey, Emanuel A. Schegloff & Gail Jefferson. 1974. A simplest systematics for the organization of turn-taking for conversation. *Language* 50 (4). 696–735.

Sierens, Sven & Piet Van Avermaet. 2014. Language diversity in education: evolving from multilingual education to functional multilingual learning. In David Little, Constant Leung

& Piet Van Avermaet (eds.), *Managing diversity in education: Languages, policies, pedagogies*, 204–222. Bristol: Multilingual Matters.

Spotti, Massimiliano. 2008. Exploring the construction of immigrant minority pupils' identities in a Flemish primary classroom. *Linguistics and Education* 19 (1). 20–36.

Storch, Neomy & Ali Aldosari. 2010. Learners' use of first language (Arabic) in pair work in an EFL class. *Language Teaching Research* 14 (4). 355–375.

Swain, Merrill & Sharon Lapkin. 2000. Task-based second language learning: The uses of the first language. *Language Teaching Research* 4 (3). 251–274.

Turnbull, Miles. 2001. There is a role for the L1 in second and foreign language teaching, but.... *Canadian Modern Language Review* 57 (4). 531–540.

Van den Branden, Kris & Koen Van Gorp. 2000. How to evaluate CLIM in terms of intercultural education. *Intercultural Education* 11 (S1). 42–51.

Van den Branden, Kris, Koen Van Gorp & Machteld Verhelst (eds.), 2007. *Tasks in action: task-based language education from a classroom-based perspective*. Cambridge: Cambridge Scholars Publishing.

Yağmur, Kutlay. 2009. Language use and ethnolinguistic vitality of Turkish compared with the Dutch in the Netherlands. *Journal of Multilingual and Multicultural Development* 30 (3). 219–233.

Appendix 1: The final coding tree

Content-related

1. Formulating ideas:
a. Proposing ideas for the story or reread pieces of what was written in order to go further.

    Example: *bir küçük Çin annesiyle* . . . (blue kami)
    Translation: A small Chinese is with his mother . . .

b. Proposing ideas for explaining hypotheses (dino) / what happened with the bubbles.

    Example: *Yo dinazorlar yenilmiş.* (blue dino)
    Translation: No, the dinosaurs were eaten.
    Example: *Bu uzun bir şeyden böyle yapınca belletjesler gelmiyor. Çünkü hava gelmiyor.*
    (green bubble)
    Translation: If we do this with the long thing, bubbles won't appear. Because there is no air.

2. Negotiation:
a. Discussing what to write, the exact meaning of pictures and co-occurring text or words.

> Example: *Ismini koyalım, cüce demeyelim isim koyalım . . . Fatih!* (blue kami)
> Translation: Let's give him a name and not call him dwarf . . . Fatih!

b. Discussing events in the case of the science tasks.

> Example: *Asitli suyun içine kuru üzüm koyduk. Soruyorlar, niye oldu bu?* (green bubble)
> Translation: We put raisins in sparkling water. They ask: Why did that happen?

3. Presenting the task product: reading out loud the story when finished creating (only in story writing-in all other tasks this happened in monolingual Dutch).

> Example: *Öcünün ismi Fatih'ti. Çocuklari korkuttu.* (blue kami)
> Translation: The monster's name is Fatih, he scared the children.

Management-related

4. Meta comments: commenting on the performance itself, or the language to be used.

> Example: *Ne biçim yazıyon ya!* (blue kami)
> Translation: You write so badly!
> Example: *Ah attım kafadan birşeyler!* (blue dino)
> Translation: I just made it up! (about his answer to the question)

5. Checking: talking about how practical matters were dealt with (looking back).

> Example: *Oké twee, siz ne yazdınız oraya?* (blue kami)
> Translation: Okay, two, what have you written there?

6. Urging: urging each other to go on, which can be explicit or implicit.

    Example: *Oké, hadi devam edelim.* (blue kami)
    Translation: Okay, come on, let's move on.
    Example: *Abo, bunlar daha var!* (blue dino)
    Translation: Hey, there are more!

7. Planning: Talking about how to deal with matters, still to come, looking forward e.g. sequencing of actions.

    Example: *Sen okumadan anlamazsın.* (blue dino)
    Translation: You won't understand it if you don't read it first.

8. Establishing roles: who will be doing what.

    Example: *Dört kişiyle beraber anlaşiyoruz sonra bir kişi de yazıyor.* (blue kami)
    Translation: We make decisions with four persons and afterwards one person writes it down.

9. Material: talking about papers, pens and so on, used for task performance.

    Example: *Kağıdımı ver.* (blue kami)
    Translation: Give me my sheet.

10. Climate: commenting on each other's behaviour: expressing annoyance and repairing conflicts (about the task performance).

    Example: *Sus! Bana bağıramazsın!* (blue kami)
    Translation: Shut up! You can't scream to me!
    Example: *Ay doğru ya bugün onun yaşgünü, bide sinirlendirdik onu ya.* (green dino)
    Translation: Ah, that's true, it was his birthday today and we made him angry.

11. Joking: about something to do with the task performance.

    Example: *Allah korusun! En çirkini demek istiyon.* (blue dino)
    Translation: God bless, you mean the ugliest. (after F says he writes the most beautifully)

Interpersonal relations: off-task

12. Joking

    Example: *Yağlı derken? Yakışıklılığımımı diyorsun?* (blue kami)
    Translation: Greasy you say? Do you mean my handsomeness?

13. Chitchatting

    Example: *Emilie sana eetzaal'da napıyordu?* (green dino)
    Translation: What did Emilie do to you in the lunchroom?

14. Quarreling

    Example: *Saçımı elleme lan.* (blue bubble)
    Translation: Don't touch my hair, man.

15. Playing

    Example: *Hartje yapcam bak hartje* (blue bubble)
    Translation: I'm going to draw a heart, look, a heart

16. Singing

    Example: *sanki bana gülüyor ...* (blue kami)
    Translation: as if she smiles at me (singing)

17. Swearing

    Example: *Orospu çocukları.* (blue kami)
    Translation: Sons of a whore.

Commenting on the research situation

18. About me: about my clothes, my Turkish skills.

    Example: *Bundan sonra öğretmene Türkçe konuşalım, sonra anlamazsa oğrensin.* (blue bubble)
    Translation: From now on, let's talk Turkish to the teacher and when she doesn't understand, she can learn it.

19. Teaching Turkish: when addressing me for teaching me Turkish words.

   Example: *Als die selâmın aleyküm zegt, moet ge aleyküm selam zeggen.* (blue dino)
   Translation: When answering "*selâmın aleyküm*" we say "*aleykumselam*".

20. Material: mostly the camera and voice recorders.

   Example: *Bu açıkmı?* (blue dino)
   Translation: Is this on?

21. Professor Orhan: he is one of the team leaders of the project I work for. He is from Turkish origin, which the pupils admire.

   Example: *Sşt, şttt. Orhaaan telefonunu bana versene?* (green bubble)
   Translation: Sst, sst. Orhan, can you give me your phone number? (talking to the voice recorder)

Appendix 2: Distribution of functions

Percentage of turns containing Turkish per category for every task performance of both groups (in the last row, turns consisting of two utterances with a different function (n=15) were counted twice. The number of turns is 96 – 198 – 36 – 522 – 176 – 408).

Category	Green group Dino task	Blue group Dino task	Green group Kamishibai task	Blue group Kamishibai task	Green group Bubble task	Blue group Bubble task	Average over groups and tasks
CONTENT	**6%**	**14%**	**19%**	**34%**	**35%**	**16%**	**21%**
Ideas	1%	3%	19%	18%	7%	5%	9%
Negotiation	5%	11%	0%	10%	27%	10%	11%
Read	0%	0%	0%	6%	0%	0%	1%
PERFORMANCE	**48%**	**38%**	**58%**	**37%**	**19%**	**49%**	**42%**
Meta	4%	3%	22%	6%	6%	6%	8%
Urging	8%	5%	0%	3%	2%	2%	3%
Checking	10%	4%	6%	4%	4%	5%	6%
Planning	1%	5%	8%	5%	0%	4%	4%
Roles	4%	4%	19%	10%	1%	12%	8%
Material	0%	2%	0%	5%	2%	14%	4%
Climate	13%	9%	0%	2%	3%	3%	5%
Joke (on)	7%	8%	3%	3%	2%	3%	4%

INTER-PERSONAL	27%	30%	19%	24%	34%	28%	27%
Joke (off)	4%	5%	3%	2%	3%	0%	3%
Chitchat	21%	18%	17%	20%	27%	20%	21%
Quarrel	0%	0%	0%	1%	0%	0%	0%
Playing	2%	4%	0%	0%	2%	2%	2%
Sing	0%	1%	0%	0%	1%	0%	0%
Swearing	0%	4%	0%	1%	2%	6%	2%
RESEARCH	15%	16%	0%	2%	11%	6%	8%
x	3%	2%	3%	2%	1%	1%	2%
TURNS containing Turkish	97	198	36	534	176	410	

Part 3: **Responses to multilingual challenges in the context of family policies and practices**

Elizabeth Lanza
5 Urban multilingualism and family language policy

Abstract: This article addresses the need to investigate family language policy in regard to issues concerning immigration in contemporary urban spaces. Family language policy is an emerging field of inquiry that bridges the gap between studies of child language and the field of language policy research in its approach to understanding language maintenance and shift in multilingual families and communities. A case study on Norway concerning the school performance of children with an immigrant background is presented to illustrate the importance of addressing language ideologies at the societal level and how they may affect language policies in the home. While Norway has been considered a sociolinguistic paradise in the widespread acceptance of dialectal variation, without diglossia, the use of other immigrant languages is not looked upon as favourably. Drawing on media data of a particular case that received considerable national attention, the article highlights how political pressures were placed on families with an immigrant background in order to promote their speaking Norwegian in the home. Such a policy would ultimately promote monolingualism in society. The study shows how family spaces, traditionally considered private domains, have essentially become public spaces through mediatised discourses. A comparison is made with other similar cases in Europe.

1 Introduction

The world is connecting in many complex ways, driven by the globally integrated nature of technological innovation and human mobility across continents. One of the most significant cultural consequences of such mobility and urban development in post-modern society is what Vertovec (2007) has called "super-diversity". While the notion of "super-diversity" has been challenged as a global process, "migration has globalized from a destination country perspective" (Czaika and Haas 2014: 283), and urban centres in Europe today reflect this pattern. This diversity has had a significant impact on language in society,

Elizabeth Lanza, Center for Multilingualism in Society across the Lifespan (MultiLing), University of Oslo, ILN, Henrik Wergelands hus, Niels Henrik Abels vei 36, N-0313 Oslo, Norway.

https://doi.org/10.1515/9781501503207-006

as argued by Blommaert and Rampton (2011), specifically concerning language policies and practices, as well as ideologies. And multilingualism, the "coexistence, contact and interaction of different languages" (Li Wei 2013: 26), is a "social, linguistic and individual phenomenon, which is fast becoming one of the core issues of current communities" (Ruiz de Zarobe and Ruiz de Zarobe 2015) and an everyday reality in cities today (Cenoz 2013).

An excellent example of such intense diversity in urban areas is the increasingly large number of transcultural families, with multilingualism as a dominant feature. Some transcultural families result from immigration and transnational movement, while others are from intercultural marriages and bonds. Some of these families are recently established, while others have existed for generations; globalisation only serves to intensify the encounters of different traditions, values and languages of the various members of the family (Lanza and Li Wei 2016). Children from families with an immigrant background may enter local school systems without the necessary proficiency in the language of the host society, presenting challenges to the educational system. Such challenges provide in turn material for media presentations and spur political pressures to propose solutions, launching various language policy efforts in the educational sector. Language policy research offers a broad array of research methods for investigating such issues in language planning and language practices (cf. Hult and Johnson 2015) and should be drawn upon to address societal issues.

Whereas language policy research focuses on language practices in schools, as well as the workplace and in society in general, the social unit of the family has received less attention (Lanza and Li Wei 2016). Yet there is a need to gain insight into linguistic practices in multilingual transcultural families as this insight may contribute to understanding why children from some ethnic backgrounds succeed in schools while others may not. While language education research has for a long time privileged the home-school relationship as pivotal to understanding educational success, much less research has started from an examination of the home context. Such insights from the home may, moreover, also reveal some of the key forces in processes that may potentially lead to the demise of regional or minority languages and culture, or to their spread. Given the urban multilingualism in European society today, there is a pressing need to understand the role of languages and linguistic ideologies at all levels of society, including the family, in order to address the interface between language policy, language planning, and actual practices in the current landscape of linguistic diversity in Europe. Such an approach can contribute to valorising multilingualism and hence promoting immigrants' social inclusion and linguistic diversity.

In this article, I will present the burgeoning field of family language policy (King, Fogle, and Logan-Terry 2008; Li Wei 2012; Schwartz and Verschik 2013; King and Lanza 2019), which investigates how multilingual families manage their linguistic and cultural heritage in contemporary urban spaces. Drawing on Norway as a case study, with a particular focus on its capital city Oslo, I will argue for the need to investigate family language policy, not only concerning the minority heritage language but also in regard to the host society's language, through an ongoing debate in Norway involving discourses of multilingualism and responsibility. In the following, I will first present family language policy as a field of study, illustrating the type of knowledge such a field can yield, invoking both language planning and language practices. Subsequently, Norway as a case will be presented, a country traditionally perceived as one with a high tolerance for linguistic diversity. A particularly hot debate arose in the fall of 2013 that brought immigrant families into the ring in the debate surrounding linguistic diversity in the schools. In conclusion, the importance of insights into family language planning will be discussed in light of urban multilingualism.

2 Family language policy as an emerging field of study

The research field of family language policy (FLP) bridges the gap between studies of child language and the field of language policy research in its approach to understanding language maintenance and shift in multilingual families and communities (King, Fogle, and Logan-Terry 2008; Li Wei 2012; Ó hIfearnáin 2013). FLP can be defined as explicit and overt, as well as implicit and covert, planning in relation to language use and literacy practices within home domains and among family members (King, Fogle, and Logan-Terry 2008; Curdt-Christiansen 2013). In line with current trends in language policy research (Shohamy 2006; Spolsky 2009; Hult and Johnson 2015), FLP involves linguistic practices, which reveal implicit language planning (Li Wei 2012; Spolsky 2012). FLP is, moreover, formed and implemented in interaction with wider political, social, and economic forces, especially important to capture in addressing urban multilingualism in Europe today. Macro-level societal phenomena play a role in language maintenance and language shift; however, as Fishman (1991) so clearly pointed out in reference to reversing language shift, it is the micro-level of face-to-face interaction and social life within the family that plays a crucial role (cf. Lanza [1997] 2004a, 2004b, 2007). Heritage language is indeed "profoundly connected to speakers' attitudes and values" (Weiyun He 2012). Lanza and Svendsen (2007) revealed that family language ideologies played a decisive role in parents' decisions to maintain the heritage language or use the societal language with their children, hence language policy at the family level.

Family language policy has been an underexplored area of sociolinguistic scholarship (Li Wei 2012). It is situated at the cutting edge of two well-established areas of sociolinguistic research: language socialisation and linguistic ideology. Language socialisation takes account of socialising *into* language to enable appropriate use of linguistic structures, and *through* language for individuals to become effective social actors and community members (Schieffelin and Ochs 1986; Duranti, Ochs, and Schieffelin 2012). The study of language ideologies investigates how particular ways of using languages reflect and (re)produce socio-cultural values, and the beliefs and assumptions that people have about language (Irvine and Gal 2000). Linguistic ideologies are outcomes of socio-historical conditions of a nation, a community or a group, as well as experiences of individuals (cf. Kroskrity 2000). Ideologies, moreover, are closely intertwined with identities. Both language socialisation and language ideologies meet in family language policies as they are formed and implemented in interaction with wider socio-political and cultural forces (King, Fogle, and Logan-Terry 2008; Li Wei 2012; Lanza and Li Wei 2016; King and Lanza 2019).

The family is a community of practice, a social unit that has its norms for speaking, acting and believing, and hence provides a focus on praxis, the cornerstone for language socialisation (Lanza 2007). Migration and ongoing changes in socio-political and cultural environments have resulted in changing linguistic configurations of families, including those in which both of the caregivers have the same immigrant background as well as those involving different linguistic and cultural backgrounds. Establishing a transcultural family resulting from an intercultural marriage or civil bond requires the negotiation of divergent cultural values and beliefs. Crippen and Brew (2007) point out that childrearing may be a significant source of conflict for intercultural couples (cf. Okita 2002). Indeed, decision-making about intergenerational transmission of language and culture is an important issue for multilingual couples (Piller 2002; Varro 2003). Families may, moreover, involve other structures, including a single parent or caregivers from different generations. Research is needed on just how these various configurations impact on family language policy and how they may relate to social inclusion and exclusion in society.

2.1 Language ideologies

Language ideologies underpin family language policies. Riley (2012: 493) points out that "[...] language ideologies are intrinsically implicated in all language socialization processes and vice versa – that is, language ideologies influence the sociocultural contexts that shape language socialization, and language ideologies are also among the many cultural values socialized through language use". De Houwer (1999: 83) refers to an "impact belief", which she defines as "[...] the parental belief that parents can exercise some sort of control over their children's linguistic functioning". These impact beliefs may be influenced by cultural as well as personal preferences and can be strong as when parents provide negative sanctioning to certain linguistic practices, and thus employ control over the child's language use; on the other hand, they may be fairly weak in that there is an attitude of anything goes. Parental ideologies will thus influence parents' linguistic practices and interaction strategies with their child, and this in turn may impact on the child's language development. Okita (2002: 232) notes that language use in bilingual families is "[...] deeply intertwined with the experience of childrearing", a finding also in King and Fogle (2006). Garrett (2007: 237) promotes the examination of cases of "bad subjects", which in a bilingual context refers to the "apparent failure or refusal of children to acquire both languages". Traditionally, in language socialisation adults are seen as socialising children; however, as Gafaranga (2011) points out "*Tout le monde est coupable*" [Everyone is guilty] since children also exert agency, or "the socioculturally mediated capacity to act" (Ahearn 2001: 133), in multilingual contexts and may even contribute to language shift (Gafaranga 2010).

Local and societal ideologies support and constrain language choices and linguistic practices in the family with potentially conflicting ideologies also coming into play, for example, when speakers attribute varying importance to language as a core value of identity (cf. Lanza and Svendsen 2007). Spolsky (2009: 18) notes that "The home language is influenced by the sociolinguistic ecology inside and outside the home and by the parents' beliefs about the best strategy". This sociolinguistic ecology may include significant persons such as grandparents (cf. Ruby 2012). In a review of the field of early child bilingualism, Romaine (1995) proposed six basic types of language choice patterns in the family according to the native languages of the parents, the language(s) of the community, and the strategy the parents employ with the child:

(1) One person – one language
(2) Non-dominant home language / One language – one environment
(3) Non-dominant home language without community support
(4) Double non-dominant home language without community support

(5) Non-native parents
(6) Mixed languages.

Romaine (1995)'s influential typology is still often cited. Other aspects of family bilingualism may, however, come into play such as the parents' and the community's ideologies of language, the language the parents use to communicate with each other, as well as peer or sibling language use (cf. Lanza and Svendsen 2007). Moreover, the sixth type concerning mixing languages actually overlaps with the other types; for example, parents claim to maintain the "one person – one language" principle yet they code-switch, that is, they use more than one language in interaction, both within and across utterances (Lanza [1997] 2004a). And finally, while Romaine (1995)'s typology highlights family members' language choice in the home, we must recall that the home is in fact not a sealed-off space for language input. For example, input from visitors, television, radio and the internet may also be present in situations in which family members only speak one language.

2.2 Language practices and language contact

The issue of language mixing or language contact has figured especially in studies of family language policy involving early childhood bilingualism. In work on Norwegian-English bilingual families in Oslo, Lanza ([1997] 2004a) presents a framework for analysing the role of parental discourse strategies in response to bilingual children's language mixing and the children's bilingual outcomes. The particular discourse strategies can, moreover, also be construed as part of identity constructions in interaction. The framework draws on language socialisation and discourse analytic approaches to studying family interaction, yet it can be applied analytically to examine any conversation involving the negotiation of language choice. Gafaranga (2010) extended Lanza ([1997] 2004a) through a focus on the bilingual children in caregiver-child interactions in Rwandan Kinyarwanda-French bilingual families in Belgium. He showed how language shift was "talked into being" in family interactions through the use of a particular discourse strategy – the "medium request" – used primarily by children to turn the language of interaction to French. Moreover, when caregivers resisted the children's language negotiation to turn to French, parallel conversations in the two languages resulted, thus with the children being allowed to use their preferred medium. Hence children may be agents of change. To what extent and how language shift occurs in families in Europe with an immigrant background deserves further attention in today's globalised society. The large-scale empirical findings on language use in the home in the volume on *Urban multilingualism in Europe* (Extra and Yağmur 2004) are now over ten years old.

The social order is produced and reproduced through linguistic practices and ideologies, and in a multilingual context, the use of code-switching has been highly documented as a strategy in identity negotiation in interpersonal communication (cf. Bucholtz and Hall 2005). Zhu Hua (2008) demonstrates through the sequential organisation of code-switching how conflicts in values and identities are negotiated, mediated and managed in bilingual Chinese-English family interactions. Contrary to the stereotype of the obedient Chinese child, children challenged their parents' positions with multilingual language use contributing to the emergence of new interpersonal relationships and social values. Studies of youth language in urban spaces outside the family point to the complex patterns of language contact in interaction involving many languages (Svendsen and Røyneland 2008), with such multilingual practices involved in identity constructions (Quist and Svendsen 2010). These practices have been attributed various names. For example, Otsuji and Pennycook (2010: 240) refer to the phenomenon as "metrolingualism" – "creative linguistic practices across borders of culture, history and politics". Others prefer "translanguaging" (García and Li Wei 2014). Makoni and Pennycook (2007) and Blommaert (2010) call for the deconstruction of the concept of "language", preferring the emphasis on "repertoires" (cf. Busch 2012), as language boundaries are at times impossible to demarcate in such linguistic practices, which have been documented especially among youth in peer-interaction in and out of school. There is a new need to investigate to what extent these multilingual practices figure within the family and the ideologies associated with them, including practices of naming languages and drawing boundaries (or not) between them.

2.3 Literacy and family language policy

Socialisation into literacy is traditionally consigned to the school (Sterponi 2012). In transcultural families, this usually implies literacy development in the societal language only, whereas multiliteracy may be a goal. Stavans (2012) demonstrates how home literacy practices can in fact contribute to literacy at school among members of a cultural group that preferred oral not written discourse as the foothold for their literacy-driven parent-child interactions. In these families, caregivers resorted to oral descriptions and folk narratives in facilitating the development of vocabulary and narrative syntax. New social media and other means of digital communication provide a platform for language maintenance, identity constructions and multiliteracies (cf. Androutsopoulos 2010). Through iPads and other similar reading tablets, even toddlers are introduced to mediated linguistic, and more generally semiotic, literacies. A strengthened knowledge base on digital competence and multiliteracies is of paramount importance. While more and more important public information goes online, the extent of digital literacies among new citizens remains to be documented. In Norway, Guthu and Holm (2010) documented that half of the immigrants in the country, and their offspring, had limited digital proficiency at a time when the country aimed to employ digital media with the goal of creating a more inclusive society. Interestingly, what country the individual came from was an important variable. Norwegian-born individuals with parents from Pakistan and Vietnam were just as digitally included as their peers with Norwegian parents. Although digital competence is taken for granted today in European society, there may still be many who have limited access and proficiency. To what extent children are socialised into digital literacy is an open question.

In sum, examining the family language policy of those with a migrant background, both from within Europe and from outside of Europe, can provide valuable information concerning the role of languages and linguistic ideologies at all levels of society and the extent of multilingualism in contemporary urban spaces.

3 The need for family language policy research: Norway as a case

In the following, I first present an overview of current immigration to Norway in order to provide a context for the presentation of the particular media coverage on immigration that ensued in November 2013. This case clearly illustrates the need to view the family in light of society.

3.1 Current immigration to Norway and national language policy

Despite traditional images of homogeneity in Scandinavia, Norway has indeed experienced immigration throughout the years; however, the rate of immigration from the 1970s has increased significantly and the origins of immigration have also changed. Statistics Norway indicated that as of 1 January 2016, 16.3% of the country's population of over 5 million were immigrants or Norwegian-born to immigrant parents. The percentage rose to 32% in the capital, Oslo.

Figure 1 from Statistics Norway[1] indicates that immigrants from Asia including Turkey as well as immigrants from EU countries, including EEA (European Economic Area), account for the large increases of immigration.

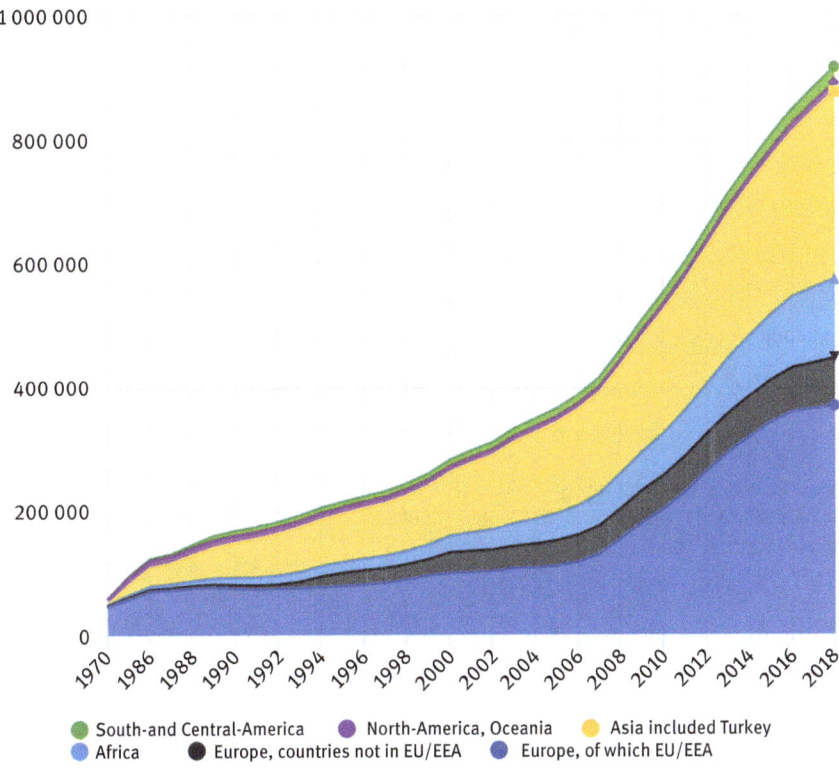

Figure 1: Immigrants and Norwegian-born to immigrant parents, by geographical area of origin.
Source: Statistics Norway.

The enlargement of the European Union can explain the latter influx, which includes a large percentage of Poles, indicated in Figure 2[2] as the largest single group in Norway today. They represent 14% of all immigrants to Norway today. Those with a Pakistani background comprise the largest group of second-generation individuals born in Norway of immigrant parents. Previously, the Pakistani were for many years the largest immigrant group in the country. The

---

1 https://www.ssb.no/en/befolkning/statistikker/innvbef (accessed 12 January 2018)
2 https://www.ssb.no/en/befolkning/statistikker/innvbef (accessed 12 January 2017)

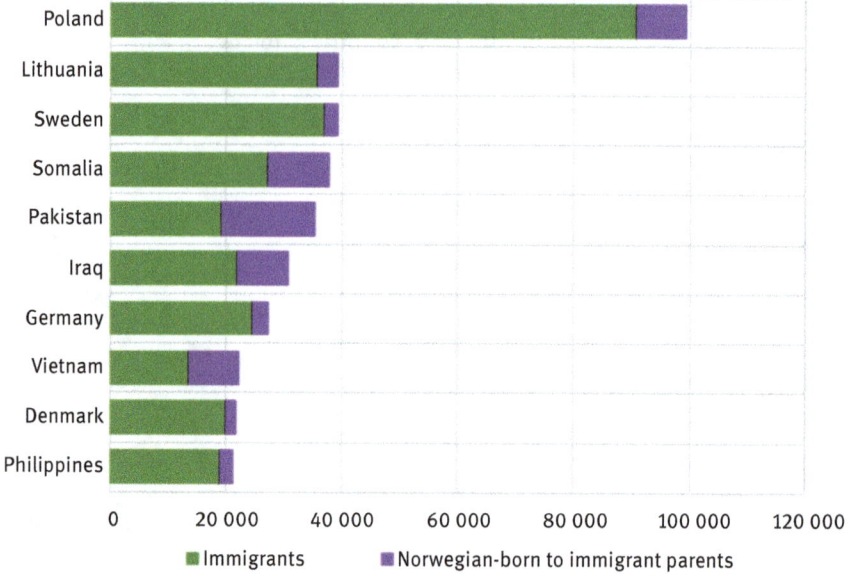

Figure 2: Immigrants and Norwegian-born to immigrant parents, by country background. The ten largest groups, 1 January 2015. Absolute numbers.
Source: Statistics Norway.

Pakistani began to come to Norway already during the late 1960s and 1970s, due to a shortage in the country's workforce. At that time there were fairly liberal immigration regulations that allowed labourers, often unskilled, to come to Norway for temporary residence. This was a situation experienced in many other European countries as well, although other ethnic groups may dominate. In Norway, stricter immigration laws were enforced in 1976 and subsequently, family reunification accounts for the influx of immigrants from Pakistan. Second generation Pakistani Norwegians, born in Norway, comprise many highly successful and influential individuals in the country. Notably, Hadia Tajik was appointed as Minister of Culture under the Labour Party government in 2012, at the age of 29, becoming the youngest as well as the first Muslim in Norwegian government.

Norway has no official language policy; however, there are documents that fulfil this function. The goal of the European Charter for Regional or Minority Languages is to protect and promote regional and minority languages in Europe, with two levels of protection. Norway signed the Charter in regards to historical minorities in 1992. The document was ratified in 1993 and entered in force in 1998. The languages covered include the Sámi languages, Kven, Romanes and Romani. The minority languages of new immigrants are not included in the Charter, nor is Norwegian Sign Language. The latter is elevated in the Norwegian White Paper (St.meld. nr. 35 [2007–2008], Innst. S. nr. 184 [2008–2009]) *Mål og meining. Ein heilskapleg norsk språkpolitikk*[3] [Goals and meaning. A holistic Norwegian language policy], an important document that outlines Norwegian language policy. It is worth mentioning that the *Språkrådet* [Language Council] is the state's consultative body on language issues; it works to strengthen the Norwegian language and linguistic diversity in Norway and it follows up Norway's language policy on assignment for the Ministry of Culture. It is important to point out that such official documents and consultative bodies involve language use in public spaces such as government and education. Language choice in the home, on the other hand, is not regulated and is rather a matter of individual choice. Yet ideologies in the public sphere also make an impact on private spheres, hence the importance of gaining insight into family language policies.

3.2 Discourses of the local and global in Norway

As noted above, urban centres in Europe today experience to various degrees the "super-diversity" Vertovec (2007) described concerning Great Britain. This has also been a significant cultural consequence of mobility and urban development in post-modern Norway. Traditionally, Norway has often been described as a "linguistic paradise" (Mæhlum and Røyneland 2012) due to the country's high degree of acceptance and tolerance of the use of dialects in all situations, as opposed to a diglossic situation found in many other countries, for example, Germany. Conversations among Norwegians of various dialect backgrounds are often "polylectal" (Røyneland 2009), that is, each one speaks her/his dialect, although some accommodation may occur. Indeed, one can find Norway presented as an exceptional case in regards to this acceptance of local dialects as a form of weak standard language ideology, as opposed to a strong standard language ideology (cf. Mesthrie et al. 2009). With a population of under 6 million inhabitants, Norway has two official written standards, which capture the various spoken dialects in the country. Moreover, Norwegian, Swedish and Danish form a dialect continuum and inter-Scandinavian conversations are also usually polylectal. In institutions of learning, all the Scandinavian languages may be used and are considered equal.

There is indeed a multiplicity of language ideologies in various social orders and these come to play especially in situations of urban multilingualism.

---

[3] https://www.regjeringen.no/no/dokumenter/stmeld-nr-35-2007-2008-/id519923/ (accessed 12 January 2017)

Ideas about language and language ideologies can, furthermore, be contradictory (Gal 1992). In an era of increasing globalisation marked by mobility of various sorts, the ideology of a liberating diversity may, thus, be at odds with conflicting ideologies proposing the challenges of this seemingly democratic approach to language use (Lanza and Røyneland 2015).

In the Oslo area, many young Swedish workers are found in the hotel and restaurant branches and they use their Swedish dialects in service encounters. Globalisation has also accentuated the role of English as a lingua franca. It is not uncommon to be confronted in a service encounter in Oslo with personnel who do not speak Norwegian but rather communicate in English. This creates a new situation for speakers of Norwegian, particularly the elderly, who may not master English that well, or would prefer not to use it in their own country. Hence with an increasing number of new speakers of Norwegian in Norway, many of whom come with their strong standard language ideologies, there is a need to consider the complete picture of linguistic diversity (cf. Røyneland and Lanza 2015). English has, moreover, taken a dominant role in academia as the greater move towards internationalisation speaks in favour of this lingua franca.

The overall picture that evolves for Norway is one of an acceptance of linguistic diversity. However, as Silverstein (2003) has reminded us, ideologies involve the "valorisation" of some languages over others, and creates an "indexical order" that "relate(s) the micro-social to the macro-social frames of analysis of any sociolinguistic phenomenon" (Silverstein 2003: 193). Moreover, sociolinguistic work has demonstrated time and again that languages do not exist on their own, they are associated with their speakers and the social status these may have in society. This is an important reminder as we now consider a particular public debate in Norway, more particularly Oslo, concerning children's school performance and families' language policies.

3.3 "Speak more Norwegian at home!"

The above appeal was an exhortation by Jan Bøhler, the leader of the Oslo Labour Party, directed at parents of minority-language speaking children in Oslo schools.[4] His comments figured highly in the media in the fall of 2013 when a

---

4 http://www.nrk.no/ostlandssendingen/_-snakk-norsk-hjemme-1.11380539 (accessed 12 January 2017) http://www.osloby.no/nyheter/Jan-Bohler-Ap-er-redd-morsmal-hjemme-gir-barna-darligere-forutsetninger-for-a-lykkes-7385154.html (accessed 12 January 2017)

debate on bilingualism[5] occurred after the publicising of poor academic results of children who have an immigrant background, particularly with a Pakistani background, and who start school without sufficient proficiency in Norwegian. Bøhler is quoted as saying that if children with an immigrant background are good in Norwegian when they begin school, then that will give them equal opportunities as everybody else. And this, he stated, is important for the future's well-integrated Norway.

As pointed out in 3.1 above, the Pakistani community is the one with the largest number of second-generation members in Norway. According to an article published in one of the country's national newspapers, one could read that seven out of ten students that have an Urdu language background in Oslo schools need special tuition, despite the fact that these students are born in Norway. Implicit in this is that they are not proficient enough in Norwegian in order to follow the normal teaching.[6] That these students get extra tuition in Norwegian language (*særskilt norskopplæring*) is in itself not a problem as such help is prescribed in Norway's Education Act.[7] Extra tuition in Norwegian is one of several measures delineated in the law for students with another mother tongue than Norwegian. In order to remediate the situation described in the newspaper article, schools may choose to engage another model of assistance for the children involved, including bilingual education. In other words, the remedy normally chosen involves measures taken at the school. The remedy proposed by the Oslo politician, however, was aimed at families. As Sollid (2013) states in a research blog, it is beyond doubt that Bøhler goes against important principles in Norwegian educational policies in which school-based solutions, not family-based ones, are the foremost proposed for promoting knowledge in the majority language for children with a minority language background. The idea that politicians can regulate language choice in the home is contrary to Norwegian traditions. As Sollid points out, the debate on minority-language speaking children in schools is not new. We are reminded of the policy of Norwegianisation that was imposed from the 1850s until the mid 1990s on the indigenous Sámi and Kven people in the north of the country, with disastrous results. This situation reminds us of the saying, "The more things change, the more they stay the same". And this applies especially to the nature of language ideologies.

---

[5] See for example: http://www.aftenposten.no/viten/Finn-fem-feil-i-debatten-om-tospraklighet-7392557.html (accessed 12 January 2017)
[6] http://www.osloby.no/nyheter/7-av-10-norskpakistanske-barn-ma-ha-ekstra-sprakhjelp-7382906.html (accessed 12 January 2017)
[7] https://lovdata.no/dokument/NL/lov/1998-07-17-61 (accessed 12 January 2017)

The political pressure on family language policies ensued in the coming months after Bøhler's exhortation. A central leader in the Progress Party of Norway (*Fremskrittspartiet*), Carl I. Hagen proposed several measures for ensuring that families heed the political appeal to speak Norwegian in the homes.[8] As the title of the article in another national newspaper, *Verdens Gang* (VG), states, Hagen proposed that either parents teach their children Norwegian, or they would lose public financial support. Moreover, he proposed that public preschool be obligatory for those children who speak poor Norwegian and that children's television from the homeland be refused. To a national television network, Hagen was quoted as saying "*Dersom foreldrene ikke sørger for at barnet kan norsk godt nok, mener jeg det er omsorgssvikt*" ('If parents do not make sure their child can speak Norwegian well enough, I think it is neglect of care for the child').[9] And in August of 2015, in another prominent article in VG, Hagen is pictured next to the Minister of Children, Equality and Social Inclusion Solveig Horne (also from the Progress Party) under the article's title: "*Barneministeren ber barnevernet gripe inn mot manglende norskkunnskaper*"[10] [The Minister for Children requests child welfare services to intervene against a lack of knowledge of Norwegian]. The "linguistic paradise" of Norway described above, which opens for an ideology of language acceptance and tolerance, appears to be at odds in these political proposals for a solution to an educational challenge. This case illustrates clearly the complexities of language ideologies. Interestingly, the notion of a bilingual approach to education never even entered the debate.

This heated debate was also engaged in across Europe. In Germany, researcher Monika Schmid (2014) argued for why forcing immigrants to speak German in their homes would not help integration. In the German case, another political figure from a more right-wing sister party (CSU) to German chancellor Merkel's CDU party had proposed legislation on the issue.

This recurring and timely debate on school success and integration, not only across Europe today but also across history, emphasises the need to examine family language policy and how this policy is affected by political and social pressures. Indeed, family language policy may become more consciously implemented in multilingual transcultural families in today's urban Europe.

---

8 http://www.vg.no/nyheter/innenriks/frp/carl-i-hagen-laer-barna-norsk-eller-mist-stoette/a/10122453/ (accessed 12 January 2017)
9 http://www.tv2.no/a/5333214 (accessed 12 January 2017)
10 https://www.vg.no/nyheter/innenriks/kommunevalget-2015/vil-tvinge-norsk-svake-barn-til-barnehagen/a/23509932/ (accessed 12 January 2017)

4 Conclusion

While there is no doubt that learning a country's language will facilitate inclusion into that country's public life, forcing this upon parents and thereby implying that they abandon their home language is a drastic measure that history has witnessed as a failure, notably in the Norwegian context concerning the Sámi and the Kven (Bull 2007; Lane 2010).

Zhu Hua and Li Wei (2016: 655) state that few attempts have been made in the existing literature on transnational and multilingual families to "understand what is going on *within* such families; how their transnational and multilingual experiences impact on the family dynamics and their everyday life; how they cope with the new and ever-changing environment, and how they construct their identities and build social relations". Li Wei and Zhu Hua (2015: 22) point out that "families and individuals' motivations for learning, maintaining and using languages often go beyond necessity and opportunity. They are tied to the families' and individuals' sense of belonging and imagination". This imagination of looking not only back nostalgically but also forward to a new home needs to be captured in our work on family language policy. Indeed, we should seek to understand how these families are impacted by societal discourses on language learning and language diversity, and what motivates their language planning and practices in the family with their children, and how this interacts with their identity constructions in their new society.

There is a growing awareness of the importance of taking family policy into account in policy making in general, as clearly argued in Bogenschneider (2014: vii–viii), including a consideration of, among others, policies and practices biased toward individual rights over family responsibilities, and how families support society and how societies support families. In this landmark volume, however, there is no analysis of the role of language in family policy, a key variable in contemporary urban policy planning and policy making in a globalised society aimed at inclusion.

A strengthened knowledge base of how transcultural families manage their linguistic and cultural heritage in contemporary urban space can, moreover, contribute to a better understanding of how children with another linguistic background than that of the majority society acquire both the home language and other societal languages. Practices in the home – for example, that of translanguaging – may be exploited in pedagogical situations with success, if teachers are aware of them (García and Li Wei 2014). Children are thus encouraged to use their full linguistic repertoires in the acquisition of knowledge. Conteh and Riasat (2014) illustrate how collaborative efforts in collecting data of bilingual children in the home, mainstream school and the complementary class reveal that their rich linguistic repertoires at home and the community are often not tapped on in assessments at school. As they state (Conteh and Riasat 2014: 601) "the aim is not heritage language maintenance as such, but to enhance the pupils' mainstream school learning and their chances for success by promoting a 'bilingual pedagogy'". In other words, although our focus may be on the school situation, we need knowledge of the practices in the home in order to better understand immigrant children's encounters with the school language.

Urban multilingualism in Europe today comprises a myriad of family configurations. As noted above, research is required on just how these various configurations impact on family language policy and how they may relate to social inclusion and exclusion in society. The presentation of Norway as a case illustrates the need to have more knowledge on the gap between practices and policies – while some children with an immigrant background start school with sufficient knowledge of the societal language, others do not. In a special issue on researching multilingualism and super-diversity, Li Wei (2014: 475) points out "the relevance of the notion of community in the age of superdiversity and the researcher's responsibility in researching multilingualism and superdiversity". Urban multilingualism in Europe today and the prognoses for the imminent future only attest to the necessity for such knowledge.

References

Ahearn, Laura. 2001. Language and agency. *Annual Review of Anthropology* 30. 109–137.
Androutsopoulos, Jannis. 2010. Localizing the global on the participatory web. In Nikolas Coupland (ed.), *The handbook of language and globalization*, 203–254. Malden: Wiley-Blackwell.
Blommaert, Jan. 2010. *The sociolinguistics of globalization*. Cambridge: Cambridge University Press.
Blommaert, Jan & Ben Rampton. 2011. Language and superdiversity. *Diversities* 13 (2). http://www.unesco.org/shs/diversities/vol13/issue2/art1 (accessed 12 January 2017).
Bogenschneider, Karen. 2014. *Family policy matters: How policymaking affects families and what professionals can do*, 3rd edn. New York: Routledge.
Bucholtz, Mary & Kira Hall. 2005. Identity and interaction: A sociocultural linguistic approach. *Discourse Studies* 7 (4–5). 585–614.
Bull, Tove. 2007. Inconsistencies and discrepancies in official approaches to linguistic diversity: The case of Norway. In Anne Pauwels, Joanne Winter & Joe Lo Bianco (eds.), *Maintaining minority languages in transnational contexts: Australian and European perspectives*, 124–140. Basingstoke: Palgrave Macmillan.
Busch, Brigitta. 2012. The linguistic repertoire revisited. *Applied Linguistics* 33 (5). 503–523.
Cenoz, Jasone. 2013. Defining multilingualism. *Annual Review of Applied Linguistics* 33. 3–18.

Conteh, Jean & Saiqa Riasat. 2014. A multilingual learning community: Researching funds of knowledge with children, families and teachers. *Multilingua* 33 (5–6). 601–622.

Crippen, Cheryl & Leah Brew. 2007. Intercultural parenting and the transcultural family: A literature review. *The Family Journal* 15 (2). 107–115.

Curdt-Christiansen, Xiao Lan. 2013. Family language policy: Realities and continuities. *Language Policy* 12 (1), 1–6.

Czaika, Mathias & Hein de Haas. 2014. The globalization of migration: Has the world become more migratory? *International Migration Review* 48. 283–323.

De Houwer, Annick. 1999. Environmental factors in early bilingual development: The role of parental beliefs and attitudes. In Guus Extra & Ludo Verhoeven (eds.), *Bilingualism and migration*, 75–95. Berlin: Mouton de Gruyter.

Duranti, Alessandro, Elinor Ochs & Bambi Schieffelin (eds.). 2012. *The handbook of language socialization*. Malden: Wiley-Blackwell.

Extra, Guus & Kutlay Yağmur. 2004. *Urban multilingualism in Europe: Immigrant minority languages at home and school*. Clevedon: Multilingual Matters.

Fishman, Joshua. 1991. *Reversing language shift*. Clevedon: Multilingual Matters.

Gafaranga, Joseph. 2010. Medium request: Talking language shift into being. *Language in Society* 39: 241–270.

Gafaranga, Joseph. 2011. "Tout le monde est coupable": Agency in language socialisation in a language shift situation. Paper presented at the International Symposium on Bilingualism/ISB8, Oslo, Norway, June.

Gal, Susan. 1992. Multiplicity and contention among ideologies: A commentary. *Pragmatics* 2 (3) [Special Issue]. 445–449.

García, Ofelia & Li Wei. 2014. *Translanguaging: Language, bilingualism and education*. New York: Palgrave.

Garrett, Paul. 2007. Language socialization and the (re)production of bilingual subjectivities. In Monica Heller (ed.), *Bilingualism: A social approach*, 233–256. New York: Palgrave Macmillan.

Guthu, Lene K. & Sigrid Holm. 2010. Mange innvandrere digitalt ekskludert [Many immigrants excluded digitally]. *Samfunnsspeilet* [Mirror of society] 4 (4). 58–64.

Hult, Francis & David Cassels Johnson. 2015. *Research methods in language policy and planning: A practical guide*. Oxford: Wiley-Blackwell.

Irvine, Judith & Susan Gal. 2000. Language ideology and linguistic differentiation. In Paul Kroskity (ed.), *Regimes of language: Ideologies, politics, and identities*, 35–83. Santa Fe: School of American Research Press.

King, Kendall & Lyn Fogle. 2006. Bilingual parenting as good parenting: Parents' perspectives on family language policy for additive bilingualism. *International Journal of Bilingual Education and Bilingualism* 9 (6). 695–712.

King, Kendall, Lyn Fogle & Aubry Logan-Terry. 2008. Family language policy. *Language and Linguistics Compass* 2 (5). 907–922.

King, Kendall & Elizabeth Lanza (eds.). 2019. Ideology, agency, and imagination in multilingual families. *International Journal of Bilingualism* 23 (3) [Special issue]. 717–723.

Kroskity, Paul (ed.). 2000. *Regimes of language: Ideologies, politics, and identities*. Santa Fe: School of American Research Press.

Lane, Pia. 2010. "We did what we thought was best for our children": A nexus analysis of language shift in a Kven community. *International Journal of the Sociology of Language* 202. 63–78.

Lanza, Elizabeth. [1997] 2004a. *Language mixing in infant bilingualism: A sociolinguistic perspective*, 2nd edn. Oxford: Oxford University Press.

Lanza, Elizabeth. 2004b. Language socialization of infant bilingual children in the family: Quo vadis? In Xoán Paulo Rodríguez-Yáñez, Anxo Suárez & Fernando Ramallo (eds.), *Bilingualism and education from the family to the school*. Munich: Lincom, 21–39.

Lanza, Elizabeth. 2007. Multilingualism and the family. In Peter Auer & Li Wei (eds.), *Handbook of multilingualism and multilingual communication*, 45–67. Berlin: Mouton de Gruyter.

Lanza, Elizabeth & Unn Røyneland. 2015. Emerging regimes of language ideologies: Discourses of the local and global in Norway. Paper presented at the conference The sociolinguistics of globalization: (De)centring and (de)standardization. University of Hong Kong, 3–6 June.

Lanza, Elizabeth & Bente Ailin Svendsen. 2007. Tell me who your friends are and I might be able to tell you what language(s) you speak: Social network analysis, multilingualism, and identity. *International Journal of Bilingualism* 11 (3). 275–300.

Lanza, Elizabeth & Li Wei (eds.). 2016. Multilingual encounters in transcultural families. [Special issue]. *Journal of multilingual and multicultural development* 37 (7).

Li Wei (ed.). 2012. Language policy and practice in multilingual, transnational families and beyond. [Special issue]. *Journal of Multilingual and Multicultural Development* 33 (1).

Li Wei. 2013. Conceptual and methodological issues in bilingualism and multilingualism research. In Tej K. Bhatia & William C. Ritchie (eds.), *The handbook of bilingualism and multilingualism* (2nd edn.), 26–51. Oxford: Blackwell Publishing.

Li Wei. 2014. Researching multilingualism and superdiversity: Grassroots actions and responsibilities. *Multilingua* 33 (5–6). 475–484.

Li Wei & Zhu Hua. 2015. Challenges of multilingualism to the family. In Ulrike Jessner-Schmid & Claire Kramsch (eds.), *The multilingual challenge*, 21–38. Berlin: Mouton De Gruyter.

Makoni, Sinfree & Alastair Pennycook. 2007. *Disinventing and reconstituting languages*. Clevedon: Multilingual Matters.

Mesthrie, Rajend, Joan Swann, Ana Deumert & William Leap. 2009. *Introducing sociolinguistics* (2nd edn.). Edinburgh: Edinburgh University Press.

Mæhlum, Brit & Unn Røyneland. 2012. *Det norske dialektlandskapet: Innføring i studiet av dialekter*. [The Norwegian dialect landscape. Introduction to the study of dialects]. Oslo: Cappelen Damm Akademisk.

Ó hIfearnáin, Tadhg. 2013. Family language policy, first language Irish speaker attitudes and community-based response to language shift. *Journal of Multilingual and Multicultural Development* 34. 348–365.

Okita, Toshie. 2002. *Invisible work: Bilingualism, language choice and childrearing in intermarried families*. Amsterdam: Benjamins.

Otsuji, E. & Alastair Pennycook. 2010. Metrolingualism: Fixity, fluidity and language in flux. *International Journal of Multilingualism* 7 (3). 240–254.

Piller, Ingrid. 2002. *Bilingual couples talk: The discursive construction of hybridity*. Amsterdam: Benjamins.

Quist, Pia & Bente Ailin Svendsen (eds.). 2010. *Multilingual urban Scandinavia*. Clevedon: Multilingual Matters.

Riley, Kathleen. 2012. Language socialization and language ideologies. In Alessandro Duranti, Elinor Ochs & Bambi Schiefelin (eds.), *The handbook of language socialization*, 493–514. Malden: Wiley-Blackwell.

Romaine, Suzanne. 1995. *Bilingualism*. Oxford: Blackwell.

Ruby, Mahera. 2012. The role of a grandmother in maintaining Bangla with her granddaughter in East London. *Journal of Multilingual and Multicultural Development* 33 (1) [Special issue]. 67–83.

Ruiz de Zarobe, Leyre & Ruiz Yolanda de Zarobe. 2015. New perspectives on multilingualism and L2 acquisition: An introduction. *International Journal of Multilingualism* 12 (4). 393–403.

Røyneland, Unn. 2009. Dialects in Norway: Catching up with the rest of Europe? *International Journal of the Sociology of Language* 196–197. 7–31.

Røyneland, Unn & Elizabeth Lanza. 2015. The dark sides of linguistic complexity. Paper presented at the conference Linguistic Complexity in the Individual and Society. NTNU, Trondheim, Norway, 15–16 October.

Schieffelin, Bambi, & Elinor Ochs. 1986. Language socialization. *Annual Review of Anthropology* 15. 163–191.

Schmid, Monika. 2014. Bid to force immigrants to speak German in their homes won't help integration. *The conversation*. http://theconversation.com/bid-to-force-immigrants-to-speak-german-in-their-homes-wont-help-integration-35212 (accessed 12 January 2017).

Schwartz, Mila & Anna Verschik. 2013. *Successful family language policy: Parents, children and educators in interaction*. Dordrecht: Springer.

Shohamy, Elana. 2006. *Language policy: Hidden agendas and new approaches*. London: Routledge.

Silverstein, Michael. 2003. Indexical order and the dialectics of sociolinguistic life. *Language and Communication* 23. 193–229.

Sollid, Hilde. 2013. Norskopplæring for minoritetselever: Gammel debatt i ny kontekst. [Norwegian education for minority students: Old debate in a new context]. Forskning.no. http://forskning.no/content/norskopplaering-minoritetselever-gammel-debatt-i-ny-kontekst (accessed 12 January 2017).

Spolsky, Bernard. 2009. *Language management*. Cambridge: Cambridge University Press.

Spolsky, Bernard. 2012. Family language policy: The critical domain. *Journal of Multilingual and Multicultural Development* 33 (1) [Special issue]. 3–11.

Stavans, Anat. 2012. Language policy and literacy practices in the family: The case of Ethiopian parental narrative input. *Journal of Multilingual and Multicultural Development* 33 (1) [Special issue]. 13–33.

Sterponi, Laura. 2012. Literacy socialization. In Alessandro Duranti, Elinor Ochs & Bambi Schiefelin (eds.), *The handbook of language socialization*, 227–246. Malden: Wiley-Blackwell.

Svendsen, Bente Ailin & Unn Røyneland. 2008. Multiethnolectal facts and functions in Oslo, Norway. *International Journal of Bilingualism* 12 (1). 63–83.

Varro, Gabrielle. 2003. *Sociologie de la mixité: De la mixité amoureuse aux mixités sociales et culturelles*. Paris: Belin.

Vertovec, Steven. 2007. Super-diversity and its implications. *Ethnic and Racial Studies* 30 (6). 1024–1054.

Weiyun He, Agnes. 2012. Heritage language socialization. In Alessandro Duranti, Elinor Ochs & Bambi Schiefelin (eds.), *The handbook of language socialization*, 587–609. Malden: Wiley-Blackwell.

Zhu Hua. 2008. Duelling languages, duelling values: Codeswitching in bilingual intergenerational conflict talk in diasporic families. *Journal of Pragmatics* 40. 1799–1816.

Zhu Hua & Li Wei. 2016. Transnational experience, aspiration and family language policy. *Journal of Multilingual and Multicultural Development* 37 (7) [Special issue]. 655–666.

Luk Van Mensel
6 Multilingual family practices: An interactional study

Abstract: Many voices in contemporary sociolinguistics profess an understanding of multilingualism as a set of (social) language practices that make up a speaker's language repertoires, rather than as a combination of separate languages seen as bounded entities. Such an interpretation of multilingualism, however, is hard to maintain from a language policy point of view, which typically, perhaps all too easily, assumes a macro-perspective. So even if policy makers include words such as "variety" and "multilingualisation" in their discourse, in practice policies evolve around top-down categories such as *Nederlandstalig* ('Dutch-speaking') and *Franstalig* ('French-speaking'), which tend to eschew (and erase) the complexity and fluidity of microlinguistic contexts. In multilingual Brussels (Belgium), for instance, these categorisations, as well as the category *anderstalig* ('other-speaking'), and combinations of all three, are frequently used.

In this Chapter, I will look into some of the language practices of parents from different (linguistic) backgrounds in Brussels. Spoken data were collected from two parent-pairs with children enrolled in Dutch-medium education in Brussels, specifically focusing on the interactions between two of these parents, in this case the fathers, and their respective children. The data consist of audio recordings made by these parents during some of their daily routines, e.g. taking the children to school or extracurricular activities, or picking them up. The findings illustrate how these parents deploy and activate their various linguistic resources in day-to-day interactions, pointing to a variety and complexity of multilingual practices that may be ill served by the top-down classifications of "named languages" commonly used.

1 Introduction

At the beginning of the 21st century, European society is characterised by increasing social and linguistic diversity. This growing diversity eludes sociological categorisations that have long been used to make sense of our social world. At the same time, this diversity also challenges the use of these same categories by institutions, policy makers and governments to "deal" with these realities.

Luk Van Mensel, UNamur, NaLTT, 61, rue de Bruxelles, 5000 Namur, Belgium.

https://doi.org/10.1515/9781501503207-007

In this Chapter my aim is to illustrate how the variety and complexity of multilingual practices by self-proclaimed "monolingual" speakers defies top-down language classifications such as those commonly used in language policy making and research. To this end, the Chapter consists of a detailed discussion of the interactions that take place between two parents from different (linguistic) backgrounds with their respective family members. By looking at the "social unit of the family" (see also Lanza in this volume), I will show how speakers-parents functionally activate their "limited" (at least from a normative point of view) set of linguistic resources in order to perform particular social roles or enhance family ties. As such, these observations lead us to seriously question the relevance of broadly defined language-based categories (e.g. "Dutch-speaking", "Spanish-speaking"), both in policy and in research.

Before turning to the analysis of the recorded interactions, I will first briefly discuss how recent definitions of multilingualism in the sociolinguistics literature contrast sharply with the continued use of language-based categorisations. Next, I present an example of such categorisation practices relevant to the context in which the data were collected, namely Dutch-medium education in Brussels (Belgium). Finally, after a detailed look into the data, some conclusions will be formulated.

2 Language repertoires and language categorisations

Since the early 1990s, two phenomena have guided societies in Western Europe toward what Vertovec (2007: 1024) has called "super-diversity", i.e. a diversification of diversity with "a level and kind of complexity surpassing anything [. . .] previously experienced in a particular society". Firstly, a change can be observed in the structure and nature of migration, from rather predictable collective flows to more diffuse and unpredictable shifts. One can now imagine people from all backgrounds leaving any place for any other, for any number of reasons. People move on, or return, at variable moments, and as such the composition of populations throughout the world is subject to hyperdiversity and flux, with obvious consequences for linguistic heterogeneity. Secondly, the rise of new technologies compels us to reconsider traditional ways of looking at language. Connectivity enables online contacts across the globe that were previously unimaginable, and new ways of communicating such as text messaging or chat-practices confront us with users' unprecedented linguistic creativity.

All of these factors have led to serious critiques among many sociolinguists (and social scientists more generally) of what (a) "language" and (a) "community" are. The main criticism can be summarised as an opposition to the use of essentialised, decontextualised notions of language and community, both in societal discourses and in research. As an alternative, it is suggested that languages can be regarded as fluid rather than fixed codes, which are framed within social practices. Such a viewpoint obviously also has consequences for how bilingualism or multilingualism can be defined. In her introduction to *Bilingualism: A social approach,* for instance, Monica Heller (2007: 1) calls for an approach to multilingualism that "privileges language as social practice, speakers as social actors and boundaries as products of social action" in order "to move discussions of bilingualism away from a focus on the whole bounded units of code and community". So rather than assuming the co-existence of two separate language systems within the individual or society ("poly-monolingualism", Blommaert 2007; "pluralisation of monolingualism", Makoni and Pennycook 2007), it is suggested that multilingualism should be seen in terms of a set of (social) language practices that make up a speaker's "language repertoires". These individual linguistic repertoires (Hymes 1974, 1996) can be seen as "a biographical complex of functionally organised linguistic resources" (Blommaert 2010), and are to be understood as built of generically and sociolinguistically restricted competences. As a result, competence in a language (or languages) can never be complete, but is always partial, dynamic, and in most cases "truncated" (Blommaert, Collins, and Slembrouck 2005; Blommaert and Backus 2011). In order to tighten our theoretical grip on this view of multilingualism, new terms have recently been proposed, such as polylingualism (Jørgensen et al. 2011) or metrolingualism (Otsuji and Pennycook 2010). García (2009: 45) favours the term "translanguaging", which she defines as "the multilingual discursive practices in which bilinguals engage in order to make sense of their bilingual worlds". She suggests that one should look at practices and describe these language practices "from the perspective of the users themselves, and not simply [...] from the perspective of the language itself" (García 2009: 45; see also García and Li Wei 2014).

Very much in contrast to the viewpoint explained above, policy-makers (and, to some extent, researchers) typically use categorisations based on "language" which then serve to delineate "groups of speakers of language L". Such conceptualisations are historically rooted in modernist ideas on language and society, in which the construction of imagined homogeneous language and speech communities (Irvine and Gal 2000) served the construction of nations as "imagined communities" (Anderson [1983] 1991). In censuses and similar population statistics, as Busch (2016: 13) aptly remarks, language is for instance often regarded as an indicator of some type of "ethnocultural" affiliation:

> Unlike questions about such things as people's commute to work, or the kind of housing they live in, the question asked in censuses about language is of the same order as questions used to enquire about 'identity markers' such as age, gender, origin, citizenship, and in some cases religion, ethnicity or 'race'. This kind of question is about who one is. Categories of linguistic affiliation gain much of their subject-constituting power from their multiple discursive interconnections, the intersectional interplay with other such 'identity categories'. (Busch 2016: 13)

So the question of "which language(s) do you speak", in censuses and surveys, although at first sight a rather straightforward one since it appears to relate to a hands-on reality, entails much more than just "language". And when the results from these censuses and surveys are embedded in official discourses, they obtain a life of their own, so to speak, and become clearly disconnected from the reality, namely the language use they purportedly describe. As Kertzer and Arel (2002) argue, rather than reflecting social reality, censuses may actually play a key role in the construction of that reality. It is certainly also what happens in the case of language-based categorisations (see also Rampton 2007; Busch 2016), as these categorisations become tools in ideological processes of "erasure" (Gal and Irvine 1995), i.e. leading one to turn a blind eye to sociolinguistic distinctions.

Let us now turn to Brussels, the context of our study, and more specifically Dutch-medium education in Brussels, for a concrete example of such categorisation practices.

3 Language categorisations and Dutch-medium education in Brussels

The political organisation of the Brussels Capital Region is based on a language duality, with political representation organised along a linguistic "divide". Despite the multilingual composition of its population (Janssens 2001, 2007, 2013), Brussels is still largely represented in the media and in political and public discourse as consisting of two "language blocks" (Sinardet 2012, 2013). Such a categorisation aligns with the general depiction of Belgium, where popular and media representations typically highlight the ethnolinguistic opposition between Dutch-speaking Flemings and French-speaking Walloons as fundamental to Belgian political dynamics (Blommaert 2011). As a result, categorisations such as *Nederlandstalig* ('Dutch-speaking'), *Franstalig* ('French-speaking') and *anderstalig* ('other-speaking'), as well as combinations of these, are frequently used. The label 'otherlingual' (*anderstalige*) is quite commonly used in the Flemish part of Belgium, and it is typically used to refer to all people who speak an immigrant language, and by extension (or reduction) to immigrants or descendants from immigrants, mostly from the less affluent socioeconomic classes. As Blommaert (2011) argues, the focus on (and literally naming of) the two categories pertaining to the "long-language ideological debate in Belgium" (Blommaert 2011: 1) as well as the remittal of all other languages into one singular "other" category, not only perpetuates the dominance of a (poly-)monolingual ideology, but also leads to a denial of both linguistic and social diversity.

As a corollary to the political duality, education (considered a "personal matter" in Belgian legislation) is organised in two parallel systems in Brussels, one using Dutch as the medium of instruction and the other one French, and all parents may opt to enrol their children in either French- or Dutch-medium education.[1] In the whole of Brussels, Dutch-medium education now hosts about 17% of the city's pupil population compared to 80% for French-medium education and 3% in educational institutions that use (an)other language(s) of instruction (e.g. European schools) (Janssens, Carlier and Van de Craen 2009). The data in Figure 1, based on estimates collected by the representative body of the Flemish government in Brussels, *Vlaamse Gemeenschapscommissie* (VGC), from the schools' principals, illustrate some of the changes that Dutch-medium education has undergone in the past three decades. It should be added that these figures are based on the school principals' interpretation of the parents' statements about their home language(s) at the time of their child's enrolment. Furthermore, the categories represented here are literally adopted from the ones used by the VGC to describe language background. As shown, the total number of pupils in Dutch-medium primary school and kindergarten in particular has grown exponentially, and the proportion of children from "homogeneously Dutch-speaking" families is now a mere 10% (in secondary education, this is 30%), with over a third of the children speaking an immigrant language (partly in combination with French) at home (in secondary education, this is 20%). However, and more important for the present discussion, we can see how the language background of the pupils is categorised in terms of top-down language-based categories ("labels") that reflect the macro-political

---

[1] For more details and other takes on language management in Brussels and in Belgium, I refer to the Chapter from Janssens (in this volume). For a historical perspective on education in Brussels, I can refer to Treffers-Daller (2002).

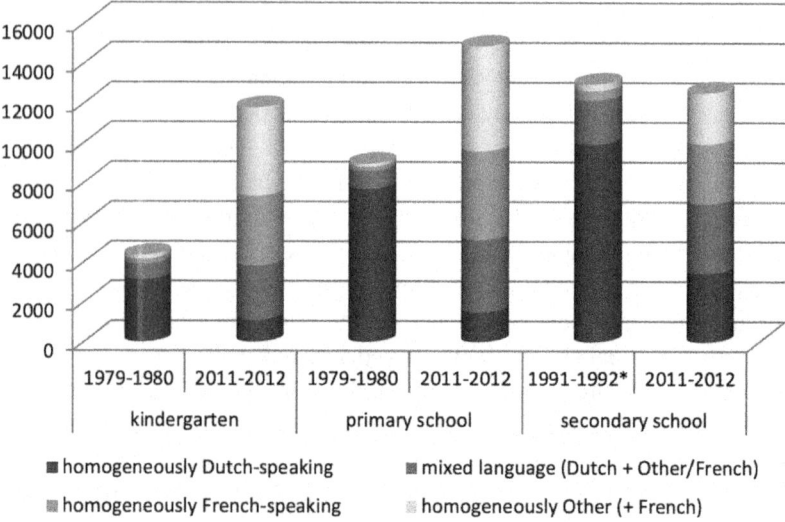

Figure 1: Dutch-medium education in Brussels: evolution of pupil population according to reported language background (VGC 2013[2]); *no figures available before 1991.

two-tier organisation of the city (i.e. combinations of Dutch, French and "other") rather than the city's (as well as the schools') multilingual reality.

The particular situation of Dutch-medium education in Brussels has led to a number of studies (for a brief overview, see Van Mensel 2014), some of which have involved the parents of the pupils in question (e.g. Deprez et al. 1982; Gielen and Louckx 1984). My own work on the topic started with a quantitative survey (Van Mensel 2007), which focused on parents who did not have Dutch as a home language. The main purpose was to identify their background and to find out what their motivations were to choose a Dutch-medium school. In order to operationalise the language background variable, however, I applied the same homogenising categories mentioned above, such as "speaker of Dutch" or "speaker of French", and a wide range of languages were assembled in a category "other". Whereas such broad categorisations are probably unavoidable in quantitative analyses, it is clear that certain aspects of social (linguistic) life are obscured rather than revealed in this way, as complexities are dismissed for the purposes of descriptive analysis. In the case of this particular study, I felt that the categorisation in terms of language background that I had

---

[2] http://www.vgc.be/Onderwijs/Onderwijsbeleid+van+de+VGC/Over+het+Brussels +Nederlandstalig+onderwijs/cijfers.htm (accessed 11 April 2018)

applied clearly misrepresented the actual language practices of the parents involved. The survey's questions on parental language use in different domains of social life (Fishman 1972) showed that these language practices were highly varied and multilingual. However, this variation was inevitably eschewed, as I aimed to provide a general(ised) picture.

In order to overcome these and other shortcomings from the quantitative study, I conducted a qualitative multiple case study (Van Mensel 2014) with a number of parents from various social and linguistic backgrounds, who had all enrolled their children in Dutch-medium education in Brussels. One of the aims of the study was to look into the language practices these parents engage in, and in what follows I will discuss some of the data collected, focusing on two individual parents, Alain and Ricardo, and their respective families.[3] Both parents (and their partners) can be seen to embody a number of "typical" labels frequently encountered in public discourse on Brussels, as outlined in the second column of Table 1. Furthermore, in terms of their language backgrounds, they would be grouped in quantitative surveys as in the third column:

Table 1: A possible categorisation of the participating parents.

Names	Labels	Language(s)
Béatrice & Alain	"Francophone Brusselers"	French-French
Ann & Ricardo	"mixed Flemish-expat"	Dutch-Other

4 Method

The data used in the remainder of this Chapter consist of a number of audio excerpts recorded by the parents themselves in various settings and circumstances, and were collected between November 2010 and September 2012 (Van Mensel 2014). The participants were requested to record short instances of language interaction, preferably during "transitional" events such as when dropping off or picking up their children at/from school or on their way to/from an extracurricular activity. I was interested in recording transitional moments because specific settings often elicit different types of language practices. By observing linguistic practices across settings a fuller picture of the participants'

---

[3] Parts of the interviews with these parents are discussed in Van Mensel (2015) and Van Mensel (2016).

language practices can be achieved. Furthermore, one would also expect to find a certain level of linguistic creativity in these transitional moments, with language users more likely to negotiate their linguistic identities as they move across multiple sites and contexts (cf. also Lamarre and Lamarre 2009). Finally, the aim was not to analyse the data from a code alternation point of view in the strict sense,[4] but to explore how the parents deploy their various repertoires in day-to-day interactions.

5 Alain "on the move"

Alain (38) and his wife Béatrice (40) originate from one (of the two) "traditional" language communities in Brussels, yet have enrolled their children in an institution that represents the other traditional language community. As such, they are labelled and/or categorised as "Francophones" (for instance in educational statistics such as the ones presented above). Obviously, their trajectory (current language use, family language background, and schooling) displays largely French language repertoires, which provides grounds for such a classification. On the basis of this reported language use, we would thus expect these parents and their children to engage in predominantly "monolingual French" language practices: Béatrice and Alain state that French is the language commonly spoken at home, as well as with relatives and most of their friends, and the children reportedly speak mostly French with each other as well. In the larger part of the data recorded by Alain, which comprises a total of seven recordings, this general picture seems to be confirmed, as he and his children speak French with each other throughout. From one of the longer recordings (total duration: 28 minutes), however, a different and more intricate picture emerges.

This particular recording was made shortly before, during, and after a twenty-minute car ride from an afternoon music lesson in another part of town to Béatrice and Alain's home. The participants are Alain, his son (Léo, age 4.5), his daughter (Sarah, age 7), a friend of hers (Emma, age 7), the music teacher, Emma's father Wim, and the car's navigating system (see Table 2).

As Alain moves from one space to another, the setting and the participants change, entailing noticeable changes to his language practices. The recording illustrates how even in a short period of less than 30 minutes, language

---

[4] See, for instance, Gardner-Chloros (2009) for an overview of research on code-switching (and the critical review of this volume by Heller [2011]). A small part of the data were analysed in this way in a bachelor paper by Vandevondele (2011).

Table 2: On the move: overview of spaces, participants, and duration.

Spaces	Participants	Duration (total: 28 mins.)
(1) In the car (1)	Alain, Léo	1:30
(2) At the music school	Alain, Sarah, music teacher, other children (incl. Emma)	1:30
(3) On the street	Alain, Sarah, Emma	1:00
(4) In the car (2)	Alain, Léo, Sarah, Emma, (GPS)	20:00
(5) Getting out of the car	Alain, Léo, Sarah, Emma	1:23
(6) At Wim's	Alain, Léo, Sarah, Emma, Wim	2:37

practices can vary considerably according to different circumstances, and this despite limited linguistic resources such as in the case of Alain's Dutch. We will divide our discussion of this recording into six episodes, which correspond to the six spaces as outlined in Table 2.

In the car (1)

The recording starts with a brief interaction between Alain and his son Léo who have just arrived in front of the music school. Léo wants to accompany his father to collect the other children, but he is not allowed to do so. The interaction is in French, and Alain clearly takes up his role as a father, speaking "parent talk", which is evidenced in a number of prosodic and interactional features, and exemplified by the following exchange:

Excerpt 1

Alain	*tu restes dans la voiture pendant que je vais vite chercher Sarah et Emma?*	you stay in the car while I go get Sarah and Emma?
Léo	*non!*	no!
Alain	*si si si, c'est juste en face, t'inquiète pas de*	yes yes yes, it's just in front, don't worry
Léo	*mais je veux aller avec toi*	but I want to go with you
Alain	*mais non non, regarde, c'est juste là en face, c'est pas la peine de sortir*	but no no, look, it's just there in front, there's no point getting out

At the music school

The next interaction takes place at the music school, and consists of two parts. In the first part father and daughter exchange greetings (see Excerpt 2). The second part is a conversation between Alain and the music teacher, in French only. It should be mentioned that the music school is largely a French-speaking space. All internal and external communication is handled in French and most teachers are monolingual French-speakers. Some of the children are from other language backgrounds, but all classes are in French.

Excerpt 2

Alain	*soir!*	((French:)) evening!
Teacher	*bonsoir*	good evening
Sarah	*dag papa!*	((in Dutch:)) hi daddy!
Alain	*dag Sarah! tu prends ta veste?*	hello sarah! ((in French:)) can you take your jacket?
Sarah	*pa, he .. heb je Chaise Musicale ((a music CD))... mag ik van voor?*	((in Dutch:)) dad, ha .. do you have Chaise Musicale ((a music CD)) ... can I go in the front?
Alain	*mag ik van wat?*	can I go what?
Sarah	*voor*	in the front
Alain	*voor wat?* <laugh>	in front of what? <laugh>
Sarah	*maar voor, in de auto*	but in front, in the car
Alain	*oh, in de auto? euh, ik denk het niet, nee*	oh, in the car? euh, I don't think so, no
Sarah	*jawel!*	yes!
Alain	*tu me parles en néerlandais, toi, maintenant?*	((French:)) you talk to me in Dutch now?
Emma	*maar allez alstublieft. allez please!*	(Dutch:)) but *allez* ((interj.)) please. *allez* ((interj.)) ((English:)) please!
Alain	*(((@Emma:)) hoe was het Emma? ja? ((@ teacher:)) ça a été?*	((@ Emma in Dutch:)) how was it Emma? yes? ((@teacher in French:)) did it go ok?
Music teacher	((in French))	((in French))
Alain	*ouais ouais et . elle traduit pas euh*	yeah yeah and . she doesn't translate euh

As we can observe, neither the language regime of the school nor Sarah's habitual way of speaking to her father prevent her from starting an interaction with her father in Dutch. This does not remain unnoticed, as Alain explicitly asks her (in French) why she is doing so. The presence of her Dutch-speaking school friend Emma causes Sarah to continue (twice) in Dutch, perhaps to show off, or because the topic of the talk is about riding shotgun in the car, i.e. to sit in the passenger seat, a privilege which is highly valued among 7-year-olds.

On the street

Next, Alain leaves the music school with Sarah and Emma and they cross the street to get to the car. Again, the language use pattern is quite mixed but here we find the first occurrences of Alain speaking in Dutch – addressing both girls – but turning to French when things have to go faster or he has to be sure everything is understood:

Excerpt 3

Alain	*wacht, we moeten niet lopen, den auto is daar*	((Dutch:)) wait, we don't have to run, the car is over there
Sarah	*moeten we lopen?*	do we have to run?
Alain	*nee . nee nee wacht, den auto is daar*	no . no no wait, the car is over there
Sarah	*maar moe- moeten we lopen?*	but do- do we have to run?
Alain	*NEE! ik ben Léo, ik ben Léo eerst gaan halen, hop! kom, attend, va sur le trottoir!, ga maar daar*	NO! I went to get Léo, I went to get Léo first, hop! come, ((French:)) wait, go on the sidewalk!, ((Dutch:)) go there

With respect to Alain's use of Dutch as observed in this excerpt, we should first mention the use of the article *den* instead of standard *de* (*den auto*, 'the car'), as well as the modal particle *maar* in *ga maar daar* ('go there'), occurrences which index Alain's access to and experience with informal spoken Dutch. Most probably, this experience derives from his previous working environment and perhaps also from contacts with his children's school friends and their parents. Nonetheless, we can also observe the limits of Alain's Dutch repertoire in this episode, which are clearly informed by a lack of fluency, and are compounded by the constraints imposed by the situation at hand, i.e. crossing (the event) a busy street (the location).

In the car (2)

The episode that follows involves the main bulk of the recording. It comprises the GPS-episode in which all participants engage in a bout of language play with the car's navigating system. The system's posh British English pronunciation is apparently the cause of great hilarity. A thorough discussion of this episode is not possible within the range of this Chapter (see Van Mensel 2014), but for the present purposes let it suffice to say that it includes a great deal of code alternation on the part of both Alain and his daughter Sarah (French, Dutch and "posh" English), mostly silence from Sarah's friend, Emma, and the continued use of French between Alain and Léo.

Getting out of the car

A brief intermezzo ensues when Alain and the children get out of the car in front of Emma's house. Rather than having a joint conversation with all the children present, Alain engages in exchanges with each of them separately. The pattern of language use established in the previous part seems to continue, though, with Alain talking Dutch to Emma and French – barring the occasional Dutch word inserted – to his own children. Sarah (and this is slightly different from the observations until now) and Léo use French in direct conversation with their father, but Dutch when the topic is somehow related to Emma. Sarah's request in Dutch to stay for a while at Emma's place is echoed by Léo's 'and me!' (*en ikke ook*), which suggests a strategic use of Dutch in order to align himself with his older sister's request and not to be excluded from her privileges. We will not get into a detailed study of the children's code alternation practices here, but these instances certainly show that Dutch has become a familiar part of this particular family's language repertoire.

At Wim's

The last episode of this recording takes place in the hallway at Wim's house. Wim is Emma's father and Dutch-speaking. The participants are the same as in the previous scenes, plus Wim, as well as Emma's two siblings. The five children's voices frequently intermingle, which makes it somewhat harder to distinguish who says what to whom, but the main discussion recorded is the one between Alain and Wim. The two men converse in French, and it is Wim himself who initiates this pattern, starting off with a French 'How's it been?' (*ça a été?*), as can be observed in the following excerpt:

Excerpt 4

Alain	*Léo, avant de traverser c'est mieux de .. de .. d'attendre que je t'aie dit que tu pouvais traverser, ok?*	((French:)) Léo, before you cross the road it's better to .. to .. to wait until I have told you you may cross, ok?
Sarah	*mais j'ai déjà sonné, mais ça marche pas*	but I already rang ((the doorbell)), but it doesn't work
Alain	*ah, wacht voilà .. hop*	((Dutch:)) ah, wait ((Dutch/French:)) here you go .. hop
Léo	*hop*	Hop
Wim	*ça a été?*	((French:)) how's it been?
Alain	*ouais, pas de problème, pas de problème*	yeah, no problem, no problem
Léo	*pas de problème, pas de problème*	no problem, no problem
Alain	*elle ((the music school teacher)) a dit euh, il y a juste un truc. attends, je rentre pour pas que tu ouvres ((the door)) trop grand. il y a juste un truc, c'est qu'il y a des mots qu'elle connait pas en néerlandais*	she ((the music school teacher)) said euh, there's just one thing. wait, I'll come in so you don't open ((the door)) too wide. there's just one thing, that there's words that she doesn't know in Dutch

At the beginning of the excerpt Alain still speaks both Dutch and French with the children, but once Wim opens the door and greets Alain (and during the conversation that follows this excerpt), the situation changes. Both Alain and Wim adhere to a strict monolingual pattern, as no Dutch insertions are found in the talk of either, an observation which is in stark contrast with what we have found in the previous episodes when Alain talks to the children.

Perhaps we could say that two different spaces are involved in this episode, each with its own specific social and language rules. In the first space, Wim and Alain are talking French (in the foreground of the recording), and in the second space the children are speaking in Dutch (in the background of the recording). The children are thus temporarily offered a "free" space that is only partly monitored by adults. Again, the physical site of the action, i.e. the place where the interlocutors find themselves (the hallway, a transitional place by definition), as well as the event in which they are engaged (equally transitional: dropping off someone), could be said to determine the rules of and constraints on possible language behaviour. This is reflected in the participants' language use, which is far more based on a monolingual format than in the previous episodes where there were no separate spaces.

To conclude this part on Alain's language practices, we have observed how Alain, beyond a classification as a Francophone, resorts to various (language) practices, the nature of which cannot just be described as instances of "Dutch" that are inserted into Alain's "French" language. In fact, Alain deploys a wide variety of registers across contexts in order to obtain certain goals and perform particular roles. While moving from one space to another, Alain activates a range of registers to a varying extent, be it in French (parent-to-child, parent-to-teacher, friend-to-friend) or in Dutch (parent-to-child). Whereas the presence or absence of a non-French speaker (Emma) as a participant in the conversation seems to trigger some of the alternation, the particular "place-cum-event" or space in which it takes place clearly co-determines the availability of particular language practices for use. For instance, the use of Dutch as an inclusionary act toward predominantly Dutch-speaking Emma is temporarily suspended when crossing the street, reminding us also of how circumstances shape possible practices, with different set-ups invoking different (linguistic) practices. This recalls Blommaert, Collins and Slembrouck (2005: 213) who suggest that multilingualism is "not what individuals have or lack, but what the environment, as structured determination and interactional emergence, enables and disables them to employ". The observation also chimes with findings by Lamarre and Lamarre (2009, *Montreal on the move*) and shows how this approach reveals a type of data that is often overlooked yet highly suitable to revealing the language experiences of multilingual social actors. In any case, from what we observed here, clearly a classification in terms of "French speaker" (or perhaps "bilingual Dutch-French speaker") only partially captures what Alain is doing here, and as such feeds into overrated assumptions about lives being led in one language.

6 Ricardo "on the move"

Ann (35) and Ricardo (36) met in Salamanca (Spain) in 1995, where she was an international student on an "Erasmus" European exchange programme. When we look at the linguistic backgrounds of Ann's and Ricardo's families, they both seem exclusively "monolingual" in nature. Ricardo grew up in Valladolid, Spain, in a Spanish-speaking environment. Ann is from Bruges, in the Flemish part of Belgium, where she spoke a dialectal variety of Dutch at home. In their present home, they claim to follow the "one parent – one language" principle, since Ann uses Dutch with the children and Ricardo Spanish. They have spoken Spanish to each other from the very beginning of their relationship, and continue to do so until the present day. The children speak Dutch with each other and their mother, and are supposed to communicate with their father in Spanish, although they are said to respond in Dutch at times, "when they are tired or lazy". Ricardo explicitly calls himself a monolingual (Spanish) and a bad speaker of any other languages, referring to French and English, and to a lesser extent to Dutch (see Excerpt 5).

Excerpt 5

Ricardo	*soy monolingüe y y hablo, el resto de los idiomas, mal. en fin, mal. el inglés, hablo el inglés como un extranjero, hablo el francés como un extranjero, y hablo, y hablo el holandés como un marroquí, ya sé.*	I'm a monolingual and and I speak, other languages, badly. well, badly, English, I speak English like a foreigner, I speak French like a foreigner, and I speak, I speak Dutch like a Moroccan, I know.

The mixed language background of Ann and Ricardo places them in a specific situation with respect to the Dutch-speaking character of Dutch-medium education in Brussels. Ann would be considered as belonging to the traditional target group, as Dutch-medium education provides language maintenance education that enables her and her children to maintain and strengthen their home language in French-speaking Brussels. At the same time, her Spanish husband Ricardo is an outsider, speaking a language that would be categorised as "Other" in typical surveys on language use in Brussels.

Generally speaking, the family language regime reported by Ann and Ricardo is indeed confirmed by the collected recordings. Ann speaks (vernacular) Dutch with her children and Spanish with her husband. Ricardo addresses his daughters in Spanish, and they mostly reply in (idiosyncratic) Spanish, although at times a Dutch word may be inserted. The children speak Dutch when interacting with each other. However, when we take a closer look at the recorded interactions, a different picture emerges.

The excerpts presented here were taken from two recordings made by Ricardo when bringing the children to school in the morning. Both recordings concern mostly interactions between Ricardo and his three daughters, which happen mostly in Spanish. At the beginning of the recordings, Ricardo and the children are about to leave the house and his wife Ann is helping them with the preparations. Although these morning events predictably happen in a rush, the exchanges seem to confirm the previously reported family language practices, as Ann and Ricardo broadly stick to the one parent-one language approach. However, exceptions to this occur, and the first example is when Ricardo engages in a leave-taking ritual in Dutch:

Excerpt 6
Ann	((@ all)) *ciao veel plezier!*	((Dutch:)) ((@ all)) ciao have fun!
Ricardo	*dag mama*	bye mummy
Ann	*veel plezier papa*	have fun daddy

In this excerpt, we observe how Ann initiates the interaction by saying goodbye to Ricardo and the children in Dutch. Ricardo then responds in Dutch, calling Ann "mummy", as if speaking from the children's point of view. Ann extends his interactional move by wishing "daddy" much fun. A plausible explanation for the fact that Ricardo responds to his wife in Dutch seems to be that the parents are showing (and teaching) their youngest daughter "how to say goodbye", enacting the ritual from her perspective, hence the use of Dutch. A similar occurrence can be observed in the second example:

Excerpt 7
| Ricardo | *dankuwel! ... di 'dankuwel' eh . dankuwel! . Daniela, qué dices . dankuwel! corre* | ((Dutch:)) thank you! ... ((Spanish:)) say ((Dutch:)) 'thank you' eh . ((Dutch:)) thank you! . ((Spanish:)) Daniela, what do you say ((Dutch:)) thank you! ((Spanish:)) go go |

Here, Ricardo urges his daughter to say "thank you" to a Dutch-speaking parent at school; first by saying it himself with an enthusiastic pitch, as if showing his daughter how to do it, then explicitly telling her to do so. By telling his daughter to say "thank you", however, Ricardo is obviously not teaching Dutch, but explaining a rule of politeness, which could be formulated in the following way: "You are supposed to say thank you to people when they do something for you, and at the entrance of a Dutch-medium school you say thank you in Dutch. I, a Spanish speaker, who insists on speaking Spanish with you, my daughter, am complying with this rule".

And in the following excerpt (Excerpt 8), Ricardo praises his youngest daughter Isabel, first in Spanish and then immediately repeating it in Dutch, including a change of her name:

Excerpt 8
Ricardo *voilà* ((interj., Spanish pronunciation)) *muy bien Isa! bravo Belleke!* ((school bell rings)) *oh Daniela, un beso. tienes que ir a tu clase, vale? te quiero mucho . aprende, hè? y concentrate, vale?*

((Dutch/French, Spanish pronunciation)) there you go ((Spanish:)) very good Isa! ((Dutch:)) well done Belleke! ((school bell rings)) ((Spanish:)) oh Daniela, a kiss . you should go to class now, ok? I love you lots . learn, right? and focus, ok?

Like in the previous examples, the Dutch elements that occur in this excerpt (the encouragement *Bravo Belleke!*) are inserted in a predominantly Spanish conversation and can be considered examples of formulaic language, formulated in the context of a "teaching-learning" event that involves Ricardo and one of his daughters. In Excerpts 6 and 7, Ricardo is teaching "how to say goodbye" and "when to say thank you", and here, he is praising the fact that Isabel has learnt a particular practice (most probably putting her school bag on her shoulders). Interestingly, the encouragement is given twice in linguistic terms, and the second instance can arguably be said to pertain to the repertoire Ann shares with the children; the use of the diminutive Dutch form of the daughter's name ("Belleke" for Isabel) is illuminative in this respect. Admittedly, the fact that in this example the event is taking place in a setting (the playground of a Dutch-medium school) that is favourable to the use of Dutch in parent-child interaction may have incited Ricardo to repeat his praise in Dutch as well. Such an interpretation, which we cannot verify on the basis of the present material, does, however, not contradict our claim that Ricardo draws on his wife's repertoire to carry out particular acts.

What we have seen so far as regards the presence of Dutch in Ricardo's language practices may suggest that the language is used in a relatively "framed" way, i.e. Dutch occurrences appear to happen "in brackets", in the context of a teaching-learning event, and are limited to the formulaic. Rather than speaking Dutch, Ricardo appears to be "doing speaking Dutch", and in a sense re-enacts his wife's practices with the children. Nevertheless, we also found instances where Ricardo resorts to words that can be linked to his wife's language repertoire rather than his own but which appear to have become internalised in his own speech patterns. This can be seen in the following excerpts:

Excerpt 9
Ricardo *Daniela cuidado en los cruces*   ((Spanish:)) Daniela watch out at the
         eh! . stop en el cruce! STOP!   crossings eh! . ((English/Dutch:)) stop ((Spanish:)) at the crossing! ((English/Dutch:)) STOP!

Excerpt 10
Ricardo ((5 seconds silence)) <sighs> .. ((5 seconds silence)) <sighs> .. *allez*
         allez ((3 seconds silence))   ((interj.)) ((3 seconds silence))

In the first example, Ricardo uses the word "stop" to make his daughter Daniela stand still at the zebra crossing, instead of the Spanish *para* or *espera*. The use of "stop" seems a habitualised practice since the utterance is pronounced relatively rapidly, most likely in response to the urgency of the situation. Obviously, using the multilingual "stop" to make children stand still on the streets of Brussels may be effective to alert possible bystanders. Furthermore, assuming it is Ricardo's aim to make his daughters react quickly, his use of the word "stop" suggests they have probably heard the word more frequently than the Spanish equivalent *para*. We know, however, from other recordings that Ricardo does use Spanish *para* with the children, though in less urgent circumstances. In a similar fashion, the relatively isolated (i.e. it is bookended by five seconds of silence before it and three seconds of silence after it) occurrence of the interjection *allez* preceded by a sigh in Excerpt 10 emerges as a habitualised expression as well, in this case of frustration, probably due to the difficulties Ricardo's daughter is having with lifting her bicycle up over the school's doorstep. What we can observe here is that Ricardo not only understands the meaning of *allez* but also uses it himself even when there are no obvious listeners around.

So, on the basis of these last observations, we must qualify our previous claim about Ricardo speaking Dutch as "drawing on Ann's repertoire with the children" for it does not give us the whole story; as observed here these Dutch elements have become part of his language repertoire as well. Therefore, I think that a more useful conceptualisation that encapsulates all observed occurrences would be the notion of a "home" or a "family" repertoire, shared by Ricardo, Ann, and the children, which consists of a number of Dutch formulae that are functionally linked to particular practices. The couple (and, by extension, the family) can be considered as a community of practice whose participants "share certain practices" to which "particular linguistic forms are associated" (see also Lanza 2007). In this sense, our findings resonate with Fogle (2012) who shows how shared language practices in the family can be harnessed to foster family membership and ties.

Such an interpretation of the observed language practices differs substantially from the one we could have made if we had adopted a normative point of view in terms of language competence. Indeed, from such a point of view, one could argue that the instances of Ricardo speaking Dutch do not reflect an elaborate linguistic competence in Dutch, as they are restricted to a few interjections and seem generally limited to the formulaic. However, these instances can also be regarded as elements that, as a product of Ricardo's ongoing (and so continuously changing) trajectory, have become part of his multilingual repertoire. In this sense, Ricardo's (but also Ann's) repertoires can be considered "indexical biographies" (Blommaert and Backus 2011: 22), as they are a reflection of their trajectories.

7 Conclusions and implications

In this Chapter, I have presented a detailed look into the language practices that the parents-informants engage in. With respect to the "multilingual" aspect of these practices, the observations show us that the participants not only use multiple languages across various contexts, but that they do so within contexts and within conversations as well. In other words, they can indeed be termed translanguaging individuals, engaging and engaged in multilingual practices "in order to make sense of their bilingual worlds" (García 2009: 45). The most illustrative example of this is Ricardo, whose use of "Dutch" is related to a "home language" repertoire that he shares with his wife and children. Alain also springs to mind, who, when moving from one space to another, deploys a wide variety of registers in order to obtain certain goals and perform particular roles. To describe these observations only as instances of "Dutch" that are inserted into Alain's "French" language or Ricardo's "Spanish" language would clearly not do justice to the complexity of the phenomena at hand. Whereas such observations may seem somewhat self-evident in view of the body of empirical and theoretical literature on the matter, they have not been made with respect to the Brussels' context (barring the exception of Declercq 2008). In his longitudinal survey research on language use in Brussels, Janssens (2001, 2007, 2013) did uncover an evolution toward more people using more languages in different domains, and Mettewie and Van Mensel (2009), for instance, talk of a "multilingualisation" of language use in companies in Brussels. However, in the data discussed in this Chapter, the variety and complexity of language practices is substantially higher than even asserted by previous researchers.

With respect to the discussion of top-down language categorisation practices above, we can go even further on the basis of these observations and problematise the issue of "which language(s) the parents speak" altogether. For instance, it was suggested that a classification in terms of "French speaker" does not adequately capture the actual range of Alain's language practices, but then probably neither would a classification as a "bilingual Dutch-French speaker". One might – provocatively – ask the question whether he can be categorised at all, and if so, how? Likewise, in the case of Ricardo, we could ask whether the occurrences of "Dutch" in his speech should be regarded as "speaking Dutch" or rather as "doing speaking Dutch". And what about the *allez*'s in his utterances? The point here, however, is that the question as to which "language(s)" one speaks in itself inevitably perpetuates a so-called monoglossic point of view (i.e. a view on language in which only linguistic practices by monolinguals are considered legitimate), hence our difficulties in providing satisfying answers to describe the observed language practices. Answers to this question inescapably depend on what we define as "speaking a language" (entailing covert and often exacting notions of proficiency), and thus necessarily involve a particular ideological point of a view of "language" as a bounded entity and of multilingualism as a combination of multiple monolingualisms (poly-monolingualism, cf. Blommaert 2007).

These reflections become particularly important when we consider how these parents are categorised in language educational policy statistics such as those presented earlier. Particularly, if we consider the social, political, and financial stakes that are involved in these and similar statistics, we should ask ourselves whether by asking questions from a language-based point of view rather than describing social phenomena, we are actually contributing to the perpetuation of these categories as such. As Busch (2016: 16) cogently argues, "the way categories are created and related to each other not only reflects social power relations, but also helps to establish them as self-evident facts, thus exerting a performative power". In fact, in the case of research on Brussels, it may be propitious to discard categories such as *Nederlandstaligen*, *Franstaligen*, or *anderstaligen* altogether (and a *mea culpa* cf. my own survey research briefly mentioned above). Of course, discarding categories that are endemic to political and public discourse will be no mean feat, but research could and should at least play a pioneering role in this regard.

Moving beyond the specific situation of Brussels or Belgium, it is clear that in many other contexts similar contrasts can be at play between on the one hand the "labelling" of people in terms of their language background for policy purposes, and on the other hand the actual language practices people engage in. Therefore, I would argue that we should be extremely careful in applying broad language categories in policy and research, not just because they unavoidably erase the complexity and fluidity of microlinguistic contexts, as illustrated in this Chapter, but perhaps even more importantly because they are in fact related to the political and the ideologically-motivated rather than the linguistic, in spite of their appearance. In light of the current linguistic superdiversity, policy makers should move away from language-based categorisations toward a real recognition of multilingual practices.

Transcription conventions

The following conventions were used when transcribing the recorded data:

((words))	Double parentheses enclose transcriber's comments.
\<laugh\>	Angle brackets enclose descriptions of vocal noises (e.g. laughter, chuckle, inhale) or other noises on the recording that are relevant for the analysis (e.g. hands clapping).
xx	x's indicate strings of talk for which no hearing could be achieved.
?	A question mark indicates a relatively strong rising intonation (interrogative).
!	An exclamation mark indicates rising intonation (exclamatory).
..	Dots indicate silence (more dots indicate a longer silence).

References

Anderson, Benedict. [1983] 1991. *Imagined communities: Reflections on the origin and spread of nationalism*, 2nd edn. London: Verso.
Blommaert, Jan. 2007. Commentaries: On scope and depth in linguistic ethnography. *Journal of Sociolinguistics* 11 (5). 682–688.
Blommaert, Jan. 2010. *The sociolinguistics of globalization*. Cambridge: Cambridge University Press.
Blommaert, Jan. 2011. The long language-ideological debate in Belgium. *Journal of Multicultural Discourses* 6 (3). 241–256.
Blommaert, Jan & Ad Backus. 2011. Repertoires revisited: "Knowing language" in superdiversity. *Working Papers in Urban Language & Literacies* 67. London: King's College.
Blommaert, Jan, James Collins & Stef Slembrouck. 2005. Spaces of multilingualism. *Language and Communication* 25 (3). 197–216.
Busch, Brigitta. 2016. Categorizing languages and speakers: Why linguists should mistrust census data and statistics. *Working Papers in Urban Language & Literacies* 189. London: King's College.

Declercq, Karolien. 2008. *Une ethnographie sociolinguistique de deux classes multiculturelles*. Louvain-la-Neuve: UCL dissertation.
Deprez, Kas, Yves Persoons, Marina Streulens & Armel Wijnants. 1982. Anderstaligen in het Nederlandstalig basisonderwijs in Brussel: Wie en waarom? [Otherlinguals in Dutch-medium primary education in Brussels: Who and why?]. In Els Witte (ed.), *Taal en Sociale Integratie* 6. 231–266. Brussels: VUBPress.
Fishman, Joshua. 1972. Domains and the relationship between micro-and macrosociolinguistics. In John J. Gumperz & Dell Hymes (eds.), *Directions in sociolinguistics*, 407–434. New York: Holt, Rinehart & Winston.
Fogle, Lyn. 2012. *Second language socialization and learner agency: Adoptive family talk*. Bristol: Multilingual Matters.
Gal, Susan & Judith Irvine. 1995. The boundaries of languages and disciplines: How ideologies construct difference. *Social Research* 62 (4). 967–1001.
García, Ofelia. 2009. *Bilingual education in the 21st century: A global perspective*. Chichester: Wiley-Blackwell.
García, Ofelia & Li Wei. 2014. *Translanguaging: Language, bilingualism and education*. Basingstoke: Palgrave MacMillan.
Gardner-Chloros, Penelope. 2009. *Codeswitching*. New York: Cambridge University Press.
Gielen, Gerda & Fred Louckx. 1984. Sociologisch onderzoek naar de herkomst, het taalgebruik en het schoolkeuzegedrag van ouders van kinderen in het Nederlandstalig basisonderwijs in Brussel [Sociological research into the origins, language use, and school choice behavior of parents with children in Dutch-medium primary education in Brussels]. In Els Witte (ed.), *Taal & Sociale Integratie* 7. 161–208. Brussels: VUBPress.
Heller, Monica (ed.). 2007. *Bilingualism: A social approach*. Basingstoke: Palgrave Macmillan.
Heller, Monica. 2011. P. Gardner-Chloros: Code-switching. *Journal of Sociolinguistics* 15 (1). 138–141.
Hymes, Dell. 1974. Ways of Speaking. In Richard Bauman & Joel Sherzer (eds.), *Explorations in the ethnography of speaking*, 433–451. Cambridge: Cambridge University Press.
Hymes, Dell. 1996. *Ethnography, linguistics, narrative inequality: Towards an understanding of voice*. London: Taylor and Francis.
Irvine, Judith & Susan Gal. 2000. Language ideology and linguistic differentiation. In Paul Kroskity (ed.), *Regimes of language: Ideologies, politics, and identities*, 35–83. Santa Fe: School of American Research Press.
Janssens, Rudi. 2001. *Taalgebruik in Brussel: Taalverhoudingen, taalverschuivingen en taalidentiteit in een meertalige stad* [Language use in Brussels: Language relations, language shifts and language identity in a multilingual city]. Brusselse Thema's 8. Brussels: VUBPRESS.
Janssens, Rudi. 2007. *De Brusselse taalbarometer* [The Brussels language barometer]. Brussels: VUBPress.
Janssens, Rudi. 2013. *Meertaligheid als cement van de stedelijke samenleving* [Multilingualism as the cement of urban society]. Brussels: VUBPress.
Janssens, Rudi, Donat Carlier & Piet Van de Craen. 2009. Het onderwijs in Brussel [Education in Brussels]. *Brussels Studies*, Synthesenota 5.
Jørgensen, Jens Normann, Martha Sif Karrebæk, Lian Malai Madsen & Janus Spindler Møller. 2011. Polylanguaging in superdiversity. *Diversities* 13 (2). 23–38.
Kertzer, David & Dominique Arel (eds.). 2002. *Census and identity: The politics of race, ethnicity, and language in national censuses*. Cambridge: Cambridge University Press.

Lamarre, Patricia & Stephanie Lamarre. 2009. Montréal "on the move": Pour une approche ethnographique non-statique des pratiques langagières des jeunes multilingues. In Thierry Bulot (ed.), *Formes & normes sociolinguistiques: Ségrégations et discriminations urbaines*, 105–134. Paris: L'Harmattan.

Lanza, Elizabeth. 2007. Multilingualism and the family. In Peter Auer & Li Wei (eds.), *Handbook of multilingualism and and multilingual communication*, 45–67. Berlin: Mouton de Gruyter.

Makoni, Sinfree & Alastair Pennycook. 2007. *Disinventing and reconstituting languages*. Clevedon: Multilingual Matters.

Mettewie, Laurence & Luk Van Mensel. 2009. Multilingualism at all costs: Language use and language needs in business in Brussels. *Sociolinguistica* 23. 131–149.

Otsuji, Emi & Alastair Pennycook. 2010. Metrolingualism: Fixity, fluidity and language in flux. *International Journal of Multilingualism* 7 (3). 240–254.

Rampton, Ben. 2007. Neo-Hymesian linguistic ethnography in the United Kingdom. *Journal of Sociolinguistics* 11 (5). 584–607.

Sinardet, Dave. 2012. Le rôle des médias dans le conflit communautaire belge: Le traitement du dossier Bruxelles-Hal-Vilvorde lors des débats politiques télévisés francophones et néerlandophones en Belgique. In Julien Perrez & Min Reuchamps (eds.), *Les relations communautaires en Belgique: Approches politiques et linguistiques des relations communautaires en Belgique*, 105–132. Louvain-la-Neuve: Academia.

Sinardet, Dave. 2013. How linguistically divided media represent linguistically divisive issues: Belgian TV-debates on Brussels-Halle-Vilvoorde. *Regional & Federal Studies* 23 (3). 311–330.

Treffers-Daller, Jeanine. 2002. Language use and language contact in Brussels. *Journal of Multilingual and Multicultural Development* 23 (1–2). 50–64.

Van Mensel, Luk. 2007. *Onderzoeksrapport: Niet-Nederlandstalige ouders en het Nederlandstalig onderwijs in Brussel* [Research report: Non-Dutch-speaking parents and Dutch-medium education in Brussels.] Brussel: BRIO.

Van Mensel, Luk. 2014. *Language labels, language practices: A multiple case study of parents with children enrolled in Dutch-medium education in Brussels*. Namur: University of Namur dissertation.

Van Mensel, Luk. 2015. Children and choices: The effect of macro language policy on the individual agency of transnational parents in Brussels. *Language Policy* 15. 547–560.

Van Mensel, Luk. 2016. Being a francophone parent in Dutch-medium education in Brussels: A tale of tensions and competing discourses. *Minorités Linguistiques et Société* 7. 195–211.

Vandevondele, Florence. 2011. *Codeswitching: Een casestudie in een Franstalig gezin in Brussel* [Codeswitching: A case study in a French-speaking family in Brussels]. Namur: University of Namur bachelor dissertation.

Vertovec, Steven. 2007. Super-diversity and its implications. *Ethnic and Racial Studies* 30 (6). 1024–1054.

Part 4: **New ways of mapping multilingual proficiency**

Giuditta Caliendo and Annarita Magliacane

7 Sociopragmatic competence and second language acquisition: Learners of English in a study abroad context

Abstract: Reflecting today's globalisation, student mobility has now become increasingly popular among university students. Such mobility programmes allow participants to expand their cultural and social knowledge of the target language community as well as to foster or learn another language during the study abroad (SA) experience. A number of Second Language Acquisition (SLA) studies situated within SA learning contexts have started to appear over the last three decades in order to analyse the linguistic development in the second language (L2) during a period of student mobility abroad. This Chapter will contribute to this research stream by focusing on the sociopragmatic competence in English as an L2 of five university students during their Erasmus programme in Ireland. In particular, their sociopragmatic competence will be analysed by focusing on their use over time of discourse markers (DMs) in the L2. The linguistic items under analysis were *yeah, like, well, ehm*, and were analysed longitudinally in order to investigate whether any differences were present over time in their frequency and use in learner language. Combining insights from the research domains of sociolinguistic variation in SLA and L2 Pragmatics, this contribution is an exploratory study aimed to investigate to what extent a temporary period of transnational mobility in Ireland affected learners' use of DMs in L2 English upon completion of SA. Data were elicited with individual sociolinguistic interviews (Labov 984). The DMs under analysis were tracked over a period of about six months and were then compared to a baseline corpus of interviews elicited from Irish English native speakers.

Note: The authors conceived this article together. Each section is the result of joint discussion, planning and revision, with the individual contribution in writing as follows: Giuditta Caliendo is responsible for sections 2, 4.2, 4.3, 5.1 and 7; Annarita Magliacane is responsible for sections 1, 3, 4.1, 5.2 and 6.

Giuditta Caliendo, University of Lille, UMR 8163 Savoirs, Textes, Langage, Domaine Universitaire du Pont de Bois, 59650 Villeneuve-d'Ascq, France.
Annarita Magliacane, School of Languages & Social Sciences, Aston University, Birmingham, United Kingdom.

https://doi.org/10.1515/9781501503207-008

1 Introduction

In a world that is increasingly mobile, a period of a temporary student mobility as part of education and training has become almost commonplace for the majority of university students. The elite Grand Tour, which allowed exclusively well-off individuals to travel around Europe in order to discover new cultures and learn new languages in the past centuries, is now almost a distant memory. Transnational student mobility among EU member states is now actively promoted among university institutions and it is also enhanced by means of inter-university agreements as an effect of the internationalisation at third-level education. Among the different types of mobility programmes now available to students in Europe (and beyond), the Erasmus programme, which will be analysed in this contribution, is presumably the most common form of student mobility at the university level. Since its inception in 1987, it has allowed thousands of students to spend part of their university studies in another European state (European Commission 2017). As a consequence, a new concept of mobility has also started to emerge in Europe. As mentioned by Murphy-Lejeune (2002), this programme has created "new strangers" (Murphy-Lejeune 2002: 230), who, unlike other types of migrants, experience mobility in somewhat more privileged circumstances. Indeed, their departure is characterised by choice and their experience is presumably less dramatic due to the transient nature of their in-between status in another culture and language (for further details, see Murphy-Lejeune 2002: 232–233).

Although their experience in another culture and language is temporary, an analysis of student mobility from a Second Language Acquisition (SLA) perspective can be extremely revealing to understand developmental patterns in the second language (L2). Indeed, during the mobility experience, the study abroad (SA) student can shift from being simply an L2 learner, who uses the language exclusively in the classroom, to a multilingual user, who uses the language in real-life contexts. Traditionally, the growing mobility in student populations around the globe seems to be linked to the possibility of improving foreign language (FL) skills while abroad (Howard 2005). However, SA research to date does not seem to provide evidence of beneficial effects for all learners and in all areas of SLA (Serrano, Tragant, and Llanes 2012). While SA students seem to outperform their "at home" counterparts in terms of fluency (see, for example, Freed 1995), less striking gains seem to emerge for other areas of L2 speakers' proficiency (for a review of the state of art, see Llanes 2011; Howard and Schwieter 2018). In addition, SA research seems to have predominantly focused on the effects of a period of mobility on the variables of "complexity", "accuracy" and "fluency" in the L2 while other skills seem to be rather under-represented in the literature. Therefore, there is a need to map other aspects of language proficiency upon completion of a period of student mobility in order to have a better understanding of the effect that a mobility experience can have on SLA. In particular, due to the possibility of being exposed to more and much varied input while abroad, it is the socio-contextual aspect of the experience that needs more investigation, as we need to better understand to what extent the possibility of being exposed to real-life language use can affect SLA.

In the analysis of socio-contextual features, the variationist perspective on SLA research (Adamson and Regan 1991; Dewaele and Mougeon 2004; Howard 2005; Regan, Howard, and Lemée 2009; Howard 2012) has begun to provide interesting findings for assessing the qualities of SA learning contexts. Traditionally, as mentioned by Howard (2012), research in SLA has focused on the acquisition of categorical features of the L2, with a focus on "type I variation" (Rehner 2002), which can be defined as: "[the] alternation between [...] forms that conform to native language norms and [...] forms that are not observable in native speech, often referred to as 'errors'" (Dewaele and Mougeon 2004: 296).

A recent wave of SLA research has also started investigating "type II variation" (Rehner 2002) or "sociolinguistic variation" (Mougeon, Nadasdi, and Rehner 2010), i.e. the learner's ability to use native-like non-standard variants (Howard, Mougeon, and Dewaele 2013), mainly belonging to a more informal and colloquial register. Since this type of variation is also conditioned by extra-linguistic factors, it presents a special challenge to L2 learners, especially for students who mainly learned the language in a classroom context and who were presumably mainly exposed to formal variants. Consequently, since in SA contexts learners may be potentially exposed to formal and informal input, the use of sociolinguistic variants upon completion of a temporary sojourn in the target language (TL) community may also be a symptom of language exposure and social participation while abroad.

This study will attempt to investigate this issue by focusing on the use and frequency of a selected number of discourse markers (DMs) in the oral production of five university students who lived on a temporary basis in an Irish university learning context. As maintained by Liao (2009), unlike other variationist studies of L2 speech that show more systematic patterns of variation on the target variable (such as *-ing* versus *-in*), there is extreme variation in the frequency and use of DMs by L2 speakers. Moreover, in the classroom, the presence of these linguistic items, mainly pertaining to the oral sphere, is rather limited and this has led some scholars (see, for example, Sankoff et al. 1997) to believe that it is NS contact which may favour the production of these linguistic items in the L2. Since learners can be exposed to a plurality of inputs while abroad, these linguistic items appear to be relevant candidates for analysis according to an SA perspective and in relation to the social participation of learners in the TL community. Indeed, recent studies, conducted predominantly on migrants, have assumed a correlation between the use of DMs in L2 users' oral production and the degree of their social participation in the TL community. According to Giuliano and Russo (2014), the functionally correct and lexically varied use of these linguistic components is a sign of intense contact with the TL. Migge (2015: 391) also affirms that the frequency of markers in conversation can function as an index of learners' level of exposure to the language. Whether similar results can be found in shorter-term mobility, is an issue that still needs to be addressed by the literature.

In this contribution, our analysis will be twofold: firstly, we will investigate the use of fillers, such as *ehm* or *yeah*, and assess their use and frequency over time. These results will be then compared to the use of other types of markers, which we will refer to, following Lafford (1995), as "native-like stalling phenomena", i.e. linguistic devices that speakers may tend to use mainly when they hesitate, fill in pauses and fumble for what to say next. Our analysis will focus on the use of *well* and *like*. The former has been claimed to be present to some extent in textbooks (Buysse 2015). Its analysis will, therefore, allow an investigation of the longitudinal use of a marker which the L2 learner is presumably familiar with. With regard to *like*, some of its pragmatic uses have been claimed to be particularly frequent in Irish English (Hickey 2007, 2015), therefore, given the setting of our investigation, the analysis of the use of this marker may allow to gauge the effect of the SA context of learning on the linguistic outcomes of the learners as well as their language exposure and social participation within the TL community during their SA experience.

2 Discourse markers and second language acquisition

DMs have been interestingly described by Crystal (1988: 48) as "[...] the oil which helps us perform the complex task of spontaneous speech production and interaction smoothly and efficiently [...]". DMs are a very functional class of words and it is impossible to imagine communication without them. They are also commonly used to signal a change in the direction the conversation is going or to react to what is said by our interlocutor, providing "instructions to the hearer [about] how to integrate their host utterance into a developing mental model of the discourse in such a way as to make the utterance appear optimally coherent" (Mosegaard Hansen 2006: 25). However, a clear-cut definition of DMs seems to be quite a controversial issue in linguistics, with no common agreement among scholars (Bazzanella 2006) who have tended to highlight the heterogeneity of those elements rather than generating precise definitions (Migge 2015). As Beeching (2015: 178) strikingly argues: "a sound basis for the classification of markers – or even what to call them – has not yet been fully established".

Indeed, the names given to these linguistic items have varied greatly and the different labels in place have often been the result of different scholarly approaches. They have been variously referred to as discourse markers (Schiffrin 1987; Jucker and Ziv 1998), pragmatic markers (Brinton 1996) and discourse particles (Fischer 2006), just to mention some of the most common labels to be found in the literature. In this Chapter, we will use "discourse markers" (DMs), following Schourup (1999), as this label seems to be the most widespread among the academic community as well as the most inclusive among other compelling ones (Schrourup 1999). With regard to their description, two main approaches have been identified: the functional-pragmatic approach (Bazzanella 2006), mainly aimed at describing the role of these linguistic items, and the contextual-semantic one (Khachaturyan 2011), which is instead aimed at identifying formal properties of DMs as a class of words. In this Chapter the analysis will be mainly focused on identifying the functions performed by DMs in conversation and their pragmatic values.

Indeed, DMs play a pivotal role at the pragmatic level and their role in communication cannot be underestimated. As effectively illustrated by Svartvik (1980), a pragmatic "failure" (Thomas 1983) in the use or even the omission of a particular marker may not be considered as an error by the interlocutor, who, instead, may misinterpret what the L2 user is attempting to convey as impolite or inappropriate behaviour: "If a foreign language learner says five *sheeps* or he *goed*, he can be corrected by practically every native speaker. If, on the other hand, he omits a *well*, the likely reaction will be that he is dogmatic, impolite, boring, awkward to talk to etc, but a native cannot pinpoint an 'error'". (Svartvik 1980: 171) [italics added]. However, despite the crucial importance of DMs for successful communication, the literature on their use in L2 seems to be rather scanty (Müller 2005; Liao 2009) and the majority of studies appear to have mainly relied on cross-sectional study designs (Liao 2009), i.e. they provided a snapshot of certain linguistic conditions at a single point in time. Although these studies have provided interesting insights into the use of these linguistic items in the L2 in comparison to NS use, they shed little light on the process of acquisition, the developmental patterns and the possible correlation between the use of these linguistic items and the features of the learning context.

3 Research questions and aims

Given that SA learning contexts allow "the instructed learner to acquire 'pseudo-naturalistic' status by engaging in more informal acquisition in the TL community, through naturalistic contact with the L2 in everyday social situations" (Regan, Howard, and Lemée 2009: 20), this Chapter will attempt to investigate whether a temporary period of student mobility in the TL community may aid the production of DMs in conversation, and consequently, be beneficial for the development of learners' sociopragmatic competence. More specifically, this Chapter will analyse how social factors affect English language acquisition in an SA context by referring to the learners' daily use of, and exposure to, the L2 and the closest social circle of the participants whilst abroad. The study starts from the general assumption that students who have more chances of interacting with local people are also more likely to develop pragmatic competence. As argued by Regan, Howard and Lemée (2009), learners may choose to reproduce native-speaker variation patterns in their speech as an attempt to integrate themselves in the target community and better identify with its speakers.

In particular, the study sets out to investigate the use of a selected number of DMs in speech productions by L2 learners of English drawing upon a corpus of interviews ("NNS data") conducted at two different points in time: upon the informants' arrival in Ireland, and six months later, just before their departure. This longitudinal approach enabled us to assess whether any change could be detected in the use of DMs in the respondents' speech production after their experience abroad and if any trends could be detected over time. Results were also analysed in the light of the informants' interaction with local community members to ascertain whether this social variable affected the frequency and typology of the DMs used.

4 Description of the study

4.1 The informants

This paper presents a pilot study conducted within the framework of a PhD research project carried out in cooperation with an Irish university. The investigation was conducted with five Italian students who all spent a semester abroad (January–June 2015) at the Irish university where the research was conducted. Participation in the study was entirely voluntary. Although all participants knew that the study was being conducted for research purposes in order to assess L2 development over time, they were not made aware of the specific items under investigation in order to avoid affecting data production. Informants were interviewed by the second author twice: the first time within their first month in Ireland and then again at the end of their stay. In order to keep personal information confidential, initials have been used throughout this Chapter to replace participants' first names.

Upon arrival, all participants had an onset proficiency level of English corresponding to the B1/B2 of the Common European Framework of Reference for Languages (CEFR). The sample was relatively homogeneous in terms of gender and age, since all informants were young female university students, either working towards their completion of the Bachelor's Degree or at the beginning of their Master's. Their university background was, on the contrary, rather diversified. As shown in Table 1, the choice of learners' accommodation was also rather diverse. C. lived in a private house, which she shared with another Italian speaker. S. was staying on campus, sharing some student accommodation with other non-native speakers of English (Chinese, Spanish), while A. lived in student accommodation off campus, which she shared with US and French students. With regard to G. and V., they both changed their place of residence over the six-month period. G. spent the first half of her SA experience in a host family, a young Irish couple with no children, and for the rest of her stay she lived in a private house, a little distant from the city centre, with three young Irish ladies in their thirties. V. moved after a few weeks from a house

Table 1: The sample.

Informant	University studies	Type of accommodation	Co-tenants*
C.	Law	Private house	NNSs of English (Italian)
S.	Modern languages	Campus accommodation	NNSs of English (Chinese, Spanish)
G.	Geology	Host family /Private house	NSs of English (Irish)
A.	Finance	Student accommodation	NSs & NNSs of English (US & French)
V.	Economics	Private house(s)	NSs/ NNs of English (Irish/ Spanish)

*Native Speaker (NS) of English; Non-Native Speaker (NNS) of English.

with Irish students to a place closer to campus, which she shared with Spanish students and with whom she ended up speaking Italian most of the time.

4.2 Instruments

The research was interview- and survey-based and included two sociolinguistic interviews, the first one conducted within the first month in the host country, hereafter referred to as "T1" (= time 1), and the second one towards the end of the students' experience abroad, hereafter referred to as "T2" (= time 2). Thus, the learners' corpus was comprised of 10 interviews. Each interview lasted on average 50 minutes, for a total of about 9 hours of spoken data and accounting for about 58,000 words. Interviews were organised following the principles of the sociolinguistic interview (Labov 1984) for the elicitation of spontaneous conversation. Topics were both formal and informal and extremely varied, ranging from university studies and future plans to cultural differences between Ireland and Italy. In order to minimise the "experimenter effect" (Labov 1984: 30), a friendly setting was reproduced for the oral interviews, which were conducted while having a coffee with the informants. The collected data were manually transcribed verbatim into standard orthography by the second author following the conventions proposed by Blanche-Benveniste and Jeanjean (1987).

In addition to their participation in the interview, students were asked to complete two questionnaires, the first upon arrival in Ireland and the second before their departure. The two questionnaires provided useful information about the informants, with specific reference to their background learning experiences, expectations about their experience abroad, desired learning outcomes and degree of interaction with people from the local community. These questionnaires, which were administered through an online survey system,[1] were devised according to the models proposed by Freed et al. (2004) and the Social Networking Questionnaire (McManus, Mitchell, and Tracy-Ventura 2014) used within the framework of the LANG-SNAP project (University of Southampton, UK). The latter was specifically aimed at investigating social networks and TL interaction in an SA context.

---

[1] The questions and the relative answers relevant for the current study have been summarised in Tables 1, 13 and 14.

4.3 Methodology

Each transcribed audio-recorded interview was analysed to assess the frequency of the markers under scrutiny used by each learner. The raw number of occurrences for each marker in the interview was normalised (per thousand words)[2] according to the number of tokens of each interview[3] to enable comparability of data across informants. Each discourse marker was then analysed in order to determine its precise function in context. The occurrences of each marker and its relevant function at T1 and T2 were compared to assess whether there had been any changes in their use in L2 over time, namely after the SA experience. Cases of increase or decrease in the use of each marker were analysed in the light of the learners' response to interviews and questionnaires, to assess to what extent their social participation and integration in the TL community may have affected their production. A comparison of the results obtained for each learner led to the identification of some common traits among the students who partook in the research.

With regard to the functions considered, we followed Lafford (1995) for the first typology of markers under analysis. According to Lafford (1995), speakers may resort to the use of connectors, fillers and backchannel signals to keep the conversation going and develop it further. Lafford (1995: 104) defines the first category, connectors, as the "elements used to connect parts of the conversation in a cohesive manner", whereas fillers are linguistic items used in conversation when speakers pause to think about what to say next. However, a clear-cut distinction between connectors and fillers is not always feasible since those items, under some circumstances, do perform the same phatic function (Lafford 1995). Hence, in this Chapter, the term "filler" will be used as a hypernym to identify linguistic items which have been referred to as "connectors" and "fillers" elsewhere, being such a distinction beyond the scope of the current study. With regard to backchannel signals, they mainly perform the phatic function of showing mutual understanding (Lafford 1995). In the analysis, other functions were also taken into account, more specifically the use of markers to introduce reformulations or to signal that the speaker is searching for the right word.

---

[2] A similar methodological approach was used by Beeching (2015).
[3] In the tables we will refer to the raw number of occurrences as "tokens" (T), whereas the normalised number of occurrences will be referred to as "rate" (R).

5 Results

5.1 Increased occurrence of discourse markers

Most of the respondents seemed to rely mainly, both at T1 and at T2, on the use of items such as *ehm*, *uhm* and *oh*, or on DMs such as *yes*, *yeah* as connectors or fillers in conversation. The analysis and the comparison of the occurrences over time showed that all learners, with the exception of V.,[4] tended to increase the use of at least one of the above mentioned markers. The breakdown of the occurrences of DMs for each learner is shown in Tables 2 to 7 below. Each column lists respectively: "T", the raw frequencies of the occurrences of the highlighted marker fulfilling a specific function; "%", the percentage of the use of the marker in that specific function out of its overall number of occurrences; and "R", the marker's normalised frequencies (ptw).

Table 2: Longitudinal occurrences of *ehm* for C.

Discourse marker	Function	T1			T2		
		T	%	R	T	%	R
Ehm	Filler	35	83.33	6.54	97	83.62	13.27
	Reformulation	0	0.00	0.00	5	4.31	0.68
	Searching for word	0	0.00	0.00	10	8.62	1.37
	Backchannel	7	16.67	1.31	4	3.45	0.55
	Total	42	100.00	7.85	116	100.00	15.88

Table 2 lists the occurrences of *ehm* for C., our first informant. As the table shows, there is a tendency towards a generally increased use of this marker in all its functions, with a slight decrease when used as a backchannel signal. Among all functions, the use of *ehm* as a filler in the conversation is the most frequent one, as shown in (1). Other functions that have been identified include the use of *ehm* to introduce reformulations or, in some instances at T2, as a filler when searching for the right word, as shown respectively in (2) and (3):

(1) [...] I want to find probably ehm - I want to find probably a work in a company [...] (NNS data)

---

4 As regards V., although some signs of improvement were noticeable, it was not always possible to find evidence of any marked differences between Time 1 and Time 2.

(2) [...] it's clear and all people know this ehm - you have to have a recommendation to work [...] (NNS data)
(3) [...] and every summer the best ehm ehm -- the best ehm - guys can go to [...] (NNS data)

This strategy may be considered particularly interesting and relevant in the case of this specific learner, as it was not at all present at T1, and may be seen as an attempt on the part of C. to try and keep the conversation going, without relying on other communication strategies, as Lafford (1995: 116) suggests, such as turning to her interlocutor for direct (*How do you say ... ?*) or indirect appeal (*I don't know the word for ...*).

Similar findings can be found in the case of G., as shown in Table 3 below. Similarly to C., the use of *ehm* as a filler increased at T2, while a slight decrease can be detected in the use of this marker to introduce reformulations or when searching for a word. These changes may perhaps be explained by the fact that G. was one of the learners to develop native-like stalling phenomena,[5] namely through the use of DMs such as *well* and *like*, which may have replaced simple fillers in her oral production by the end of her SA experience.

Table 3: Longitudinal occurrences of *ehm* for G.

Discourse marker	Function	T1			T2		
		T	%	R	T	%	R
Ehm	Filler	48	72.73	10.78	92	92.93	21.57
	Reformulation	1	1.52	0.22	0	0.00	0.00
	Searching for word	12	18.18	2.69	3	3.03	0.70
	Backchannel	5	7.58	1.12	4	4.04	0.94
	Total	66	100.00	14.82	99	100.00	23.21

With regard to S. and A., significant changes were reported in the longitudinal use of *yeah*. As shown in Table 4 and 5 below, an increase was detected in the use of marker *yeah* at T2 with respect to all its functions. For both speakers, *yeah* was mainly used as a filler, and in some occurrences it introduced reformulations of thoughts. The use of *yeah* as a backchannel signal tended to be more frequent at T2. As far as V. is concerned, although the occurrences of *yeah* remain rather

---

5 The use of native-like stalling phenomena will be further explored in subsection 5.2.

Table 4: Longitudinal occurrences of *yeah* for S.

Discourse marker	Function	T1			T2		
		T	%	R	T	%	R
Yeah	Backchannel	2	15.38	0.42	12	6.00	2.13
	Reformulation	0	0.00	0.00	6	3.00	1.06
	Filler	11	84.62	2.33	182	91.00	32.30
	Total	13	100.00	2.76	200	100.00	35.49

Table 5: Longitudinal occurrences of *yeah* for A.

Discourse marker	Function	T1			T2		
		T	%	R	T	%	R
Yeah	Backchannel	7	38.89	2.67	26	23.64	6.35
	Reformulation	0	0.00	0.00	2	1.82	0.49
	Filler	11	61.11	4.20	82	74.55	20.03
	Total	18	100.00	6.86	110	100.00	26.87

Table 6: Longitudinal occurrences of *yeah* for V.

Discourse marker	Function	T1			T2		
		T	%	R	T	%	R
Yeah	Backchannel	1	100.00	0.38	20	83.33	5.85
	Reformulation	0	0.00	0.00	0	0.00	0.00
	Filler	0	0.00	0.00	4	16.67	1.17
	Total	1	100.00	0.38	24	100	7.02

low at T2, the data might still be revealing as *yeah* did not occur at all at T1, with the exception of a single instance as a backchannel signal. The examples (4)–(6) which follow are taken from the interview with S. at T2 and are, respectively, examples of the use of backchannel signal (4), reformulation (5) and filler (6):

(4) I: what about your classmates - is there a special person you will miss?
S: yeah - I also - ehm will miss them - but I don't know - they - ehm ehm -- we are not so close [...] (NNS data)

(5) [...] because I lived in - yeah I am living in C⁶[...] (NNS data)
(6) [...] because - yeah usually I think maybe so much - about things and these days I had the opportunity to think ehm - yeah - to realise that I am leaving (NNS data)

According to Lafford (1995), the use of fillers, such as *ehm* or *yeah*, can be considered as a feature peculiar to L2 learners who tend to use them to overcome difficulties in conversation, or, following Canale and Swain (1980), as an instantiation of the learner's strategic competence. With regard to our analysis of *ehm* and *yeah*, the data revealed that this feature is also shared by our group of NSs, as illustrated in Tables 7 and 8 below. However, the use of *ehm* and *yeah* as a filler seems to be more frequent among our learner informants (with the sole exception of V.), especially at T2.

Table 7: Occurrences of *ehm* in the NS control group*.

Discourse marker	Function	T (average)	%	R (average)
Ehm	Filler	55.33	93.26	10.15
	Searching for word	4.00	6.74	0.73
	Total	59.33	100.00	10.88

* With regard to the control group, the average value of "T" (number of raw occurrences) and "R" (normalisation ptw) has been considered as a parameter of assessment.

Table 8: Occurrences of *yeah* in the NS control group.

Discourse marker	Function	T (average)	%	R (average)
Yeah	Filler	36.00	61.30	6.60
	Backchannel	22.67	38.70	4.16
	Total	58.67	100	10.76

The control group was comprised of three speakers, with similar mean age to that of the learners (NS mean age = 25, NNS mean age = 24). The NSs interviewed were all Irish speakers born in Cork and who were living there at the time of the interview. The data were collected following the same principles and under the same conditions as the data collection for the learners. Since, as

---

6 The initial of the name of the place has been provided in order to respect the confidentiality of personal information provided in the interviews.

mentioned by Beeching (2016), the use of a particular marker can indicate a sense of belonging to a particular social group, as well as the idiolect of the speaker, mean values for the control group will be considered in the analysis as a parameter of reference.

5.2 Development of native-like stalling phenomena

The second trend detected among the interviewees is the emergence of some native-like stalling phenomena for some of the participants. The term "native-like stalling phenomena" is used in Lafford (1995) in order to distinguish simple fillers from other items which are typical of NSs' oral production. As previously mentioned, as instances of "native-like stalling phenomena", we will focus on the marker *well* and two pragmatic uses of *like*, namely the use of *like* as a focuser and its use to introduce a quotation. Such uses of *like* have been claimed by Hickey (2007, 2015) to be extremely frequent in Irish English and common all over Ireland and all age groups.

5.2.1 *The use of* well

With regard to *well*, our data show that two of the participants, i.e. S. and G., started using this discourse marker more frequently by the time they completed their experience abroad, as illustrated in Table 9. With the exception of a single occurrence (7) for participant S. at T1, the use of this marker became more consistent at T2:

Table 9: Use of *well* for S. and G.

Discourse marker	S.				G.			
Well	T1		T2		T1		T2	
	T	R	T	R	T	R	T	R
	1	0.21	23	4.08	0	0.00	20	4.69

(7) [...] well - there is a courtyard in ehm -- where there are different ehm -- yes apartments [...] (NNS data)

The occurrences in the oral production of these two learners (Table 9) were then compared with the average use of *well* by the members of the control group (Table 10) and, as evident in Tables 9 and 10, learners' production of *well* at T2 was relatively higher when compared with the reference group (NS mean: 2.93). It can therefore be assumed that, once acquired, this DM became a characteristic of these two learners' speech and they tended to use it rather frequently in their oral production at T2, even more frequently than average NS use.

Table 10: Use of *well* in the NS control group.

Discourse marker	T (average)	R (average)
Well	16.00	2.93

5.2.2 *The use of* like

Particularly relevant, especially in terms of social participation, is the development to some degree of what we may refer to, following Lafford's (1995) label of "native-like stalling phenomena", as "TL stalling phenomena". In her study, Lafford hints at some differences in the development of some markers in Spanish, depending on the host country where the learners lived, i.e. whether it was in Mexico or in Spain, without, however, providing a specific label for markers typical of the host community. Nonetheless, the language variety to which learners are exposed to may be particularly relevant, especially if the outcomes are analysed according to an SA perspective. With regard to Irish English, for instance, Hickey (2007, 2015) provides an insightful analysis on the most frequent markers in Ireland.

Among these markers, *like* seems to be the most frequent one (Hickey 2007). In particular, Hickey (2007, 2015) affirms that *like* is used all over Ireland and, in particular, it seems to be commonly used in these two pragmatic functions:

(i) to introduce a quotation or an inner thought ("quotative like") as it occurs in (8). This use is particularly frequent among young people and, according to Hickey (2007, 2015) and Beeching (2016), it has been traditionally considered to be imported from American English;
(ii) as a focuser, i.e. as a highlighting device, especially in explanatory contexts, to introduce new information (Dailey-O'Cain 2000), as shown in (9) and (10). This use of *like* is detected to be frequent in all age groups (Hickey 2007) in Ireland.

(8) I'm, like, "No way my parents will pay for that!" (in Hickey 2007: 376).

(9) He's producing, like, we'll say, at a lesser expense. (in Hickey 2007: 376).
(10) I'm just telling you what I heard, like. (in Hickey 2007: 376).

Hickey's (2007) analysis is based on spoken data collected all over Ireland. The data drawn from the interviews collected in County Cork, confirm that *like* is also a very common feature in this area, as this short passage, taken from our corpus of interviews, shows:

(11) [...] Ireland is a good place to - for people to come for learning English - ehm because what - ok - I know we have accents and I know we speak quite fast - but we love to talk - the Irish - *like* - we have a reputation *like* - we love - you know *like* - we are quite friendly *like* - I'm being so vain here now! - but you know what I mean *like*? We are *like* - you know - they're always very welcoming *like* and - you know - that's great practice for foreign people - to come over cause you're always going to be talking to somebody *like* [...] (NS data) [our emphasis]

With regard to the production of this marker by our learner participants, as Table 11 shows, S. and G. started using *like* as a focuser more frequently at T2. With regard to participant G., a limited number of occurrences of "focuser *like*" were found also at T1, although this use became more consistent (44 raw occurrences and a rate of 10.31) at T2. In addition to a more consistent use of *like* at T2, in comparison with the spoken data of participant S., the values for focuser *like* for participant G. were found to be above the control group average values (10.31 *versus* 6.36). The fact that she tended to use *like* quite often at T2 may be explained by the fact that she acknowledged that it was a specific feature of Irish English, as she clearly stated in extract (12) below. Thus, it may be assumed that she started producing it consciously for a sense of group inclusion.

Table 11: Use of *like* for S. and G.

	S.				G.			
	T1		T2		T1		T2	
Functions	T	R	T	R	T	R	T	R
Focuser	0	0.00	15	2.66	3	0.67	44	10.31
Quotative	0	0.00	8	1.42	0	0.00	1	0.23

Table 12: Use of *like* in the NS control group.

Functions	T	R
Focuser	34.67	6.36
Quotative	23.33	4.28

(12) [...] sometimes *is not the slang that I find difficult to remember and understand completely but - but *is the way of saying something and the way of *emphasise everything that I find more - like - interesting and funny - like I don't know how if I can say like -- Jesus Christ - something like this [*laugher*] - and I don't know - yeah -- it's very funny - I can't remember now but there was something else - ehm- ehm --- oh! they always say like like like - like like like - just just just-you know you know - you know what I mean [...] (NNS data).

6 Discussion

The results emerging from the pilot study show that the effects of a semester abroad were certainly beneficial for the production of DMs in learner language, although the increase in use of DMs was not homogeneous among all the participants in the study. With regard to *well* and *like*, their use at T2 become more consistent for only two of the learners involved in the project. These linguistic findings may be related to the participants' exposure to the TL and to their degree of interaction with the members of the TL community. Throughout the oral interviews, students were asked information about their daily life, their social network(s), and the degree of interaction with NSs, in particular with Irish people. All students mentioned that it was extremely hard for them to get acquainted with Irish nationals and, although during their stay in Ireland, they attended classes with Irish students, their interaction with them was limited to short conversations or greetings. These findings were then compared with the responses given in questionnaires, where respondents were also asked to self-assess their use of the English language on a daily basis. The data are summarised in Table 13.[7]

---

[7] Students were asked to assess (in hours, per day) the amount of time they would spend interacting with native speakers, non-native speakers of English and their housemates. The options given were: "> 5"; "4–5"; "2–3"; "0–1".

Table 13: Language interaction.

Language use on a daily basis					
	C.	S.	G.	A.	V.
How many hours per day did you speak English with native speakers?	0–1	4–5	2–3	4–5	0–1
How many hours per day did you speak English with non-native speakers?	4–5	> 5	4–5	> 5	4–5
How many hours per day did you speak English with your housemates?	0–1	> 5	2–3	> 5	0–1

As Table 13 shows, all students mentioned that during their experience abroad they tended to speak English mostly with non-native speakers of English and that for all of them the number of hours spent talking to L2 users every day was quite high ("4–5" or "> 5"). This corroborates recent scholarly findings that consider immersion in the TL to be a myth since "exchange students are likely to be engaged socially in international Erasmus communities" (Mitchell, McManus, and Tracy-Ventura 2015: 119), where English is the lingua franca.

In order to understand more about their social networks while abroad, students were also asked to mention three of their closest contacts during their semester in Ireland (Table 14). These people would probably be those they interacted with the most during their experience abroad:

Table 14: Informants' closest social network.

Closest contacts during the experience abroad					
	C.	S.	G.	A.	V.
Person 1	NNS	NNS	NNS	NNS (Italian)	NNS (Italian)
Person 2	NNS (Italian)	NNS	NNS (Italian)	NNS	NNS (Italian)
Person 3	NNS	NNS	NS	NS	NNS (Italian)

As shown in Table 13 and 14, C. and V. did not use English profusely while living abroad but while the inner circle of C.'s friends also comprised non-Italian speakers, V. tended to interact mainly with Italians and this may explain why her linguistic data did not show significant differences between T1 and T2. The speakers who seemed to have used English the most in their daily interactions were S. and A. However, S.'s circle of friends was mainly composed of non-native speakers of English, which may be related to the fact that she was a member of many student societies or associations on campus, which gave her the chance to meet numerous peers, not necessarily of her same nationality. The fact that she was able to develop some native-like stalling phenomena may be linked to the fact that, as Howard (2012) puts it, "[...] learners who engage in extracurricular activities demonstrate higher rates of use of informal variants than their counterparts who do not" (Howard 2012: 21). With regard to A., although she mentioned in the questionnaire that one of her closest friends was an NS of English, which turned out to be one of her housemates, she also acknowledged in the interview before departure that interactions with this person were not that frequent and often limited to short conversational exchanges, as it is possible to see from the following passage:

(13) [...] I -- have a more confidence with the French girl - and we go out together - we *are friends together - ehm the same friends - and with American - it's ok - but one has her friends and the other one is a - sometimes * goes out with us - yes - she is a little bit shy and so [...]

With regard to participant G., the learner who mainly developed TL stalling phenomena, it is worth noticing that her closest circle of friends encompassed native and non-native speakers of English, including speakers of her mother tongue. As regards her interaction with NSs, it is particularly interesting that the answer to the questions "How many hours per day did you speak English with native speakers?" and "How many hours per day did you speak English with your housemates?" was the same: "2–3 hours". This may lead us to believe, as she also confirmed retrospectively, that her interaction with NSs coincided with the time spent with her housemates, who happened to be also members of the local community. Additionally, her contact with her housemates was not limited to small talk, but she actually spent a significant amount of time with them, engaging in different and varied activities, from going to the university together to going out at the weekend. Thus, she was not exclusively exposed to a greater amount of input while abroad, but also she engaged in different types of conversation while abroad.

7 Conclusions

This Chapter investigated the effects of a period of student mobility on the production of a number of DMs in the L2 by SA learners of English who spent a semester in the South of Ireland. As previous studies have shown, DMs are particularly relevant at the pragmatic level in oral L2 production and may be a symptom of social participation in the TL community. Our data revealed that the experience abroad resulted in some beneficial, though heterogeneous, effects in terms of use of DMs by our subjects. We suggest that the heterogeneous results may be mainly linked to the students' different degree of exposure to the TL and interaction with the target community members.

Two trends have emerged from the analysis:

– an increase in the use of fillers for most participants;
– the use of native-like stalling phenomena for some of the participants. The sub-category of TL stalling phenomena has also been suggested for some functions of the marker *like*.

The linguistic data have also been related to some social factors that may have triggered the acquisition of some markers. Although the study is based on a small-scale exploratory study, some conclusions, albeit tentative, can be drawn from the discussion presented in the previous section. Type of accommodation appeared to play an important role in the creation of social networks while abroad, as well as on the linguistic outcomes in relation to the linguistic items under investigation in the current study. One of the students, G., who mainly lived with local people, produced at T2 a more widespread use of the DMs under scrutiny.

However, another student, namely S., also produced many native-like or TL stalling phenomena despite the fact that she lived with non-native speakers of English. Thus, motivation, personality and even curiosity towards the TL and culture may also have played a role in the development of sociolinguistic and sociopragmatic competence. In fact, not all learners abroad might develop the same competence, simply because of living in, or being in close contact with the TL community. This was clearly evidenced by the different beneficial outcomes of the learners interviewed in the present study. Thus, as Freed, Segalowitz and Dewey (2004) also illustrate, it is not "the context per se that promotes various types of learning but rather [...] the nature of the interactions, the quality of the experiences, and the efforts made to use the L2" (Freed, Segalowitz, and Dewey 2004: 298).

This study presented the findings of an exploratory study conducted within the framework of a broader doctoral project. Due to its nature of pilot study, limitations are inevitably present and should therefore be taken into consideration when analysing the results. With regard to the number of learners under scrutiny, data collection was circumscribed to five participants only. The relatively small sample can be ascribed to the longitudinal design of the study, and the consequent level of commitment required from each participant in terms of data collection and the efforts on the part of the researcher in the participant retention over time. However, this limitation can be minimalised by the amount of data elicited from each participant (about 1.5 hours for each speaker) and the information regarding the social networks of each informant, which allowed us to analyse the spoken data with insights into the SA experience of each learners.

Another limitation of the current study can be the sex of the participants. Indeed, the informants were exclusively female speakers. While this aspect guaranteed homogeneity among respondents, it prevented us from assessing whether a difference in the use of DMs might be gender-bound. Moreover, as also previously mentioned, variables such as motivation and personality can also play a role in the quantity and quality of social bonds that learners can create during an SA experience. In addition, this contribution enabled to analyse the effects of an Erasmus programme from an SLA perspective. However, today students can avail themselves of different types of experiences abroad, and this aspect seems to be still rather under-represented in current research on SA (cf. Magliacane 2018 on the au pair placement). A comparative analysis on different types of experiences can therefore help deepen our understanding of the correlation between input/exposure conditions while abroad and the language gains during different types of mobility programmes (also see Magliacane 2017; Magliacane and Howard 2019). Taken together, the above limitations can be considered as desiderata and possible developments for future research.

References

Adamson, H. Douglas & Vera Regan. 1991. The acquisition of community speech norms by Asian immigrants learning English as a second language: A preliminary study. *Studies in Second Language Acquisition* 13 (1). 1–22.
Bazzanella, Carla. 2006. Discourse markers in Italian: Towards a "compositional" meaning. In Kerstin Fischer (ed.), *Approaches to discourse particles*, 449–464. Amsterdam: Elsevier.
Beeching, Kate. 2015. Variability in native and non-native use of pragmatic markers: The example of "well" in role-play data. In Kate Beeching & Helen Woodfield (eds.), *Researching sociopragmatic variability: Perspectives from variational, interlanguage and contrastive pragmatics*, 174–197. New York: Palgrave Macmillian.
Beeching, Kate. 2016. *Pragmatic markers in British English: Meaning in social interaction*. Cambridge: Cambridge University Press.

Blanche-Benveniste, Claire & Colette Jeanjean. 1987. *Le français parlé: Transcription et édition*. Paris: Didier.
Brinton, Laurel J. 1996. *Pragmatic markers in English: Grammaticalization and discourse function*. Berlin: Mouton de Gruyter.
Buysse, Lieven. 2015. "Well it's not very ideal..." The pragmatic marker "well" in learner English. *Intercultural Pragmatics* 12 (1). 59–89.
Canale, Michael & Merrill Swain. 1980. Theoretical basis of communicative approaches to second language teaching and testing. *Applied Linguistics* 1. 1–47.
Crystal, David. 1988. Another look at well, you know... *English Today* 13. 47–49.
Dailey-O'Cain, Jennifer. 2000. The sociolinguistic distribution of and attitudes toward focuser "like" and quotative "like". *Journal of Sociolinguistics* 4 (1). 60–80.
Dewaele, Jean-Marc & Raymond Mougeon. 2004. Preface. In Jean-Marc Dewaele & Raymound Mougeon (eds.), Patterns of variations in the interlanguage of advanced second language learners [Special Issue]. *International Review of Applied Linguistics* 42. 295–301.
European Commission. 2017. *Erasmus: Annual report 2016*. Luxembourg: Publications Office of the European Union. https://publications.europa.eu/en/publication-detail/-/publication/b0250d33-fcce-11e7-b8f5-01aa75ed71a1 (accessed 28 May 2019).
Fischer, Kerstin. 2006. Towards an understanding of the spectrum of approaches to discourse particles. In Kerstin Fischer (ed.), *Approaches to discourse particles*, 1–20. Amsterdam: Elsevier.
Freed, Barbara F. 1995. What makes us think that students who study abroad become fluent? In Barbara Freed (ed.), *Second language acquisition in a study abroad context*, 123–148. Amsterdam & Philadelphia: John Benjamins Publishing Company.
Freed, Barbara, Dan P. Dewey, Norman Segalowitz & Randall Halter. 2004. The language contact profile. *Studies in Second Language Acquisition* 26 (2). 349–356.
Freed, Barbara, Norman Segalowitz & Dan P. Dewey. 2004. Context of learning and second language fluency in French. *Studies in Second Language Acquisition* 26. 275–301.
Giuliano, Patrizia & Rosa Russo. 2014. L'uso dei marcatori discorsivi come segnale di integrazione linguistica e sociale. In Paolo Donadio, Giuseppe Gabrielli & Monica Massari (eds.), *Uno come te*. 237–247. Milano: Franco Angeli.
Hickey, Raymond. 2007. *Irish English*. Cambridge: Cambridge University Press.
Hickey, Raymond. 2015. The Pragmatics of Irish English and Irish. In Carolina P. Amador-Moreno, Kevin McCafferty & Elaine Vaughan (eds.), *Pragmatic markers in Irish English*, 17–36. Amsterdam & Philadelphia: John Benjamins Publishing Company.
Howard, Martin. 2005. Second language acquisition in a study abroad context: A comparative investigation of the effects of study abroad and foreign language instruction on the L2 learner's grammatical development. In Alex Housen & Michel Pierrard (eds.), *Investigations in instructed second language Acquisition*, 495–530. Berlin & New York: Mouton de Gruyter.
Howard, Martin. 2012. The advanced learner's sociolinguistic profile: On issues of individual differences, second language exposure conditions, and type of sociolinguistic variable. *The Modern Language Journal* 96 (1). 20–33.
Howard, Martin, Raymond Mougeon & Jean-Marc Dewaele. 2013. Sociolinguistics and second language acquisition. In Robert Bayley, Richard Cameron & Jean-Marc Dewaele (eds.), *The Oxford handbook of sociolinguistics*, 340–359. New York: Oxford University Press.

Howard, Martin & John Schwieter. 2018. The development of second language grammar in a study abroad context. In Cristina Sanz & Alfonso Morales-Front (eds.), *The Routledge handbook of study abroad research and practice*, 135–148. New York: Routledge.

Jucker, Andreas H. & Yael Ziv. 1998. Discourse markers: Introduction. In Andreas H. Jucker & Yael Ziv (eds.), *Discourse markers: Description and theory*, 1–12. Amsterdam: John Benjamins Publishing Company.

Khachaturyan, Elizaveta. 2011. Una classificazione dei segnali discorsivi in italiano. In Elizaveta Khachaturyan (ed.), *Discourse markers in Roman languages. Oslo Studies in Languages* 3 (1). 95-116.

Labov, William. 1984. Field methods of the project on linguistic change and variation. In John Baugh & Joel Scherzer (eds.), *Language In Use*, 28–53. Eagle Cliffs: Prentice Hall.

Lafford, Barbara. 1995. Getting into, through and out of a survival situation. In Barbara Freed (ed.), *Second language acquisition in a study abroad context*, 97–121. Amsterdam & Philadelphia: John Benjamins Publishing Company.

Liao, Sylvie. 2009. Variation in the use of discourse markers by Chinese teaching assistants in the US. *Journal of Pragmatics* 41 (7). 1313–1328.

Llanes, Àngels. 2011. The many faces of study abroad: An update on the research on L2 gains emerged during a study abroad experience. *International Journal of Multilingualism* 8. 189–215.

Magliacane, Annarita. 2017. Sociopragmatic development in study abroad contexts: The role of learner status in the use of second language pragmatic markers. Naples & Cork: University of Naples Federico II & University College Cork PhD dissertation.

Magliacane, Annarita. 2018. Family members or workers? Insights into sociopragmatic development and the au pair experience in an SA context. In Ariadna Sánchez Hernández & Ana Herraiz (eds.), *Pragmatics beyond traditional contexts*, 285–314. Berlin: Peter Lang.

Magliacane, Annarita & Martin Howard. 2019. The role of learner status in the acquisition of pragmatic markers during study abroad: The use of "like" in L2 English. In Anne Barron (ed.), Pragmatic development and stay abroad. [Special issue]. *Journal of Pragmatics* 146. 72–86.

McManus, Kevin, Rosamond Mitchell & Nicole Tracy-Ventura. 2014. Understanding insertion and integration in a study abroad context: The case of English-speaking sojourners in France. *Revue Française de Linguistique Appliquée* 19 (2). 97–116.

Migge, Bettina. 2015. "Now" in the speech of newcomers to Ireland. In Carolina P. Amador-Moreno, Kevin McCafferty & Elaine Vaughan (eds.), *Pragmatic markers in Irish English*, 390–407. Amsterdam & Philadelphia: John Benjamins Publishing Company.

Mitchell, Rosamond, Kevin McManus & Nicole Tracy-Ventura. 2015. Placement type and language learning during residence abroad. In Rosamond Mitchell, Nicole Tracy-Ventura & Kevin McManus (eds.), *Social interaction, identity and language learning during residence abroad*, Eurosla monographs.

Mosegaard Hansen, Maj-Britt. 2006. A dynamic polysemy approach to the lexical semantics of discourse markers (with an exemplary analysis of French "toujours"). In Kerstin Fischer (ed.), *Approaches to discourse particles*, 21–41. Amsterdam: Elsevier.

Mougeon, Raymond, Terry Nadasdi & Katherine Rehner. 2010. *The sociolinguistic competence of immersion students*. Bristol: Multilingual Matters.

Müller, Simone. 2005. *Discourse markers in native and non-native English discourse*. Amsterdam/Philadelphia: John Benjamins Publishing Company.

Murphy-Lejeune, Elizabeth. 2002. *Student mobility and narrative in Europe: The new strangers*. London & New York: Routledge.
Regan, Vera, Martin Howard & Isabelle Lemée. 2009. *The acquisition of sociolinguistic competence in a Study Abroad context*. Clevedon: Multilingual Matters.
Rehner, Katherine. 2002. The development of aspects of linguistic and discourse competence by advanced second language learners of French. Toronto: OISE/University of Toronto PhD dissertation.
Sankoff, Gillian, Pierrette Thibault, Naomi Nagy, Hélène Blondeau, Marie-Odile Fonollosa & Lucie Gagnon. 1997. Variation in the use of discourse markers in a language contact situation. *Language Variation and Change* 9. 191–217.
Schiffrin, Deborah. 1987. *Discourse markers*. Cambridge: Cambridge University Press.
Schourup, Lawrence. 1999. Tutorial overview: Discourse markers. *Lingua* 107. 227–265.
Serrano Raquel, Elsa Tragant & Àngels Llanes. 2012. A longitudinal analysis of the effects of one year abroad. *The Canadian Modern Language Review* 68 (2). 138–163.
Svartvik, Jan. 1980. "Well" in conversation. In Sidney Greenbaum, Geoffrey N. Leech & Jan Svartvik (eds.), *Studies in English linguistics for Randolph Quirk*, 167–177. London: Longman.
Thomas, Jenny. 1983. Cross-cultural pragmatic failure. *Applied Linguistics* 4. 91–112.

Patrizia Giuliano
8 The building of textual cohesion in the narrations of bilingual children: Implications for bilingualism and multilingual societies

Abstract: The paper investigates a less widespread type of bilingualism, that acquired by young learners attending foreign schools in their own country, in our case the French School in Naples, Italy. Pupils attending this institute are daily exposed to French, at school, and Italian, at home. Their bilingualism is the expression of a new way of looking at foreign language acquisition. In our contemporary world, increasingly characterised by cultural diversity and multilingualism, monolingual families are starting to realise the importance of raising their children bilingually by sending them to foreign or international schools: a modern practice made possible in certain urban settings. From a linguistic perspective, the paper investigates the way the bilingual pupils under scrutiny manage textual cohesion when producing oral narrative tasks. We aim at testing our data with respect to the following questions: Is there any difference in the way our bilingual speakers exploit language specific patterns vis-à-vis their monolingual counterparts (in French and Italian) for textual cohesion? Does one of the two patterns prevail by virtue of the possible strong character of one of the two languages? To what extent are these issues relevant to a multilingual society? These research questions will be addressed by relating them to matters of intercultural pragmatics within the two cultures involved. This means that, although the purpose of our study is primarily cognitive and linguistic in nature, it also tries to explore the possible influence of extra-linguistic factors on the bilingual speaker's mental and verbal dimension.

1 Introduction

The paper investigates a less widespread type of bilingualism, that acquired by young learners attending foreign and international schools. More specifically,

Patrizia Giuliano, Università degli Studi di Napoli Federico II, Dipartimento di Studi Umanistici, Via Porta di Massa 1, 80133, Naples, Italy

https://doi.org/10.1515/9781501503207-009

this paper deals with the case of the French School in Naples, Italy. Pupils attending the French School of Naples are daily exposed to two languages: French at school, with their teachers, and Italian at home, with their family members. This type of bilingualism is the expression of a new way of looking at foreign language acquisition. In our contemporary world, increasingly characterised by cultural diversity and multilingualism, monolingual families are starting to realise the importance of raising their children bilingually or multilingually by sending them to a foreign/international school, also to make them more sensitive to different ways of conceiving human interaction. The new type of bilingualism that ensues can be seen as a modern practice made possible in certain urban settings.

In particular, the paper investigates the way young bilingual learners attending the French School in Naples manage textual cohesion when producing an oral narrative task. Our informants' bilingualism is precocious since their second language, namely French, intervened at the age of about three. We studied three groups of subjects: a group of bilingual speakers and two reference groups of monolingual speakers, that are necessary for the evaluation of the bilinguals' narrations.

French is only used by these bilingual speakers at school (they have been attending the branch of the French School in Naples since kindergarten), since they exclusively use Italian at home. Though precocious, their bilingualism has not been simultaneous (Italian preceded French).[1]

As for the reference groups, one consists of French speakers and the other of Italian speakers, interviewed in France and Italy respectively. They are rigorously monolingual and only use their mother tongue in their daily life.

All the data were elicited using the video clip *The finite story* (cf. Dimroth 2006) – made up of 30 film segments – in which three characters (also referred to as "entities" in the terminology of the Quaestio theory) repeat the same actions or do the opposite of another character in different moments of the story (cf. §2). Our groups of informants were asked to watch the video clip and retell the story, segment by segment. Since the stimulus involves a non-prototypical flow of information, the informants have to exploit different linguistic devices in order to convey contrasts in the entity domain and the time domain or to maintain the predicative information. The bilingual subjects performed the task both in Italian and in French.

---

[1] The term bilingualism is often used to refer to different types of linguistic knowledge: simultaneous bilingualism (two languages learned since birth), precocious bilingualism (two languages learned before the age of six or even three), late bilingualism (two languages learned after childhood). In the present work bilingualism will refer to the precocious acquisition of a second language (from the age of three on).

The starting point of our analysis is represented by the works by Dimroth et al. (2010), Giuliano (2012) and Andorno and Benazzo (2014), authors who analysed *The finite story* narrations of German, Dutch, French, English and Italian adult native speakers, identifying some specific patterns of textual cohesion in each of the above languages. As a matter of fact, the construal of textual cohesion by our bilingual subjects is the main focus of this paper.

Our data will be discussed and interpreted through a crosscultural perspective such as the one adopted by Giuliano and Di Maio (2008), Giuliano (2012) and Giuliano and Musto (2016), according to which the referential mechanisms of interpretation which are typical of a specific language for a given textual genre cannot be wholly understood unless they are related to matters of intercultural pragmatics. Speakers having at their disposal very similar linguistic means – such as native speakers of French and Italian – can make different linguistic and textual cohesion choices with respect to the content that they have to convey in the same experimental conditions (cf. *The finite story* experiment described above), which can happen for reasons that the grammars of the languages alone cannot always explain. Patterns of interaction and perspective-taking habits together with grammars can, conversely, explain this state of things in a more satisfactory manner. So a way of becoming bilingual and "acculturated" (namely absorbing a different culture, cf. Diaz-Rico and Weed 2006) in two languages lies in the ability to "absorb" the implicit cultural facts conveyed by the dimension of language through interaction and text genre rules. While building a text, a speaker selects content and linguistic means and builds up cohesion mechanisms according to an unconscious preferential "perspective" that prompts them to focus on some aspects of reality rather than others. It is possible to state that each language and culture induces individuals to adopt a specific cognitive-linguistic perspective (cf. Carroll and von Stutterheim 2003; Carroll and Lambert 2005; Carroll et al. 2008; Giuliano and Di Maio 2008; Giuliano and Musto 2016). As a consequence, the evaluation of the proficiency level of bilingual subjects should involve a careful consideration of the mastering of interactional and textual mechanisms and not just of sentence grammar and lexicon.

2 Framework and stimulus

In the last two decades several authors have shown that adult advanced second language learners master the grammar of the target language at utterance level but not at discourse level, since their way of establishing anaphoric linkage, and consequently textual cohesion, still reflects their mother tongue perspective-taking (cf., among others, Carroll et al. 2000; von Stutterheim, Nüse, and Murcia Serra 2002; Carroll and von Stutterheim 2003; Carroll, von Stutterheim, and Nüse 2004; von Stutterheim and Carroll 2006; Giuliano and Di Maio 2008; Giuliano 2012; Giuliano and Musto 2016). These authors have investigated the way native speakers and second language learners organise and structure information when producing a cognitively complex task. Such a task refers to the elicitation of texts involving formal and logical complexity, namely restrictions of various types in the way information is introduced, maintained and reintroduced. Most of the authors agree that discourse patterns of textual cohesion depend on grammatical core principles of the language in question and act since very early childhood, forcing speakers to adopt a peculiar "perspective" on the world they talk about (cf. Slobin 1987, 2003). Giuliano and Di Maio (2008), Giuliano (2012) and Giuliano and Musto (2016), nevertheless integrate the grammatically driven reasons with pragmatic habits of interaction, indicating the necessity of taking cultural factors into account.

Despite the possibility of applying the aforementioned framework to the study of bilingual subjects, this has rarely been done and generally only for very young children (cf. Jisa 1995, 1999; Álvarez 2005; Schneider 2008), for whom the production of cognitively complex tasks is not always possible. The focus of our paper is, conversely, on bilingual teenagers of Italian and French living in Italy (cf. §3), who performed a narration ideated by Dimroth (2006): *The finite story*.

The finite story is a video clip about three men, Mr Blue, Mr Green and Mr Red, living in three different flats but in the same building, which one night catches fire. It is subdivided into several segments, the content of which is illustrated in Table 1. We will focus on six information structures (IS: I, II, III, IV, V and VI), each of which is repeated two or three times during the story (listed in bold in Table 1), and especially on the possible anaphoric linkages that can be exploited to build textual cohesion.

As to the first information structure (cf. segments 4, 5 and 8 of the story), this is the prototypical configuration for setting up an addition in the domain of the entities, since it involves a shift in the entity domain but maintenance of the levels of polarity and predicate; so we expect informants to use additive particles both in French and Italian (cf. It. *anche, pure*; Fr. *aussi, également* corresponding to Engl. *also, too, as well*) or to employ verbal periphrases such as It. *fare la stessa cosa/lo stesso*; Fr. *M. Rouge fait la même chose/de même*; in Engl. *to do the same*). Furthermore, at least theoretically, it is possible to signal the change of the entity simply by prosodic prominence (It. *Il siGNOR ROsso va a letto*; Fr. *M. ROUge va se coucher*), thus avoiding any other linguistic marking.

Table 1: *The finite story*: information configuration in segments selected for analysis.

Nr	Content of film segment	IS	Information configuration with respect to the antecedent segment	Relevant antecedent segment	Possible structure markings
01	Introduction characters				
02	Introduction house and flats				
03	Mr. Blue going to bed, sleeping				
04	Mr. Green going to bed, **sleeping**	I	Different entity, same polarity	03	*Anche il Signor Verde va a letto* / *M. Vert va se coucher aussi*
05	Mr. Red going to bed, **sleeping**	I	Different entity, same polarity	03/04	*Il Signor Rosso fa lo stesso* / *M. Rouge fait de même*
06	Fire on the roof				
07	**Mr. Green sleeping**	IV	Same entity, same polarity	04	*Il Signor Verde continua a dormire (dorme sempre / ancora)* / *M. Vert continue à dormir (dort toujours / encore)*
08	**Mr. Red sleeping**	I and IV	Different entity, same polarity	07	*Anche il Signor Rosso continua dormire/ Neanche il Signor Rosso si sveglia* / *M. Rouge continue à dormir aussi / M. Rouge ne se reveille non plus*

(continued)

Table 1 (continued)

Nr	Content of film segment	IS	Information configuration with respect to the antecedent segment	Relevant antecedent segment	Possible structure markings
09	**Mr. Blue not sleeping**	II	Different entity, opposite polarity	07/08	*Solo il Signor Blu non dorme* / *M. Bleu, lui il ne dort pas* / *M. Bleu s'est bien réveillé*
11	Mr. Blue calling fire brigade				
12	Fireman in bathroom, not answering				
13-15	M. Blue leaves his room to wake up his friends but does not manage				
16	M. Blue goes back to his place	V	Same entity, same polarity	13	*Il Signor Blue ritorna (torna di nuovo) nella sua stanza* / *M. Bleu remonte dans sa chambre*
17	M. Blue calling fire brigade	VI	Same entity, same polarity	11	*Il Signor Blu richiama (chiama di nuovo/ ancora) i pompieri* / *M. Bleu rappelle (appelle à nouveau / encore) les pompiers*
18	Fireman answering the phone	III	Same entity, opposite polarity	12	*Questa volta il pompiere risponde al telefono / Cette fois-ci le pompier répond au téléphone*

8 The building of textual cohesion in the narrations of bilingual children — **197**

22	Arrival of fire engine			
24	Rescue net: Mr. Green not jumping			
25	Mr. Red not jumping			
26	Mr. Blue jumping	II	Different entity, opposite polarity	24/25	*Il Signor Blu invece salta Par contre M. Bleu saute / M. Bleu, lui il saute*
27	Mr. Green jumping	III	Same entity, opposite polarity	24	*Alla fine il Signor Verde salta Finalement M. Vert saute*
28	Mr. Red not jumping	IV	Same entity, same polarity	25	*Il Signor Rosso continua a non voler saltare M. Rouge continue à ne pas vouloir sauter / ne veut toujours pas sauter*
29	Mr. Red jumping	III	Same entity, opposite polarity	28	
31	The happy end			

For Configuration II (segments 9 and 26 of the story), speakers have to convey that a situation applying for the first two entities does not apply for the third one, since we have a change in the domain of the entities, an opposite polarity but the mantainance of the predicate. For this configuration, speakers can either mark the contrast on the entity or highlight the change of polarity. If they opt for the entity contrast, they cannot of course use additive particles in order to mark the contrast between entities because of the change of polarity; nevertheless, they can apply other means such as lexical modifiers (It. *invece, in compenso, diversamente da Mr X*; Fr. *en revanche, par contre, différemment de M. X*; in Engl.: *on the other hand, instead, differently from Mr X*) or restrictive particles (It. *solo, solamente, soltanto*; Fr. *seul, seulement*; in Engl.: *only, just*). As to the change of polarity, in Italian and French it can be marked, theoretically, by a prosodic stress on the lexical verb (It. *Il Signor Blu si è sveGLIAto*; in French the prosodic stress can go along with the adverb *bien*: *M. Bleu s'est bien REveillé*), but it is not a common strategy for Romance languages (conversely, it is common in Germanic languages, cf. Engl. *Mr Blue DOES jump* or *Mr Blue JUMPS*).

As for the third configuration (segments 18, 27, 29), speakers can either mark the change of polarity or the temporal shift. As a matter of fact, the temporal shift linking devices are crucial for the third information configuration since, ideally, they are the only alternative to the polarity change markings that speakers can use to mark the contrast and they can do so by means of adverbials such as It. *questa volta, alla fine* etc. and Fr. *cette fois(-ci), finalement* etc. (to Engl. *this time, eventually* etc.).

The fourth, fifth and sixth configurations, finally, involve temporal continuation (segments 7 and 28 of the story), restitution[2] (segments 16) and iteration (segment 17), respectively, which demand the recourse to adverbs and aspectual periphrasis such as It. *ancora* ('still'), *sempre* ('always'), *continuare a* ('to continue to') and Fr. *encore* ('still'), *toujours* ('always'), *continuer à* ('to continue to'), for continuation; It. *di nuovo* ('again'), *nuovamente* ('again'), *un'altra/ancora volta* ('once again'), *prefix ri-* and Fr. *de/à nouveau* ('again'), *une autre/nouvelle fois* ('once again'), *prefix r(e)-* and synonyms, for restitution and iteration.

The conclusion that we can draw from the comment of the segments that we shall focus on during the analysis of our data is that Italian and French speakers have very similar means to express the contents of the story in ques-

---

[2] Restitution is a special case of iteration: it involves that an initial situation (for ex. Mr Blue is in his room) is reestablished after an interruption (Mr Blue is again in his room).

tion. In §5 we will provide the results concerning monolinguals, which will be our point of reference for the evaluation of the bilingual perspective of our informants (cf. §6).

3 The informants

Our French-Italian bilingual subjects are between 12 and 13 years old, come from Italian families and live in Naples (Italy), where they have spent their whole life except for short holidays abroad. Almost all of their parents have a university degree and highly qualified jobs. They only speak to their children in Italian.

Our subjects began learning French at the age of three at the French School in Naples, where they attended the nursery and primary school and were attending the middle high school at the time this investigation was taking place.

At the French School all teachers are French L1 native speakers and all of the disciplines are taught in French. Nevertheless, for some topics students also have lessons in Italian with Italian L1 teachers: three hours a week from nursery to primary school, distributed between history, grammar and geography; six hours a week in the junior high school, where mathematics is added to the subjects just quoted.

Regarding the native monolingual speakers of French and Italian, or reference groups (cf. Dimroth et al 2010; Giuliano 2012; and Andorno and Benazzo 2014), they have a university education and live in France and Italy, respectively. They are monolingual and only use their L1 in their daily life.

4 Research aims

The discussion of our findings will add to the debate on "the perspective-taking" when building a text from the point of view of bilingual subjects. In particular, we aim at testing the results of Dimroth et al. (2010), Giuliano (2012), and Andorno and Benazzo (2014) for French and Italian monolinguals on our bilingual productions in order to answer the following questions:
a. Is there any difference in the way these bilingual speakers exploit language specific patterns vis-à-vis their monolingual counterparts (in French and Italian) for textual cohesion?
b. Alternatively, do they mix the above cohesion patterns when using Italian or French?

c. Does one of the two patterns prevail by virtue of the possible "strong" character of one of the two languages?
d. To what extent are these issues relevant to a multilingual society?

The questions above will be answered by relating them to matters of intercultural pragmatics within the two cultures involved, Italian and French. So, although the purpose of our study is primarily cognitive and linguistic in nature, as it aims at exploring the mental and verbal dimensions of the bilingual subject, it also explores the possible influence of extra-linguistic factors on these two dimensions as well as the cross-cultural influences of the two societies involved.

5 The narrations of French and Italian monolinguals

The configurations commented in §2 (some or all of them) have been studied by: Benazzo and Andorno (2010), Dimroth et al. (2010), Andorno and Benazzo (2014) with respect to native speakers of Dutch, German, Italian and French; Giuliano (2012, 2015) with respect to English and Italian; Giuliano and Musto (2016) with respect to Spanish. By virtue of their results, the authors identify several patterns according to which the native speakers of each language tend to build textual cohesion when narrating *The finite story* stimulus. For French and Italian, on which we focus in this paper, some micro-typological differences have been observed; we shall comment on them through the examples reported below (cf. Dimroth et al. 2010, Giuliano 2012, Andorno and Benazzo 2014).

(1) Information Structure II (contrast of entities and actions)
It. Il   Signor Blu   invece   si   sveglia   / Solo
    The Mr   Blue   instead   himself wakes-up / Only
    il   Signor Blu   si   sveglia
    the Mr   Blue   himself wakes-up
'Mr Blue instead wakes up'
It. Il   Signor Blu   è il   primo / solo   che
    The Mr   Blue   is the first / only (one) who
    si   sveglia
    himself   wakes-up
'Mr Blue is the first / only one who wakes up'

Fr. L'incendie est déclaré chez M. Bleu,   donc *lui*   il
    The fire   is burst-out at   M. Bleu ('s place), so   him he
    n'   hesite   pas,   il   saute
    NEG hesitates NEG,   he   jumps
    'The fire has burst out in Mr Blue's place, so he doesn't hesitate, he jumps'
Fr. M. Bleu a   *bien*   vu   l'incendie / M. Bleu a
    Mr Blue has certainly seen the fire   / Mr Blue has
    VU   l'incendie
    SEEN   the fire
    'Mr Blue did see the fire'

(2) Information Structure IV (temporal continuation)
    It. Il   Signor Verde *continua* *a* dormire / Il   Signor
        The Mr   Green continues   to   sleep.INF / The Mr
        Verde dorme *ancora*
        Green sleeps still
        'Mr Green continues to sleep / Mr Green still sleeps'

    Fr. M. Rouge dort   *toujours*
        Mr Red   sleeps always
        'Mr Red continues to sleep'

(3) Information Structure V (temporal restitution)
    It. Il   Signor Blu *torna*   *(di nuovo)* nella   sua stanza
        The Mr   Blue goes-back (again)   in-the his room
        'Mr Blue goes back to his room'

    Fr. M. Bleu *r*emonte   dans sa   chambre
        Mr Blue again-goes-up   in   his room
        'Mr Blue goes up to his room again'

(4) Information Structure VI (temporal iteration)
    It. Il   Signor Blu *chiama di nuovo* / *ri*chiama   i   pompieri
        The Mr   Blue calls   again   / again-calls   the firemen
        'Mr Blue calls the firemen again'

    Fr. M. Bleu *r*appelle   les   pompiers
        Mr Blue again-calls   the   firemen
        'Mr Blue calls the firemen again'

The examples from (1) to (4) illustrate the prototypical ways of realising the observed information structures in Italian and French by adult monolingual speakers with a high education. This does not mean that these are the only possible ways of expressing the information configurations concerned, but rather the preferential patterns selected by the speakers. So for IS II, Italian speakers tend to select either the adverbial *invece* ('conversely', 'instead', 58% of the means employed), or the restrictive particles *solo / solamente* ('only'), the latter sometimes combined with a cleft structure (37%; Dimroth et al. 2010 define the use of *solo / solamente* as "the uniqueness strategies"); this same structure can contain the adjective *primo* ('first') instead of *only*, which leads to the "primate strategy" (Dimroth et al. 2010). With respect to French speakers' narrations, the uniqueness and primate strategies never apply, since they definitively prefer to mark the contrast by the exploitation of French strong pronouns (cf. *lui* ['him'] in example (1) above, corresponding to the 68% of the means exploited); other alternatives occur but are clearly a minority: *en revanche* and *par contre* ('conversely', 'instead') account for 18%; the adverb *bien* and the prosodic accent on the lexical verb, highlighting the polarity contrast, are even more uncommon: 16%.

As to IS IV, Italian speakers' preferred pattern is the aspectual periphrasis *continuare a* + verb (63% of the means exploited), sometimes alternating with the particle *ancora* (30%); conversely, French speakers preferentially exploit the adverb *toujours* (62% of the means exploited), more rarely *continuer à* + verb (24%) and almost never *encore* (1 occurrence).

Concerning IS V, in French retellings the restitution is marked by the prefix *r(e)-* in 60% of the occurrences; 40% is given by *retourner* ('go-back'), a verb in which the prefix in question is fossilised since one can no longer see the relationship with the base verb *tourner* ('to turn'), so the choice of *retourner* can be seen as a lexical strategy. For Italian narrations, the exploitation of the prefix *ri-* is less frequent than in French (45% of the linguistic means used); other means are felt to be more natural: as a matter of fact, the restitution is expressed above all by lexical strategies, namely through the verbs *tornare* and *ritornare* ('go back') – the semantics of which implies the return to the place of departure with a clear fossilisation of *ri-* in *ritornare* – and the adverbial expression *di Nuovo* ('again') (3 occurrences).

As far as IS VI is concerned, in French the repetition of the same action is mainly expressed by the prefix *re-* (67% of the markings), used with a variety of verbs; adverbial means such as *à/de nouveau* are more rare. In Italian the relation between the morphologic means and the adverbial means is more balanced (*ri-* prefix + verb: 30% of the markings; adverbial markings: 53%; combination of the two means: 17%).

Concerning IS I and III, there are no remarkable differences between the results obtained for the two languages. Nevertheless, a few things need to be pointed out for IS I: French additive particle *aussi* has a very different syntax with respect to It. *anche/pure* (cf. the positions 1 and 2 in example (5)); the Italian equivalent of Fr. *également*, namely *ugualmente*, is never used.

(5) Information Structure I (addition of entities)
It. *Anche/pure* il Signor Verdi va a letto
   Also   the Mr Green   goes to bed
'Mr Green also goes to bed'

Fr. M. Vert s'   est *également* couché
   Mr Green himself is equally   gone-to-bed
'Mr Green has also gone to bed'

Fr. M. Vert aussi (1) s'   est couché   aussi (2)
   Mr Green also   himself is gone-to-bed too
'Mr Green has also gone to bed'

6 The narrations of the bilinguals

6.1 The first configuration

For the Information Structure I, the frequency of *aussi* is lower in Fr L1 (13 occurrences) with respect to Fr Lb (Language b; 24 occurrences), but in Fr Lb *également* never appears and *non plus* is a bit less productive; the same predicate means (It. *fare lo stesso*; Fr. *faire de même* and similar) are also less frequent than in Fr L1. Regarding It L1 with respect to It Lb, the productivity of *anche(/pure)* is high in both varieties (35 occurrences in It L1; 22 occurrences in It Lb), while means such as *neanche, nemmeno* and *fare la stessa cosa* are less frequent. So on the whole, for the first configuration, we identified a difference between It L1 and Fr L1 in terms of the attention that speakers give to entities by employing additive particles, since their frequency is high or very high in It L1, It Lb and Fr Lb but low in Fr L1. A dominance of the Italian perspective in the bilingual data could explain these results.

Continuing with the first configuration, we indentified some means as being typical of the only bilingual group in Fr Lb: the scalar particle *même* (with or without the negation *pas*) and the pitch accent on the noun phrase referred to the entity involved in the anaphoric link, as in the following examples:

(6) Fr Lb, IS I
La troisième scène montre que M. Bleu va à dormir
The third scene shows that Mr Blue goes to sleep.INF
// la quatrième scène montre que M. Vert
// the fourth scene shows that Mr Green

va à dormir // Et la cinquième scène
goes to sleep.INF // and the fifth scene
raconte que M. ROUge va à dormir
tells that Mr RED goes to sleep.INF

'The third scene shows that Mr Blue goes to sleep // the fourth scene shows that Mr Green goes to sleep // the fifth scene is about Mr RED going to sleep'

(7) Fr Lb, IS I
Pendant la nuit la maison prend feu // M. Vert il dort
During the night the house catches fire // Mr Green he sleeps
encore // *même* M. Rouge
still // even Mr Red

'During the night the house catches fire // Mr Green is still sleeping // even Mr Red'

(8) Fr Lb, IS I
Le bonhomme vert il ne se réveille pas // *Même*
The puppet green he NEG himself wakes-up NEG // even
pas le bonhomme rouge
NEG the puppet red

'The green puppet does not wake up // not even the red puppet'

The employment of *même*, in particular, sounds strange in the contexts under scrutiny, which do not seem to justify the presence of a scalar means.

6.2 The second configuration

Concerning the Information Structure II, a difference emerges from the comparison between Fr L1 and Fr Lb because of the more crucial role played by the strong pronoun *lui* in the first variety (74%) with respect to the second one (23%). Here is a passage from Dimroth et al. (2010: 3337):

(9) L'   incendie est déclaré   chez M. Bleu #   donc *lui* il
    The fire   is burst-out at Mr Bleu ('s place) so   him   he
    n' hésite   pas   il saute
    he NEG   hesitates he jumps
    'The fire has burst out in Mr Blue's place, so he doesn't hesitate, he jumps'

The use of *lui* as a contrasting device in the entity domain is less frequent in Fr Lb but Fr Lb speakers sometimes mark this type of contrast in a failing or relatively deviant way, as in the following extracts, where the speaker either omits the strong pronoun *lui* (examples 10 and 11) or the weak pronoun *il* (ex. 12) (this last solution does not work in French).

(10) Fr Lb, IS II
    Monsieur Bleu il   s'   aperçoit de l'   incendie
    Mr   Blue he himself   realises of the   fire
    'Mr Blue realises that there's a fire'

(11) Fr Lb, IS II
    Et   M. Vert   il   se   réveille   pas // non plus M. Rouge //
    And   Mr Green he   himself   wakes-up   NEG // neither   Mr Red   //
    M. Bleu il   s'   en   est aperçu
    Mr Blue he   himself   of-it is realised
    'And Mr Green does not wake up // Neither does Mr Red // Mr Blue has realised (that there's a fire)

(12) Fr Lb, IS II
    Les pompiers disent à   M. Vert   de descendre   mais il   ne
    The firemen say   to   Mr Green to go-down.INF   but he   NEG
    veut pas   descendre... Ils   disent à   M. Bleu de descendre
    want NEG   go-down.INF... They say   to   Mr Blue to go-down.INF
    et: *lui* descend
    and: him   goes-down
    'The firemen tell Mr Green to go down but he does not want to go down... they tell Mr Blue to go down and he does'

The first two passages are pragmatically less marked but completely acceptable in French; the third one (ex. 12), conversely, sounds like a (non acceptable) calque from Italian, which is clearly demonstrated by the following extract:

(13) It L1, IS II
      Poi   vanno   dal   Signor Blu   e   dato   che   casa   sua
      Then   go-3rd.pl.   to-the   Mr   Blue and   since that house his
      andava: già   a   fuoco   *lui* decide di saltare
      go-past.imp   already to   fire   *him* decides to jump
      'Then they go to Mr Blue and since his house was already catching fire *he* decides to jump'

The other differences, as exemplified below, concern the use of the "uniqueness strategies", namely the adverb *seulement* ('only') and the cleft structure *le seul qui* + verb + *c'est* ('the only one who ... it's ... ') and the use of the contrasting adverb *alors que* in in Fr Lb. These means are never used in Fr L1.

(14) Fr Lb, IS II
      Seulement M.   Bleu   s'   est   réveillé   et   il   a   aperçu
      Just   Mr   Blue   himself   is   woken-up   and   he   has   seen
      qu'   il y   avait   un   incendie
      that it there had   a   fire
      'Only Mr Blue has woken up and he has seen that there was a fire'

(15) Fr Lb, IS II
      Le   seul   qui   se   jette   c'est   M.   Bleu
      The   only-one   who   himself   throws   it's   Mr   Blue
      'The only one who throws himself it's Mr Blue'

(16) Fr Lb, IS II
      M. Vert   ne   s'   aperçoit pas   qu'   il   y   a   un   incendie
      Mr Green   Neg   himself   realises NEG   that it   there has a   fire
      //   et   non plus   M.   Rouge   //   *alors que*   M.   Bleu   s'   en
      //   and   neither   Mr   Red   //   whereas   Mr   Blue   himself   of-it
      aperçoit
      realises
      'Mr Green does not realise that there is a fire // and neither does Mr Red // whereas Mr Blue realises this'

If we compare the results in both languages and varieties (Fr L1, It L1, Fr Lb, It Lb), we deduce that, for the second information structure, in Fr Lb, the bilinguals tend to adopt a sort of mixed perspective between French and Italian, since they balance the exploitation of the French structure SN + *lui* + *il* + verb and the adverbial expression *par contre* with the French translation of Italian typical means such as *seulement, le seul qui ..., alors que*.

Again for the second configuration, some other means are completely lacking in Fr Lb, which is the case for polarity markings, namely *bien* (ex.: M. Bleu a *bien* sauté) and the prosodic pitch accent on the verb (ex. M. Bleu a *VU* le feu); however, their productivity is very low in Fr L1 as well. Conversely, once more in Fr Lb, bilinguals can exploit the pitch accent on the SN involved in the contrast in order to highlight the latter (cf. ex. 6 in § 6.1).

For the comparison It L1 vs. It Lb, the uniqueness strategies being productive in both varieties, this clearly shows the closeness of It Lb to the Italian of monolinguals.

Another feature typical of bilinguals for the second configuration is the more frequent use of generical means such as *ma* and *però* ('but') in Italian Lb (7 occurrences), which are not often employed by It L1 speakers (2 occurrences). In Fr Lb, the item *mais* is less frequent than its It Lb equivalent (2 occurrences). This same item is not used at all by Fr L1 speakers.

6.3 The third configuration

For the Information Structure III the differences between Fr L1 and Fr Lb lie in the lack of *aussi* in Fr L1 as a means to mark addition on the entity level and that of *quand même* and *tout de même* in Fr Lb, by which French L1 speakers try in a way to highlight the polarity strength (5 occurrences, e.g. *finalement il saute quand même*).

(17) Fr Lb, IS III
      La   maison de M. Vert   prend   feu et   donc M. Vert   decide
      The   house of Mr Green catches fire and so   Mr Green   decides
      lui   *aussi* de sauter   par la   fenêtre
      him   too   to jump.INF by the   window
      'Mr Green's house catches fire and so Mr Green also decides to jump out of the window'

(18) Fr L1, IS III[3]
Finalement il saute *quand même*
Finally he jumps however
'Finally he jumps'

The use of the additive particle *anche* is very frequent in It L1 data but only relatively frequent in It Lb; in both varieties the highlighting of polarity is conversely completely absent. These results show, once again, the influence of Italian on Fr Lb. Again probably due to Italian influence is the expression *à la fin* ('at the end') in Fr Lb, which is lacking in Fr L1 but used in It L1 by its equivalent form (cf. *alla fine*).

6.4 The fourth configuration

As far as the fourth configuration is concerned, this has to do with temporal continuation, as is the case with the addition of temporal spans, similarly to the fifth one (restitution) and the sixth one (iteration) (cf. §§6.5 and 6.6).

For this information structure, the situation of "continuing to sleep" referred to Mr Red and Mr Green (scenes 7, 8 and 28) is not always mentioned by the speakers. As we saw in §5, both It L1 and Fr L1 speakers could employ temporal adverbs (Fr. *toujours* and *encore*; It. *ancora* and *sempre*), the aspectual periphrases *continuer à* and *continuare a*, verbs expressing the persistence of a state (Fr. *rester*, It. *rimanere*: ['stay', 'remain']) and (for the scene 28) verbs marking both continuation and volition (Fr. *s'obstiner* ['obstinate']; It. *Insistere* ['insist'], etc.).

For French L1, Andorno and Benazzo (2014) state that *toujours* is crucial to express the continual function (62% of the used markings), followed by the periphrasis *continuer à/de* (24% of the markings) (cf. also §5 above). For Italian L1, the periphrase *continuare a* is, conversely, the most frequent means used to mark the information structure in question (63%); though less frequently, verbs marking both continuation and volition are also found: *ostentare* ('flaunt'), *essere reticente* ('be reticent'), *temporeggiare* ('temporise') (7%); among adverbs, It L1 speakers exclusively exploit *ancora* (30%).

---

[3] The expression *à la fin*, though never used by Fr L1 speakers, can have the meaning of *enfin*, *finalement*, by which the bilinguals use it.

Concerning the bilingual subjects in It Lb, the results are much closer to that of It L1 speakers: the aspectual periphrasis *continuare a* (67%) is predominant and followed, in terms of occurrences, by *ancora* (28%). Nevertheless, bilinguals also employ the particle *sempre* (1 occurrence) but never exploit volition verbs; the use of *sempre* could be a transfer from French (cf. results for Fr L1 *supra*), whereas the absence of volition verbs is probably a reflex of the bilinguals' young age.

For Fr Lb, similarly to other analysed configurations, the information configuration under scrutiny is less marked by bilinguals than by monolinguals; concerning the means, the Italian perspective is transferred into French through the high frequency of *continuer à*, in alternation with which we find just one occurrence of *toujours* and one of *encore*. The employment of *toujours* sounds like a feeble expression of the Fr L1 perspective; as far as *encore* is concerned, it is less frequent than in It L1, but it is questionable if that could be a reflex of the French perspective (Fr L1 speakers produce just 1 occurrence).

6.5 The fifth configuration

Regarding the fifth configuration, concerned with restitution, for French L1 Andorno and Benazzo (2014) state that speakers only use the *re-* prefix, which is exploited with a variety of verbs (*remonter* ['go upstairs again']; repartir ['leave again']; *revenir* ['come back again']; *repasser* ['pass by again']; *rentrer* ['go into again']); it is necessary to remember that for *retourner* the prefix is fossilised since the relationship with the base verb *tourner* is not evident any more.

For Italian L1 data, *ritornare* – for which the prefix *ri-* is also fossilised – is the most frequent lexical means to mark restitution (cf. §5 above), whereas the exploitation of the prefix *ri-* on other verbs is lower than in Fr L1 (45%); the second most exploited device is the verb *tornare*, that, differently from Fr. *tourner*, has a restitution (or iteration) inherent meaning and, as a matter of fact, It. *ritornare* can be considered as a case of "double marking". Italian speakers also employ the adverbial expression *di nuovo* (2 occurrences).

For bilingual subjects, the results are closer to It L1 than to Fr L1 both for It Lb and Fr Lb. As a matter of fact, in It Lb, the *ri-* prefix is exploited just with *ritornare*.

6.6 The sixth configuration

Concerning the sixth information structure, also in this case, Fr L1 speakers exploit the *re-* prefix most of the time (12/18 = 66.6%); the most frequent verb is of course *rappeler* ('call again') followed by *redécrocher le telephone* ('pick up the phone'), *recomposer un numéro* ('to dial a number again') etc. The other means consist of adverbial means such as *à/de nouveau* ('again'). When using the *re-* prefix, Fr L1 speakers do not combine it with the latter.

Regarding Italian L1 data, there is a relative balance between the *ri-* prefix strategy (6 out of the 11 occurrences are given by the verb *richiamare:* 'call again') and the use of the adverbials *di nuovo* (9 occurrences) and *nuovamente* (1 occurrence), which confirms the lower exploitation of the *ri-* prefix device by It L1 speakers with respect to Fr L1 speakers.

When it comes to the data on bilingual subjects in Fr Lb, the results seem closer to the Italian perspective than to the French L1, since we find a balance between the adverbial strategy and the *re-* prefix strategy. Nevertheless, in French the bilinguals exploit both *à nouveau* – a means similar to It. *di nuovo* – and the expression *une autre fois*. For It Lb, these same informants almost exclusively exploit the *ri-* prefix, mostly with *richiamare* ('call again') (8 occurrences) and less frequently with *riprovare a chiamare* ('try to call again') (4 occurrences); there is just one alternative to the *ri-* prefix, given by the iterative use of *di nuovo* (1 occurrence). A sort of paradox emerges from the bilinguals' data: the Fr Lb narrations are closer to the It L1 data, and the It Lb narrations are closer to the Fr L1 data!

7 Findings

From the conceptual viewpoint, the comparison between the different groups of monolinguals and bilinguals shows that the entity oriented perspective – which is related to the first three configurations – is particularly strong in Italian L1, and certainly stronger in Fr Lb and It Lb than in Fr L1. As a matter of fact, in the first three varieties, the exploitation of additive particles (in the first and third ISs) is more frequent with respect to the same predication means (cf. *to do the same*, acceptable for the first IS) and the highlighting of polarity strategies (for the second and third ISs), which implies a greater focalisation on the entity with respect to other conceptual domains.

As to the type of means exploited by the groups, some means typical of It L1, but absent in Fr L1, appear in Fr Lb as well (cf. "the uniqueness strategies" in IS2). Some other means typically ascribed to Fr L1 retellings are less frequent in Fr Lb (cf. the strong pronoun *lui*). Some more strategies seem exclusively typical of Fr Lb (cf. the use of the scalar particle *même* and the prosodic accent on the NP, for IS1; the use of the generic means *ma, però* and *mais*).

As far as the fourth, fifth and sixth configurations are concerned, from a conceptual viewpoint we find no real differences between the ways the groups mark them in Italian and French, since all the groups tend to mark the same type of concepts. Nevertheless, as we pointed out in § 1, the means they select for each IS can be different. For the fourth IS, the employment of *toujours* is predominant in French L1 but not in Fr Lb (1 occurrence); the use of the periphrases *continuare a / continuer à* are the most exploited strategies in It L1 and It Lb; *encore* appears just once in French L1, whereas *ancora* is definitively more frequent in It L1 and It Lb. The closeness of bilinguals to the Italian choices is evident for the fifth and sixth configurations as well, with respect to which, in It Lb, they opt for both lexical and adverbial strategies (*tornare, ritornare* and *di nuovo, nuovamente, un'altra volta*). As to Fr Lb, bilinguals seem closer to Fr L1 for the fifth IS; mixed tendencies emerge instead for the sixth IS both in Fr Lb and It Lb (cf. §6.6).

8 Implications for the debate about bilingualism

In this paragraph we will go back to the research questions stated in §3, which are repeated here:
(a) Do our bilingual subjects exploit the language specific patterns exploited by the monolingual subjects of the two languages in question for textual cohesion?
(b) Alternatively, do they mix the cohesion patterns in question when using Italian or French?
(c) Does one of the two patterns prevail by virtue of the possible "strong" character of one of the languages?

Our study seems to confirm the results of Giuliano (2013), according to which bilingual subjects tend to either overgeneralise the perspective of the dominant language or to adopt a sort of "mixed perspective" rather than a perspective totally consistent with the language they are using. If we conceive the perspective, as we have done in this study, as the ability to shape a text by the cohesive strategies specific to a certain language, we are then forced to admit that bilingual subjects, even when initiated into a second language very early in life (before five years old age), have trouble in dropping the cohesive modalities of the dominant language. That Italian is the dominant code emerges from at least two clues: the narrations in Italian are completely lacking in grammatical mistakes, which conversely show up, though rarely, in French retellings. Italian is the language they use with Italian classmates. The dominant language seems to encourage both the cognitive domains on which to focus (entities, in particular) and the linguistic means with which they are verbally expressed (uniqueness strategies, adverbial devices etc.); these domains and means tend to show up in a lesser or stronger way in the weak language as well. Nevertheless, bilinguals sometimes also transfer the perspective of the latter into the strong language (cf. the second and the sixth ISs), which demonstrates that transfer is bidirectional and probably depending on a single processing system.

However, bilinguals do not simply transfer from one language to the other but, in a similar way to late second language learners, their data can also give rise to creative results which are not really consistent with either of the languages involved.

9 Implications for a multilingual society

In this closing section we will answer our fourth research question: to what extent can such a study be relevant to a multilingual society?

The languages investigated in this paper are typologically and culturally close, which explains the identification of micro-typological and micro-conceptual differences rather than astonishing discrepancies between the narrations of our groups. This may not be the case, of course, for languages which are typologically and conceptually very distant from each other, as often happens in modern societies because of immigration. The capacity of adopting different perspectives on reality is linked to specific ways of building textual cohesion and of interacting, which implies focusing on some referential domains rather than others (entities, time, polarity, space etc.) according to implicit principles acting unconsciously on individuals since early childhood. In our opinion, these different perspectives cannot depend only on the grammatical systems, as some authors state (cf. §1). If this were the case, the speakers of typologically very close languages would make the same choices in the same experimental conditions, which is not the case (cf. also Giuliano and Di Maio 2008; Giuliano 2012; Giuliano and Musto 2016). As a matter of fact, interaction habits can push the speaker to referential preferences during the construction of a text even when the means at his disposal in L1 are not deeply grammaticised: the highlighting of polarity, for instance, is not grammaticised either in French or Italian but whereas Fr L1 informants have sometimes recourse to *bien* and *quand même* or the prosodic accent on the lexical verb, It L1 speakers never try to highlight positive polarity (by using, for instance, *effettivamente* ['actually'], or *sì che* ['yes that']); in English the highlighting of polarity is grammaticised thanks to the *do auxiliary*, and yet, in the *Finite story* experiment the latter is extremely rare (cf. Giuliano 2012); Spanish is a Romance language with no grammaticised means for polarity highlighting but Giuliano and Musto (2016) show that Sp L1 speakers often mark it (by *sì (que)* ['yes that']) in the *Finite story* experiment. So, in some way independently of grammar, the textual choices that a speaker makes are oriented on what in his community is seen to be relevant when talking to another speaker; the lack of respect for these choices can make the interaction more or less a failure. For this reason, patterns of interaction and perspective-taking habits on reality need to be more deeply explored in modern society with respect to autochthonous languages as well as to immigrant languages. A way of becoming bilingual and of being "acculturated" (namely absorbing another culture, cf. Diaz-Rico and Weed 2006) and of evaluating the proficiency level of bilingual subjects should involve, in our opinion, a careful consideration of the mastering of interactional and textual mechanisms and not simply of sentence grammar and lexicon.

Symbols and acronyms

Fr L1	French of monolingual
It L1	Italian of monolingual
Sp L1	Spanish of monolingual
Fr Lb	French of bilingual
It Lb	Italian of bilingual
IS	information structure
//	refers to the barrier between a scene and the following one
INF	the inflection of Fr. infinite
NEG	negative particle
(...)	in the examples it indicates an addition of the investigator

Acknowledgements: The author thanks the French School in Naples for their crucial help, without which this paper could have never been conceived and written.

References

Álvarez, Esther. 2005. Aprender a narrar: Formas temporales y sus funciones en un niño de siete a nueve años de edad. *Barcelona English Language and Literature Studies* 14. http://www.publicacions.ub.edu/revistes/bells14/PDF/sec_lan_01.pdf (accessed 28 May 2019).

Andorno, Cecilia & Sandra Benazzo. 2014. L'acquisition L2 de langues proches: L'expression de la continuation et de l'itération en français et en italien L2. In Marguerita Borreguero Zuloaga & Sonia Gómez-Jordana Ferary (eds.), *Marqueurs discursifs dans les langues romanes: Une approche contrastive*, 424–448. Limoges: Lambert Lucas.

Benazzo, Sandra & Cecilia Andorno. 2010. Discourse cohesion and topic discontinuity in native and learner production: changing topic entities on maintained predicates. *Eurosla Yearbook* 10. 92–118.

Carroll, Mary & Monique Lambert. 2005. Crosslinguistic analysis of temporal perspectives in text production. In Henriëtte Hendricks (ed.), *The structure of learner variety*, 203–230. Berlin: Mouton de Gruyter.

Carroll, Mary, Monique Lambert, Christiane von Stutterheim & Antje Rossdeutscher. 2008. Subordination in narratives and macrostructural planning: Taking a comparative point of view. In Cathrine Fabricius Hansen & Wiebke Ramm (eds.), *"Subordination" versus "coordination" in sentence and text*, 161–184. Amsterdam: John Benjamins.

Carroll, Mary, Jorge Murcia Serra, Marzena Watorek & Sandra Bendiscioli. 2000. The relevance of information organisation to second language acqusiition studies: The perspective discourse of advanced adult learners of German. *Studies in Second Language Acquisition* 22. 87–129.

Carroll, Mary & Christiane von Stutterheim. 2003. Typology and information organisation: Perspective taking and language specific effects in the construal of events. In Anna Giacalone Ramat (ed.), *Typology and second language acquisition*, 365–402. Berlin: Mouton de Gruyter.

Carroll, Mary, Christiane von Stutterheim & Ralf Nüse. 2004. The thought and language debate: A psycholinguistic approach. In Thomas Pechman & Christopher Habel (eds.), *Multidisciplinary approaches to language production*, 184–218. Berlin & New York: Mouton de Gruyter.

Diaz-Rico, Lynne T., & Kathryn Z. Weed. 2006. The crosscultural, language, and academic development handbook (3rd edn.). Boston: Allyn and Bacon.

Dimroth, Christine. 2006. *The finite story*. Nijmegen: Max-Planck-Institut for Psycholinguistics. http://corpus1.mpi.nl/ds/imdi_browser?openpath=MPI560350%23 (accessed 28 May 2018).

Dimroth, Christine, Cecilia Andorno, Sandra Benazzo & Josje Verhagen. 2010. Given claims about new topics: The distribution of contrastive and mantained information in Romance and Germanic languages. *Journal of Pragmatics* 42. 3328–3344.

Giuliano, Patrizia. 2012. Contrasted and maintained information in a narrative task: Analysis of texts in English and Italian as L1s and L2s. *EUROSLA Yearbook* 12. 30–62.

Giuliano, Patrizia. 2013. Comparaison de phénomènes complexes en italien et en français chez des adolescents bilingues et monolingues: Focus sur le texte narratif. *Travaux de Linguistique* 66. 73–96.

Giuliano, Patrizia. 2015. How children "add" or "restrict" entities and temporal spans in narrations: Evidence from Italian and English native children. *Linguistik Online* 71. 29–50.

Giuliano, Patrizia & Luca Di Maio. 2008. Abilità descrittiva e coesione testuale in L1 e L2: Lingue romanze e lingue germaniche a confronto. *Linguistica e Filologia* 25. 125–205.

Giuliano, Patrizia & Salvatore Musto. 2016. Assertive strategies in English and Spanish: A contribution to the debate on assertion in Romance and Germanic languages. *Testi e Linguaggi* 9. 228–242.

Jisa, Harriet. 1995. L'utilisation du morphème "be" en anglais langue faible. *Acquisition et Interaction en Langue Etrangère* 6. 101–127.

Jisa, Harriet. 1999. Some dynamics of bilingual language development. *Acquisition et Interaction en Langue Etrangère* [Special issue] 1. 7–32.

Schneider, Ricarda. 2008. Récits d'expériences personnelles versus récits fictifs: Analyse interactionnelle des productions narratives d'un jeune enfant bilingue français-allemand. In Jacqueline Feuillet (ed.), *Les enjeux d'une sensibilisation très précoce aux langues étrangères en milieu institutionnel*, 51–71. Université de Nantes: CRINI.

Slobin, Dan Isaac. 1987. Learning to think for speaking. *Pragmatics* 1 (1). 7–25.

Slobin, Dan Isaac. 2003. Language and thought online: Cognitive consequences of linguistic relativity. In Dedre Gentner & Susan Goldin-Meadow (eds.), *Advances in the investigation of language and thought*, 157–192. Cambridge: MIT Press.

Stutterheim, Christiane von & Mary Carroll. 2006. The impact of grammatical temporal categories on ultimate attainment in L2 learning. In Heidi Byrnes, Heather Weger-Guntharp & Katherine A. Sprang (eds.), *Educating for advanced foreign language capacities*, 42–53. Washington: Georgetown University Press.

Stutterheim, Christiane von, Ralf Nüse & Jorge Murcia Serra. 2002. Crosslinguistic differences in the conceptualisation of events. In Hilde Hasselgård, Stig Johansson, Bergljot Behrens & Cathrine Fabricius-Hansen (eds.), *Information structure in a cross-linguistic perspective*, 179–198. Amsterdam & New York: Rodopis.

Elizabeth Lanza, Giuditta Caliendo, Rudi Janssens, Stef Slembrouck and Piet Van Avermaet
Conclusion

Urban multilingualism in Europe: Policies and practices at the crossroads

Contemporary urban life in Europe has been transformed by increased mobility and technological advances in communication, spearheaded by globalisation and displaying the complexities of contemporary urban multilingualism. Increasing numbers of new speakers and new languages contribute to new forms of social and cultural diversity in the modern city (Duarte and Gogolin 2013; Pennycook and Otsuji 2015) and transform not only society at large but also educational systems and even families. Transnationalism engenders new linguistic practices and policies, the understanding of which forces us to (re)conceptualise how individuals and communities fit in and function in society (King and Lanza 2019). Issues of inclusion and exclusion are central in this regard.

Inclusion in current European discourses is not only about the human dimension of citizenship in which individuals feel a sense of attachment and loyalty to their territory. Rather inclusion in society is also channelled through the lens of the market economy, presented as leading to a better social market economy. Indeed the *Europe 2020 strategy*[1] is the agenda put forth by the European Commission for growth and jobs in the current decade that comprises an overview of key targets for the coming years. Social inclusion figures prominently in this vision – inclusion in education, in the labour market, and in society in

---

[1] https://ec.europa.eu/info/business-economy-euro/economic-and-fiscal-policy-coordination/eu-economic-governance-monitoring-prevention-correction/european-semester/framework/europe-2020-strategy_en#featuresofthetargets (accessed 28 May 2019)

Elizabeth Lanza, Center for Multilingualism in Society across the Lifespan (MultiLing), University of Oslo, Oslo, Norway.
Giuditta Caliendo, Université de Lille, Domaine Universitaire du Pont de Bois, Villeneuve-d'Ascq, France.
Rudi Janssens, Vrije Universiteit Brussel, VUB-BRIO, Brussels, Belgium.
Stef Slembrouck, Piet Van Avermaet, University of Ghent, Department of Linguistics, Faculty of Arts and Philosophy, Ghent, Belgium.

https://doi.org/10.1515/9781501503207-010

general. Diversity – both cultural and linguistic – is a vital issue in this regard in contemporary Europe as countries strive for the inclusion of all of their citizens in order to attain a social market economy, according to the EU strategy.

The notion of inclusion, furthermore, underlies institutional policies of various kinds, involving language policies, which is the focus of this volume. In the European context, how policies are actually practiced reveals deeply rooted ideologies and there are numerous examples in history of how language has united and divided territories and communities. Language policies may officially condone exclusion of certain languages and hence their speakers from society, but more often than not implicit exclusion prevails, not only institutionally but also in daily interpersonal relations. Language practices may be in line with official policy but grassroots language policy may evolve through language practices (Shohamy 2006; Hult and Johnson 2015). Many language policies support monolingual approaches to diversity – "parallel monolingualisms" (Heller 1999: 5) – and suppress linguistic diversity despite good intentions. A challenge we face in our attempts to bridge the gap between language policies and language practices concerns fundamentally how we view language. There is a need to reappraise our view of language and we need to reframe the policies based on this reappraisal.

The contributions to this book address this complex relationship between policies and practices at the crossroads from the macro national level to the micro individual level. The articles are divided into four parts, with clear links between them. Part 1 deals with tensions between language policies and language practices, illustrated through a language conflict situation and through multilingual classrooms. Part 2 addresses responses to multilingual challenges in the field of practice, by examining language ideologies in community interpreting and interactive group work. Part 3 focuses on the multilingual family and highlights the tensions between language practices in the home and language policy, bringing into focus and questioning what proficiency in a language actually means in contemporary Europe. Part 4 pursues the issue of language proficiency and presents novel ways of mapping multilingual proficiency in a study abroad context and in bilingual children's narratives. A closer look at the contributions and their implications for urban multilingualism can shed light on potential research directions to take in efforts to bridge the gap between language policies and language practices.

Part 1 deals with the tensions that evolve between language policies and language practices. The impact of globalisation on everyday life, increasing mobility and migration, accelerating technological evolution, and free movement and residence for EU citizens within the member states have all had a cumulative impact on language practices in most European cities. Brussels and Milan are two examples of such urban contexts that are described in depth in this volume by Janssens, and Catenaccio and Garzone, respectively. While both cities of large multilingual urban spaces, each country – Belgium and Italy – developed a totally different language policy. The pacification of the language conflicts in Belgium led to a policy based on territorialism with three official languages but no national language for the country as a whole, and the rejection of the concept of "linguistic minority". While the Belgian Constitution stipulates the official language(s) for all municipalities in the country, in Italy the use of Italian is taken for granted while the country additionally safeguards the languages of some historical (regional) language minorities. More recently (2007), under pressure from a growing linguistic diversity, the Italian Parliament voted that the Italian language is the official language of the Republic, while for the implementation of language policy, local municipalities play an important role. Both contributions illustrate a defensive language policy strategy designed to deal with language contact situations from the past. Despite the differences, language policies in both countries are based on the nation state ideal of monolingualism with bilingualism or multilingualism as the exception, providing a solution for historical language conflicts. These countries adhere to a static view of society, where one official language and a shared history are promoted as the base for social cohesion and for the identity of their population. Languages other than the historical official languages seemingly have no place in language policy. The only exception in some cases (for instance in higher education) is English, a language that is rather a school language and neither a traditional language of the original population nor the home language of the newcomers. Newcomers are expected to assimilate in the local language and culture in such a language policy that neglects to address critical issues of inclusion. It is no coincidence whatsoever that both contributions to Part 1 refer to linguistic diversity in education to illustrate the current language policy in both cities. "Other" languages spoken by newcomers are not mentioned in the school curriculum, unless as a threat to social cohesion. It is also striking that in both countries, initiatives bridging the home language of the newcomers and the school language are the first to be cut for budgetary reasons.

A critical view of language policy in relation to language practice continues in Part 2. Slembrouck's main conclusion is that "scale" can be useful at the heart of language policy, the analyses that inform it, as well as a framework for formulating advocacies. Spatio-temporal considerations of scale are not only useful when our efforts are directed at understanding the decision-making dynamics of multilingual provisions. Scalar analysis may also usefully underpin the development of multilingual policy. It offers a way of being reflexive and explicit in contexts where policy has to demonstrate flexibility and context-sensitivity – for example, in terms of which level of social organisation a measure is being addressed at. "Re-scaling" also provides a way of understanding capacity building. It would appear then that a scalar approach is useful not only from the point of view of describing and interpreting complex multilingual realities, but that it also comes with the potential of suggesting particular configurations oriented to successful communication strategies. One of the challenges in such an exercise continues to be that of determining the relative weight of particular factors which do not apply in the same way for each individual, language background, interactional situation, functional purpose, and so forth. Jordens, Van den Branden and Van Gorp refute three misconceptions about mother tongue use in classrooms with children with immigrant backgrounds: that pupils would resort to it all the time, that the mother tongue would be mainly used off-task, and that a lack of proficiency in their L1 would prevent pupils from discussing school-relevant subject matter. Pupils were perfectly able to interact in a mix of Turkish and Dutch during task performance, and found meaningful solutions to the complex problems they were exposed to. Moreover, they were able to present their results in Dutch only, the prescribed medium of interaction. While noting such flexibility, the authors conclude that the mother tongue fulfills an important role for cognitive as well as for socio-affective purposes. What are the implications of this for pedagogical effort and for how multilingualism is organised and stimulated in classrooms? Does the importance of L1 point to a consideration that is to be weighed against that of observing flexibility and fluidity? How does one conceptualise what counts as "mother tongue use"? Linguistic diversity in education is a recurrent theme in studies of urban multilingualism in which language policy and language practices can at times be at odds with one another.

Multilingual challenges are also a theme in Part 3. Lanza calls for the need to investigate family language policy in regards to burning issues concerning linguistic diversity in the classroom. Through case studies in a European sociopolitical context, she illustrates how the traditionally conceived private family space has become public as political actors and pressures attempt to coerce families with an immigrant background into monolingualism in the country's societal language. In public discourse, inclusion is often viewed from the perspective of the state, with proficiency in the national language being viewed as the main indicator of inclusion or integration. However, such a view fails to capture the complexity of real life experiences in culturally and linguistically diverse family settings. The family has gained centre stage in public discourses in many European countries and merits more focused research attention as a public space in a mediatised world, which in turn requires critical and innovative investigations through a cross-country comparative lens. Through investigations of language policies and practices in the home we may better understand children's learning at school, a challenge in urban multilingualism. Van Mensel addresses multilingual family practices in an interactional study. He fully engages with the implications of translanguaging and very importantly raises the challenges of categorisation in language policy efforts. The term translanguaging is much needed to make sense of the realities of language use in bilingual worlds (Garcia and Li Wei 2014). His passages on the "multilingualisation" of language use underlines how multilingualism is cutting deeper than the realities of singular language choices being associated with particular activities and domains. However, it is top down language categorisation that mostly proves to be problematic. How is "speaking a language" being defined? And what are the implications of this for how, for example, educational provisions are being organised? The question of categorisation, however, inevitably takes us further: if the current era is one recognising diversity and monitoring the allocation of resources in accordance with this, then one can begin to see the growing importance and central role of categorisations in today's governance-driven policymaking contexts. It is important to emphasise this. In addition, Van Mensel cautions us against naive uses of "broad language categories" in policy and research. By implication, his Chapter raises the question of what counts as a realistic and workable alternative – one that recognises the realities of contemporary multilingual practices.

The last section of this book, Part 4, sets out to investigate new ways of mapping multilingual proficiency in a Europe that has become more and more diversified. Contemporary society is becoming increasingly mobile and is characterised by a growing number of students, workers, and retirees opting for short-term stays abroad. These practices give rise to new needs of communication and language proficiency, resulting in alternative ways of language learning. The articles in this part focus on new strategies for second language learning, building the necessary repertoires to function in such multilingual contexts. In this respect, this final part is essential, exploring forms of language learning that bridge the individual's needs and new societal demands: acquiring essential language skills depending on new contexts and new forms of language learning. Caliendo and Magliacane examine sociopragmatic competence and second language acquisition of learners of English in a study abroad context, investigating the effects of student mobility on the production of discourse markers in a second language, which are important linguistic features facilitating communication. This perspective is innovative in the field of Second Language Acquisition as the few studies carried out on discourse markers in a second language have exclusively focused on longer-term experiences abroad (that is, migrants). However, as stressed in the Chapter, due to the intrinsic features of these linguistic items, their analysis can shed more light on the speakers' acquisition of the socially relevant communicative aspects of interaction in a second language during a period of mobility. This research, albeit exploratory and preliminary in nature, has therefore an enormous potential for future spin-offs. Some of the possible future developments of the research could deal with different types of experiences abroad. Indeed, the EU's education programme Erasmus has been the object of an extensive body of literature, while other forms of mobility still seem to be under-explored. A comparison with another learner cohort with a different L1 or with a different level of proficiency could also help investigate the effects of these variables in the production of discourse markers in conversation. Finally, if a specific length of stay abroad is needed for discourse markers to emerge in a second language, it would also be interesting to conduct a comparative analysis of experiences that differ in length. Taken together, all these factors can help to map different aspects of multilingual proficiency in an increasingly mobile world. Giuliano's study also examines the micro-context of language learning and discusses its implications for bilingualism and multilingual societies. She focuses on the building of textual cohesion in the narrations of bilingual children, and observes how, over the last decade, new language practices have been promoted throughout Italy. Among them *Content and Language Integrated Learning* (CLIL) has been increasingly emphasised by the Italian Ministry of Public Education in line with some requirements of the European Framework for Languages. The CLIL strategy has, therefore, been introduced as an obligatory part of the curriculum in secondary education and as optional and experimental in primary schools, and even preschools. Against this new scenario, realities such as the French School in Naples embody one of the *ante litteram* maximal expressions of the CLIL strategy, but also one of the oldest to be found in Italy (along with other similar schools, such as the German and Anglo-American Schools in the same city). At present, this type of institution in Italy is still limited to large urban conglomerations (such as Milan, Rome, and Naples), but they are supposed to involve an increasing number of learners and, hopefully, fight off some pre-existing and persistent prejudices about bilingualism. Italian society has only recently been experiencing multiculturalism and multilingualism at close hand, due to the increasing immigration waves of the last three decades. Hence the intellectual and cultural benefits deriving from bi/multilingualism still clash with some old and widespread misconceptions about it. Both Chapters highlight the importance of examining specific linguistic features and text structures in the speaker's repertoire in order to ground local language practices in light of societal language policies.

The way forward

The Chapters in this volume as a whole resonate with the ontological shift in sociolinguistics as to how we as linguists conceive of language based on the sociolinguistic reality of linguistic practices and multilingual repertoires. The sociolinguistic study of language in the age of globalisation stresses the unboundedness of language, with language no longer being seen as a discrete entity. Hence we no longer focus on the languages of a speaker per se, but rather the speaker's linguistic repertoire with scale as an important dimension. The deployment of a linguistic repertoire in one setting may not have the same value as in another setting. Language ideologies are at the core for such distinctions.

As we see so clearly in this volume, language policies are never neutral nor objective; they are there to legitimise ideological choices and are thus powerful instruments. Polices are implemented through educational curricula, language tests and programmes, yet there are, as demonstrated, challenges and indeed problems in the definition of multilingualism in policy documents. There are new forms of multilingualism in Europe, as clearly shown in the case studies illustrated in this volume, and these must be captured by current policy making in order to ensure inclusion in society. As noted above, policies generally support monolingual approaches to diversity – "parallel monolingualisms" (Heller 1999) – and actually suppress linguistic diversity, despite any good intentions. This static approach to managing languages contrasts with the linguistic dynamics in urban daily life. There is no lack of scientific research describing urban multilingualism in cities, but there is a need to analyse ways in which to bridge the gap between daily linguistic reality and the politics of language. In this respect, three elements seem crucial. First, a bottom-up approach is an initial research direction that needs to be explored further. Citizens in super-diverse cities develop their own way of communication, not only locally but also taking transnational contacts into account, which have become an important part of communication in everyday life. Research should, therefore, focus on language practices within different spaces, looking for workable ways of communication which might refer to face-to-face communication or to different forms of technological support. This type of analysis is grounded in "spontaneous" language practices that arise in a context in which language politics do not apply. The way in which different languages are used and gain their own function form the basis for this type of research. A second line of inquiry is situated at the political level. In the European context, there is a growing tension between the free movement of individuals as one of the fundamental rights of European citizenship (referred to as "mobility") on the one hand, and the attempts to avoid so called third-country-nationals to enter the EU (referred to as "migration"), on the other. Mobility is considered a positive aspect of European integration and supported by, for instance, the Erasmus programme, and initiatives to support labour mobility. Language issues are seldom discussed, although in general, multilingualism is promoted. The European "2+1" rule in education is rather vague and compulsory language lessons for adults go against the equal treatment of EU nationals. On the other hand, EU policy towards migration puts the emphasis on cultural assimilation and language courses to obtain a strong commitment to the host society. More research on a more converging policy is a second scientific focus that needs to be addressed. A last research area that needs to be explored in this context is social inclusion in multicultural and multilingual contexts. The monolingual ideal is based on the ideology that social inclusion can only be obtained based on a single language and a shared set of values and beliefs. The Brussels situation shows that a multilingual city can only function with multilingual citizens. For example, although almost 90% of Brussels residents claim to speak good to excellent French, mutual communication is increasingly multilingual. The way in which people deal with language also changes, which is clearly illustrated in all of the contributions in this book.

A recurrent trend and challenge we face in our attempts to bridge the gap between language policies and language practices is the need to go beyond the idea of static languages. Taking a translanguaging approach, and truly embracing multilingualism, is a promising direction in this regard – that we take translanguaging, as illustrated in studies in this volume, as a reality, in pedagogy and assessment. This would also challenge us to reappraise our view of language and the need to reframe policies based on this reappraisal. The Chapters in this volume provide us with the incentive and the inspiration to move forward on this mission, which would surely contribute to more inclusion in European societies.

References

Duarte, Joana & Ingrid Gogolin (eds.). 2013. *Linguistic superdiversity in urban areas: Research approaches*. Amsterdam: Benjamins.

García, Ofelia & Li Wei. 2014. *Translanguaging: Language, bilingualism and education*. New York, NY: Palgrave.

Heller, Monica. 1999. *Linguistic minorities and modernity: A sociolinguistic ethnography*. London: Longman.

Hult, Francis & David Cassels Johnson (eds.). 2015. *Research methods in language policy and planning: A practical guide*. Oxford: Wiley-Blackwell.

King, Kendall & Elizabeth Lanza (eds.). 2019. Ideology, agency, and imagination in multilingual families. *International Journal of Bilingualism* 23 (3) [Special issue]. 717–723.
Pennycook, Alastair & Emi Otsuji. 2015. *Metrolingualism: Language in the city*. London: Routledge.
Shohamy, Elana. 2006. *Language policy: Hidden agendas and new approaches*. London: Routledge.

Index

About-task 93, 105, 106
Academic skills 50, 63
Additive particle 194, 198, 203, 208, 210
Assessment 62
– final assessment 50
– national assessment 45, 49, 50
– national assessment exam 55, 57

Backchannel signals 175
Bilingual 91, 92, 94, 95, 97, 99, 108, 109
Bilingualism 14

Categorisations 143
Change of polarity 198
Change of the entity 194
Code-switching 93, 94
Cognitive 191, 193, 200, 212
Cohesion mechanisms 193
Communication strategies 177
Competences 46, 49, 50, 54–56, 59, 60
– academic competences 48
– disciplinary competences 61
– language competences 62
– linguistic competences 47, 48
– metalinguistic competences 48
– multilingual competence 46
Connectors 175
Conversational exchanges 184
Crosscultural perspective 193

Discourse Markers 169–171
Dutch-only policy 92, 95, 108

Educational segregation 50
Educational systems 19
Ehm 176
Erasmus programme 167, 168, 186
Experimenter effect 174
Exposure 183
Extra-curricular courses 58

Family 123–126, 128, 130, 133, 135, 136
Family language policy 121, 123, 127, 128, 132, 134, 136

Fillers 175
Flanders 73, 81, 82, 87, 88
Focuser 181
Foreign school 191, 192
Function 92–95, 97, 99–101, 105, 107, 108
Functions mother tongue 109

Guidelines 47–50, 52, 61, 63

Headmaster 53, 55, 57–59, 61, 62
Heritage language 37, 38, 40, 46, 56, 59, 61–63
High school 37, 38, 45
Home languages 25

Identity 21
Immigrant languages 37, 38, 40–42, 60, 64
Input 185
Integration 37–39, 45–47, 51, 53–56, 62–64
– cultural integration 51, 60, 62
– linguistic integration 38, 41, 42
– school integration 64
– social integration 50, 60, 62
Interaction 183, 186
Intercultural education 47, 49
Intercultural pragmatics 191, 193, 200
International school 191, 192
Irish English 170, 180
Iteration 198, 208, 209

Junior high school 37, 38, 45, 49, 50, 52–55, 60–61, 63, 64

Language and culture mediators 53
Language-based categorisations 144, 161
Language border 13
Language categorisation 160
Language censuses 17
Language community 13, 19
Language conflict 17
Language diversity 135
Language ideologies 121, 125, 131–134
Language mediation 51, 52, 55, 56
Language mediator 37, 38, 49, 58, 59, 61–64

Language policy 15, 122, 194
Language practices 147, 159, 160
Language repertoires 143
Language skills 49, 51, 54, 62, 63
Language socialisation 124–126
Languaging 33
Like 181
Lingua franca 22
Linguistic and cultural mediators 52
Linguistic assistance 65
Linguistic diversity 122, 131, 132, 194
Linguistic practices 123, 154
Linguistic repertoire 95, 108, 109

Mediatori a scuola 59
Medium of instruction 92–95, 98
Migration 13
Minority languages 37–42, 64
Mobility 168
Mother tongue 92–96, 102, 104–109
Mother tongue functions 100
Multilingualism 128, 131, 136
Multilingual practices 140, 161

Narration 191, 194, 203, 212
Native-like stalling phenomena 179
Non-territorial languages 39

Official languages 16
Off-task 92–94, 101, 102, 104–109
On-task 93, 95, 102, 105, 106, 108

Pacification 13
Perspective 193, 194, 199, 203, 207, 209–213
Placement 51, 52, 55
Polarity 202, 207, 208, 213
Polarity change 198
Polarity strategies 210
Pragmatic "failure" 171
Pragmatic markers 171
Pre-school 52, 54
Primary school 45, 52–54, 61, 63, 64
Primate strategy 202
Professional skills 64

Quotative like 181

Referential mechanisms 193
Resource 92, 95, 98
Restitution 198, 202, 208, 209
Restrictive particles 198, 202

SA research 168
Scale 71, 73–78, 80, 83–86, 88, 89
School
– comprehensive school 53
– vocational high school 57
Schooling 56, 58, 65
Secondary school 45, 50, 57
Semi-structured interview 52
Skills 62
Social cohesion 28
Social inclusion 124
Social networks 184
Social participation 170, 185
Sociolinguistic interview 174
Sociolinguistic variation 169
Strategic competence 179

Teacher
– head teacher 52, 54, 58, 60–63, 65
Teaching staff 51, 52, 60, 62, 63, 65
Temporal continuation 198, 208
Temporal shift 198
Territoriality principle 14
Textual cohesion 191, 193, 194, 199, 200, 211, 212
Transcultural families 122, 127, 134
Translanguaging 127, 135
Type II variation 169

Uniqueness strategies 202, 206, 210

Vocational courses 45, 57, 61

Well 180

Yeah 177

www.ingramcontent.com/pod-product-compliance
Lightning Source LLC
Chambersburg PA
CBHW061938220426
43662CB00012B/1948